# China Resurrected

# China Resurrected

## A Modern Geopolitical History

*Frans-Paul van der Putten*

BLOOMSBURY ACADEMIC
LONDON • NEW YORK • OXFORD • NEW DELHI • SYDNEY

BLOOMSBURY ACADEMIC
Bloomsbury Publishing Plc, 50 Bedford Square, London, WC1B 3DP, UK
Bloomsbury Publishing Inc, 1385 Broadway, New York, NY 10018, USA
Bloomsbury Publishing Ireland, 29 Earlsfort Terrace, Dublin 2, D02 AY28, Ireland

BLOOMSBURY, BLOOMSBURY ACADEMIC and the Diana logo are trademarks of
Bloomsbury Publishing Plc

First published in Great Britain 2025

Copyright © Frans-Paul van der Putten, 2025

Frans-Paul van der Putten has asserted his right under the Copyright, Designs and Patents Act, 1988, to be identified as Author of this work.

For legal purposes the Acknowledgements on p. xi constitute an extension of this copyright page.

Cover design by Chris Bromley
Cover image © BJI / Blue Jean Images via Getty Images

All rights reserved. No part of this publication may be: i) reproduced or transmitted in any form, electronic or mechanical, including photocopying, recording or by means of any information storage or retrieval system without prior permission in writing from the publishers; or ii) used or reproduced in any way for the training, development or operation of artificial intelligence (AI) technologies, including generative AI technologies. The rights holders expressly reserve this publication from the text and data mining exception as per Article 4(3) of the Digital Single Market Directive (EU) 2019/790.

Bloomsbury Publishing Plc does not have any control over, or responsibility for, any third-party websites referred to or in this book. All internet addresses given in this book were correct at the time of going to press. The author and publisher regret any inconvenience caused if addresses have changed or sites have ceased to exist, but can accept no responsibility for any such changes.

A catalogue record for this book is available from the British Library.

A catalog record for this book is available from the Library of Congress.

ISBN: HB: 978-1-3505-3659-3
PB: 978-1-3505-3658-6
ePDF: 978-1-3505-3661-6
eBook: 978-1-3505-3660-9

Typeset by Newgen KnowledgeWorks Pvt. Ltd., Chennai, India
Printed and bound in Great Britain

For product safety related questions contact productsafety@bloomsbury.com.

To find out more about our authors and books visit www.bloomsbury.com and sign up for our newsletters.

*To my parents*

# CONTENTS

*List of Figures* viii
*Preface* x
*Acknowledgements* xi
*Note on Pronunciation and Names* xii

Introduction 1

1 Under attack (1840–2) 5

2 New realities (1842–1912) 21

3 Entering the world stage (1912–25) 43

4 Emancipation (1925–43) 67

5 From big four to big three (1943–79) 93

6 Wait and observe (1979–2008) 129

7 Confrontation (2008–24) 157

Epilogue 195

*Notes* 203
*Recommended Reading* 211
*Index* 215

# FIGURES

1   Aisin Gioro Minning, the Daoguang Emperor 17
2   Lord Viscount Palmerston, from *The Illustrated London News*, 1850 18
3   Signing of the Treaty of Nanjing on 29 August 1842, aboard HMS *Cornwallis* anchored at Nanjing, to mark the end of the First Opium War, by John Platt, 1846 19
4   Chinese officials pulling down the British flag on the *Arrow* on 8 October 1856 37
5   Li Hongzhang during a visit to England, 1896 38
6   Sir Robert Hart, Inspector General of Chinese Customs, in his den in Beijing, from *The Illustrated London News*, 1891 39
7   Official portrait of Empress Dowager Cixi by court photographer Yu Xunling, *circa* 1895 40
8   US troops in the Forbidden City, Beijing 1900 41
9   Sun Yat-sen and his wife Song Qingling 62
10  President Yuan Shikai surrounded by his staff, 1912 63
11  The German surrender to Japan at Qingdao, 1914 64
12  A British soldier sharing a cigarette with a Chinese labourer in France during the First World War, *circa* 1916 65
13  Gu Weijun (also known as Wellington Koo) and his wife Oei Hui-lan 66
14  Aisin Gioro Puyi, former emperor of China, with his wife Wanrong, Tianjin *circa* 1925 90
15  Zhang Xueliang and Chiang Kai-Shek, 1930s 91
16  Chiang Kai Shek, Franklin Roosevelt, Winston Churchill and Song Meiling, Cairo 25 November 1943 92
17  Mao Zedong proclaiming the founding of the People's Republic of China, Beijing 1 October 1949 125
18  Chiang Ching-Kuo with Chiang Kai-Shek and Song Meiling, Taiwan *circa* 1955 126
19  Communist soldiers and captured American soldiers during the Korean War, Wonsan, North Korea 1951 127
20  The film star Lan Ping with her mother, *circa* 1936. She would later marry Mao Zedong and become known as Jiang Qing 127
21  US National Security Advisor Henry Kissinger and his entourage visiting the Summer Palace in Beijing, 1971 128

22 President Nixon meeting Chairman Mao, Beijing 21 February 1972 128
23 Soviet leader Mikhail Gorbachev and his wife Raisa Gorbacheva meeting Deng Xiaoping, Great Hall of the People, Beijing 16 May 1989 155
24 The Chinese military deploying tanks against protesters, Beijing, the night of 3 to 4 June 1989 155
25 Flag lowering ceremony during the handover of Hong Kong by the United Kingdom to the People's Republic of China, 30 June 1997 156
26 Prime Minister Vladimir Putin speaking with President George W. Bush before the start of the Opening Ceremony for the 2008 Beijing Summer Olympics at the National Stadium, Beijing 8 August 2008 191
27 Vice President Xi Jinping meeting US Secretary of State Hillary Clinton, US Treasury Secretary Timothy Geithner and other delegates, Diaoyutai State Guesthouse, Beijing 3 May 2012 192
28 President Donald Trump and his wife Melania Trump with President Xi Jinping and his wife Peng Liyuan, Mar-a-Lago, Palm Beach, Florida, 6 April 2017 192
29 Aircraft carrier *Liaoning* sailing into Hong Kong harbour, 7 July 2017 193
30 President Vladimir Putin meeting with President Xi Jinping at the Diaoyutai State Guesthouse, Beijing 4 February 2022 193
31 Speaker of the US House of Representatives Nancy Pelosi and Taiwan's President Tsai Ing-wen at the president's office, Taipei, 3 August 2022 194

# PREFACE

When I first visited China in the spring of 1991, the country certainly did not give the impression of being an emerging world power. China hardly even seemed involved in the process of globalization. Chinese multinationals did not yet exist, and the presence of foreign companies was very limited. The country was seen in the West as an ancient but now decayed civilization and as part of the communist world during the Cold War. But what struck me were Shanghai's many historical Western-style buildings. On the boulevard stood, and still stand, the imposing former offices of foreign companies. In the meantime, those buildings had been given new uses. In 1991, for example, the former office of the British bank HSBC functioned as Shanghai's city hall. The previous wave of globalization had largely died down, but its traces were still visible. Both domestic and international processes have shaped, and continue to shape, China's identity and behaviour within the world order. This book stems from my belief that the story of China's rise as a global power cannot be told without understanding the history of foreign influence in China and the Chinese response to it.

# ACKNOWLEDGEMENTS

Many people have helped me in one way or another when I was preparing this book. I am very grateful to Joep den Teuling, Megan Harris, Paige Harris, Balasuwathiga and her colleagues at Newgen, Suzan Kemps-Mentrop, Saartje Schwachöfer, Martin Jacques, James Pullen, Job Lisman, Nikki Verkerk, Mirela Petkova, Graham Hutchings, Leonard Blussé, Albert Kersten, Hans van de Ven, Joanna Godfrey, Xinran Xue, Rebecca Solheim, Luuk van Middelaar, Monika Sie Dhian-Ho, Frank Pieke, Ties Dams, Berdina de Boer, Susann Handke, Liang Wai Chan, Friso Stevens, Ko Colijn, Xiaoxue Martin, Marcel Baartman, Frans Stoks, Sophie Bakker, Eric Werkhoven, Peter Boorsma and Lily Sprangers.

In particular I would like to thank Elsabé Willeboordse, Mai Spijkers, Maddie Smith, Jürgen Osterhammel, Vincent Chang and Bijan Omrani, without whom the publication of this book would not have been possible.

# NOTE ON PRONUNCIATION AND NAMES

The pronunciation of some letters used when Chinese words are written in Latin script is very different from English. The most unusual letters are x (pronounced 'sh') and q ('ch'). For example, Xi'an, the name of an ancient capital and well-known tourist destination in northern China, is pronounced 'Shee-ahn', and Qing, the name of China's last imperial dynasty, as 'Ching'. It is also important to know that in China the family name comes before the personal name. So in the case of Xi Jinping, for example, Xi is the family name and Jinping is the given name.

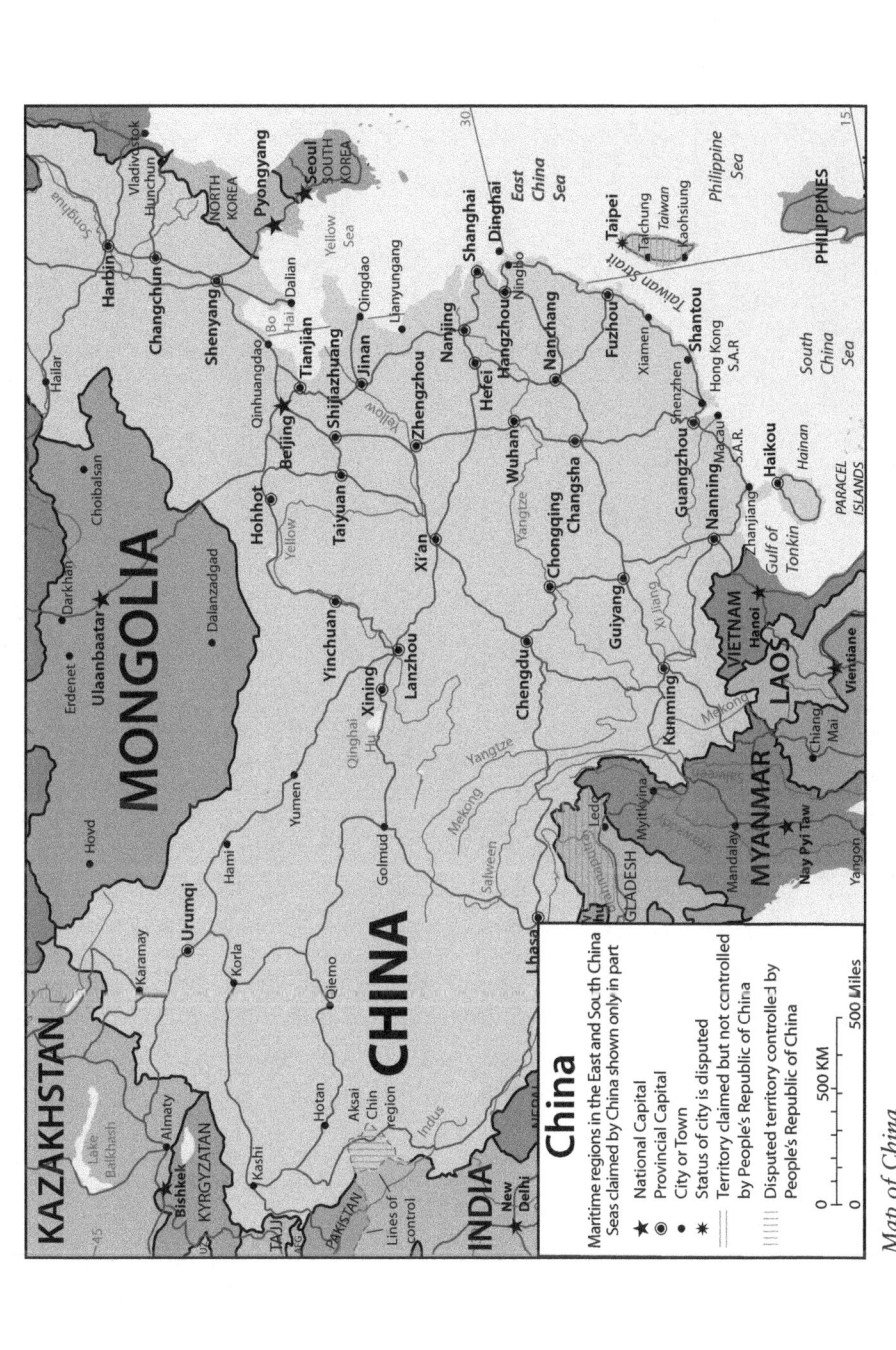

Map of China

# Introduction

On 13 August 2018, Donald Trump, as President of the United States, signed a new law for the US defence budget. It stated that competition with China for international influence is now a priority for the United States. According to the new law, to win the geopolitical rivalry with China, the United States must use all the resources at its disposal, including its economic and military might. It was the first time since the Cold War that America had expressed such emphatic and open concern that its position as the most powerful country in the world was under threat. China's growing international influence is the source of this concern. Never before has a non-European, non-Western country played such a major role in politics at the global level.

China's leader Xi Jinping says no one should worry about his country's rising power. China has always been peace-loving, Xi has said, and the stronger it gets, the more opportunities there are for the rest of the world.[1] According to him, China does not strive for global dominance but for the great revival (or 'rejuvenation') of the Chinese nation (in Chinese *Zhonghua minzu weida fuxing*). In 2012, shortly after becoming China's top leader, Xi Jinping explained what he meant by that. After visiting an exhibit at the National Museum of China on Chinese history from the First Opium War, which began in 1840, he said:

> Our struggles in the over 170 years since the Opium War have created bright prospects for achieving the rejuvenation of the Chinese nation. We are now closer to this goal, and we are more confident and capable of achieving it than at any other time in our history. Reviewing the past, all Party members must bear in mind that backwardness left us vulnerable to attack, whereas only development makes us strong. ...
>
> Looking ahead at the future, all Party members must bear in mind that we still have a long way to go and much hard work to do before we can turn our blueprint into reality. ...

> Achieving the rejuvenation of the Chinese nation is both a glorious and an arduous mission that requires the dedicated efforts of the Chinese people one generation after another. ...
> I firmly believe that ... the goal of building China into a modern socialist country that is prosperous, strong, democratic, culturally advanced and harmonious can be achieved by 2049, when the People's Republic of China marks its centenary; and the dream of rejuvenation of the Chinese nation will then be realized.[2]

The exhibition Xi had visited was called 'The Road to Rejuvenation.' Central to both the exhibition and the speech is the idea that China fell into decline as a result of the Opium Wars and that it has been trying to recover its old status ever since. Xi calls the desire to achieve this goal the Chinese dream of national rejuvenation. With his museum speech, he made it clear that striving to realize this dream is a top priority during his leadership.[3] Xi has since repeated the same message in many other speeches. He always emphasizes that China's revival only brings benefits to the rest of the world and does not pose a threat.

But not everyone is convinced of that. After all, China is a country in which no political opposition is allowed and where citizens have very limited protection against the power of the state. As an emerging global power with increasing influence abroad, why should China respect the rights and interests of non-Chinese more than those of its own citizens? On the other hand, not everyone feels as threatened by China as the US government does. Many people are inspired by China's rich culture and history. Moreover, the rise of China has brought many opportunities in the economic field. This became visible when China was single-handedly responsible for a large part of global economic growth in the years following the 2008 financial crisis.

If we want to get a good idea of what an increasingly powerful China means for the world, we need to look at the actual behaviour of the country, especially of its political leaders, government and businesses. Much has been written about China's international role. In fact, there is so much information about China – and so much is added every day – that it is difficult to keep track of it and to see the coherence between the many aspects of China's growing influence. The effects of China's rise are manifesting themselves in all parts of the world, in very different domains and at an ever-increasing pace. China has quickly become a prominent global player, especially in the areas of trade, investment and lending. But also as a diplomatic partner and supplier of technology, China is of fast-growing importance to many countries. As a result, more and more journalists and academics around the world are researching and writing about the many new and ever-changing aspects of China's rise. With this deluge of information, it is hard to obtain an overview and to separate main and side issues.

An approach completely different from looking at current events is to study how China behaved towards other countries in the two millennia before the Opium Wars. After all, the country was often very powerful for long periods at that time, and this historical perspective can therefore provide insight into how China could position itself as a world power in the future. However, one problem is that not only China but also the international context have changed fundamentally since 1840. It is difficult to know which elements of China's historical behaviour are unique to the pre-1840 situation and which may reappear in the future. China used to see itself as the centre of the world and treated its neighbours as tribute states. Does this mean that China will adopt the same attitude in the future, and what should we imagine in the twenty-first century as 'centre of the world' and 'tribute state'? These kinds of questions cannot be answered properly on the basis of a purely historical analysis.

This book gives historical context to current events. The focus is on the development of China's international role since the First Opium War. Only then did China begin to participate in a global system of international relations. Before that, China was part of the world economy, but not of world politics. By painting a picture of the period from 1840 to the present, this book shows what the constant factors are in the relationship between China and the world. This helps to contextualize the great diversity of current data. It also helps to better understand to what extent, and how, the traditional attitudes of pre-1840s China play a role in modern China.

The book traces the international role China has played from 1840 to the early 2020s from a geopolitical perspective, as the aim is to understand the significance of China as a global power. The term geopolitical refers to the competition for international influence between two (or more) actors in relation to third parties or domains. Great powers, those countries who have the most influence in a regional or global setting, are the most significant geopolitical actors. After 1840, China became less influential internationally, until the country's international status reached an all-time low in the years surrounding the First World War. By that time, China had changed from being a regional great power to being the object of geopolitical competition between other powers. From the First World War, China began to become more active as a participant in the international system. For a long time, this process was gradual and largely unnoticed. Only in recent decades has it become clearly visible how far China has come. The Chinese economy grew larger than that of countries such as Germany and Japan. It also became clear that the country had very quickly acquired considerable diplomatic and economic clout in Asia, Africa and Latin America. In a short time, China has emerged as a new world power.

Various books have been written about China's relationship with the rest of the world since the nineteenth century. A particularly thorough historical analysis of China's integration in the world is Jürgen Osterhammel's *China und die Weltgesellschaft: Vom 18. Jahrhundert bis in unsere Zeit*, which was published in 1989. Major publications in English include *China at the Centre: 300 Years of Foreign Policy* by Mark Mancall (1984) and Jonathen

D. Spence's *The Search for Modern China* (1991). More recent books on the historical background of China's international role include Henry Kissinger's *On China* (2011) and Odd Arne Westad's *Restless Empire: China and the World since 1750*, from 2013. In addition to these historical overviews with an eye for current issues, there is a much larger body of, mostly American, publications that address the relevance of China's rise to power for the United States or the West from a contemporary perspective. The historical context usually plays a role, but is not central to these publications.

What this book adds to the longer-existing literature is that it focuses on the relationship between China and great powers since 1840. More emphatically than other historical overviews, this book is a geopolitical analysis. And unlike publications that focus on contemporary geopolitical relations, this book explains how China's current relations with the United States, Russia, Japan and the European Union have formed, from the nineteenth century to the present. The story of China's demise and resurrection as a great power is told in this book against the background of the confrontation with other powerful countries.

## About China

This book covers China from the mid-nineteenth to the early twenty-first century. China's political identity has changed radically twice in that period. The first time this happened in 1912, when China changed from an empire led by the Qing dynasty to the Republic of China. The second major change took place in 1949, when the republic was split into two parts as a result of civil war. By far the largest part of the country has since been part of the communist People's Republic of China. The original Republic of China continues to exist on Taiwan, an island that was ruled from the mainland in the periods 1683–1895 and 1945–9 (and that was formerly known as Formosa). The two rival republics do not recognize each other as legitimate forms of the Chinese state, and the People's Republic strives to return the island, which it considers a renegade province, to the rule of the mainland. As for the period from 1949 onwards, the name China in this book refers to the People's Republic of China and the name Taiwan to the Republic of China. Finally, it is also important to distinguish between the Chinese population on the one hand and the government of China on the other. Unless otherwise stated, 'China' in this book refers to the country's government and political leadership.

# 1

# Under attack (1840–2)

On 2 July 1840, a group of British warships entered the harbour of Dinghai. This city is located on an island off the east coast of China, just south of Shanghai. The events that followed the appearance of the British ships have been reconstructed by Chinese historian Mao Haijian.[1] After two days without incident, the Chinese district administrator in Dinghai received a written message from the commander of the British squadron. It must have been with some hesitation that he received the message. This was because it was not drafted with the expressions of respect and submission required for written messages from foreigners to Chinese government officials. Against protocol, but somewhat understandable given the imposing presence of foreign warships in the harbour, the message was accepted and read. It turned out to be a demand for the surrender of the city. Highly alarmed, the district manager boarded the British flagship to ask what this meant.

The British navy had come to China as a result of a dispute over the opium trade in the city of Guangzhou (then known as Canton), in southern China. At the time, Guangzhou was the only place in China where foreigners were allowed to trade with the Chinese. A likely reason why the Chinese government considered Guangzhou a suitable place for this as early as the eighteenth century was that the city was located inland.[2] Most other Chinese seaports were on the coast, but to reach Guangzhou, ships arriving from abroad had to pass through the Pearl River Delta. The main responsibility of the Chinese emperor was to maintain order in his empire. Therefore, local officials all over China knew that their performance was primarily judged by their ability to prevent civil unrest in their district.

Guangzhou being at some distance from the sea made it easier for the local government, if needed, to block the departure route of foreign traders. In addition, the authorities could cut off the supply of food and water if necessary. With these means of pressure at hand, the government was assured that it had a handle on the behaviour of the foreign merchants, who during their stay were forced to remain at a designated location outside the city. So-called factories (buildings that served as warehouses, offices and homes) were located on that site. In addition, the foreigners were only allowed to trade with a limited number of Chinese merchants, who were responsible for the conduct of their foreign business partners. Outside of the annual trading season, the foreigners had to leave Guangzhou. These measures also served to give the authorities more control over foreign visitors.

For a long time, foreign trade through Guangzhou ran largely in accordance with the wishes of the Chinese government. Trade was a source of government revenue because it was taxed and the volume of trade increased. Gradually, the number of foreigners coming to Guangzhou to trade had increased. Initially, mainly the British and Dutch East India companies came to China. Similar trading companies from France, Belgium, Denmark and Sweden followed later. And eventually many smaller trading companies, often British or American, also came to Guangzhou. The Chinese authorities increasingly lost their grip on foreigners. This was a problem because some of them smuggled opium, which could be brought ashore unseen in the extensive Pearl River Delta. The trade in opium was banned in China, but outside of opium, there was no great demand for foreign products on the Chinese market. Opium from British India was a luxury product in China that gave status to its users.[3] It was mixed with tobacco and then smoked in a pipe. The smuggling trade in opium was particularly lucrative for British traders and for the British East India Company, which produced it in India.

In Guangzhou in 1839, a senior Chinese official, Lin Zexu, had a large quantity of opium seized from the foreigners and destroyed. To force the merchants to hand over their opium, Lin had forbidden all foreign merchants to leave their factories. He had cut off the supply of water and food. The pressure worked, and soon the merchants were handing over their opium. The blockade of the factories was lifted, and a number of traders who were regarded by the Chinese government as the main opium smugglers were made to promise to leave China and never to return. So far, Lin's anti-drug policy seemed to be a success. However, among the foreigners who had been temporarily imprisoned in the enclave, there were also people who had nothing to do with the opium smuggling. In particular, the representative of the British government who oversaw his country's trade interests in Guangzhou, Charles Elliot, had also been imprisoned. To end the crisis, Elliot had promised British opium smugglers that his government would reimburse the cost of the seized opium. The conflict between China and foreign opium smugglers thus became a conflict between China and Britain.

Dinghai's district administrator Yao Huaixiang knew about the problems in Guangzhou but considered it a local problem with smugglers some 1,200 kilometres away from his city. Yao's main concern was that the foreign traders might try to smuggle their opium into the country through alternative ports such as Dinghai, as this was no longer possible through Guangzhou. But by the time the British fleet entered his city's harbour, the matter had escalated considerably. On 20 February 1840, the British Foreign Secretary, Lord Palmerston, had written a letter to 'the Prime

Minister of China' (which did not exist, as the Emperor personally headed the government). Palmerston was not just another foreign minister from just any European country. His father had prepared him from early childhood for the profession of a diplomat, and for many years he served as foreign secretary at a time when Britain was at the height of its power. Palmerston was also highly regarded personally. A few months before writing his letter to the Chinese government, he had married the sister of the British Prime Minister, Lord Melbourne, the mentor of the young Queen Victoria. Like no other, Palmerston thought he knew what was best for British interests in the world, and he was generally prepared to take great risks to get his way.

In his letter to the 'Prime Minister' of China, Palmerston wrote that the British government had a number of demands in connection with the Guangzhou incident.[4] Firstly, return of the seized opium or, if that was not possible, financial compensation. Secondly, reparation for the offence done to the British Crown by the imprisonment of the British representative and assurances that British government officials would henceforth be treated with due respect. Thirdly, the ceding to Great Britain of one or more islands off the Chinese coast. And, fourthly, the paying off of debts that now bankrupt Chinese trading houses had with British traders. Moreover, Palmerston had decided that China should allow British traders access to more ports than just Guangzhou, but he had not included that in his letter. He also did not mention any specific requirement with regard to the opium trade, but he did advise the Qing government to do something about the inadequate and, in his view, inconsistent enforcement of the Chinese opium laws. If enforcement could not be improved, he suggested, it would be better to legalize the trade in opium.

To force the Chinese government to comply with his demands, Palmerston sent a fleet of warships and ground troops to China along with the letter. This strike force, composed of units from Great Britain and British India, was instructed to blockade the main Chinese ports immediately upon arrival and to occupy 'an appropriate part of Chinese territory' until all demands had been met. An additional requirement was that the costs of this military expedition were to be reimbursed by China. All of this was in Palmerston's letter, which was effectively a declaration of war from Great Britain against the Chinese Empire.

The letter had not yet been handed over to the Chinese government when Yao, the district administrator, visited the British flagship to ask what was going on. The letter was still with Charles Elliot, who around this time tried to hand it over to the Chinese authorities via Xiamen, another port city. However, officials in that city did not accept the letter because they were not authorized to do so. All communication with foreigners from overseas was ordered by the emperor to go through Guangzhou. At Dinghai's harbour, Yao was verbally informed of the situation by the British commander. This commander, James Bremer, in accordance with his instructions, intended to occupy Dinghai in order to carry out the blockade of Chinese seaports from there. Yao suggested to Bremer that it did not make sense for the British navy to attack his city while Britain's problems were related to the situation in Guangzhou. Wouldn't it make more sense for them to attack Guangzhou? Bremer was not impressed by this reasoning and gave the magistrate until the next day to surrender.

When this demand was not met, Bremer gave the order to open fire at half past two on 5 July 1840. According to Mao Haijian, the historian, it took the British just nine minutes to knock out the shore batteries and Chinese warships in the harbour. British ground troops then went ashore and deployed field guns to prepare for storming Dinghai. When they attacked the city the next day, they found that the garrison had fled during the night. Dinghai and the island on which it was located, Zhoushan, were in British hands. On the Chinese side, at least thirteen had been killed, while the British had suffered no losses. The Chinese casualties included the regional military commander, who was injured and later died, and district administrator Yao, who committed suicide.

The battle of Dinghai was not the first exchange of gunfire of the Opium War, as skirmishes between British and Chinese naval units had already broken out at other locations. But Dinghai was the beginning of the systematic British attack on the Chinese empire that Palmerston envisioned. From its new base on Zhoushan, the British navy set up blockades at various points along the Chinese coast. The Opium War had begun.

## China's international position before the war

Since 1820, Aisin Gioro Minning had been the emperor of China. In the seventeenth century, Minning's ancestors had conquered all of China from Manchuria and founded a dynasty they called Great Qing (after *qing*, clear). Since then, all emperors of China came from the Aisin Gioro clan. After seizing power in China under the leadership of the Aisin Gioro, the Manchus merged Manchuria and China into a single empire, with China as the economic and political centre. They also added Mongolia, Taiwan, Tibet and much of Central Asia to the empire of the Great Qing. The China of the Qing dynasty was therefore considerably larger than the China of the Ming dynasty, the predecessor of the Qing.

Han Chinese were by far the largest ethnic group in the Chinese Empire of the Qing dynasty. The Manchus not only ruled over, but also with the Han Chinese. Most of the civil servants and military personnel were Han. At the time of the Qing dynasty, the male part of the Han population had to adopt the traditional hairstyle of the Manchus as a sign of submission. This meant that they had to shave their foreheads and wear the rest of their hair in a braid. Although the Aisin Gioro clan was Manchu, it presented itself as a traditional Chinese imperial dynasty. The Manchus chose the former Ming capital of Beijing (also known as Peking) as the centre of their new empire.

Stability and effective governance have traditionally been deep-rooted political values in the Chinese empire. The Heavenly Mandate played a central role in China's traditional political system. According to that concept, the emperor's task was to maintain social and natural order on earth (*tianxia*, that which is under heaven) on behalf of heaven.[5] Therefore, the emperor of China was also called the Son of Heaven, and the ruling dynasty was called the Heavenly Dynasty. Order was a sign of imperial prowess and therefore of legitimate government. Serious disturbances of order, such as major natural disasters and uprisings, on the other hand, were signals that the emperor had lost his mandate. In such a situation, if someone from outside the dynasty seized power and managed to restore order, he could claim to be the new legitimate ruler and hold the Heavenly Mandate. In this way, a new dynasty could be created.

Chinese emperors are usually not referred to by their own name, but by the name of their reign period. Minning's reign was called *daoguang*, after the Chinese words for 'way' and 'light'. He has therefore become known as the Daoguang Emperor. Although he was not a great strategic thinker or bold innovator, as emperor, he did his best to preserve the empire and the administrative system he had inherited from his predecessors.[6] The Qing dynasty's most intensive foreign relations were those with various neighbouring states in East Asia and Southeast Asia, such as Korea, Vietnam, Ryukyu (now part of Japan), Siam (Thailand) and Burma (Myanmar). These neighbouring countries were considered vassal states by the Qing government. Diplomatically and ceremonially, they generally recognized the Chinese emperor as the most authoritative ruler in a hierarchical system of Asian monarchs. They remained autonomous in a political-administrative sense. What the Qing dynasty expected from these vassal states was that they would recognize the supremacy of the Chinese emperor and would not do anything that could threaten China's security. In return, the Chinese Empire provided legitimacy to the vassal rulers and the ability to trade with China and safeguarded the geopolitical status quo in East and Southeast Asia.

In addition to these vassal states, of which Korea and Vietnam were the most important, there were other states that surrounded the Chinese empire in the first half of the nineteenth century. To the east was Japan, which had no diplomatic relations with China. Japan was once a vassal state of China, but that was many centuries ago. At the end of the sixteenth century, the Japanese warlord Toyotomi Hideyoshi, who had risen to power in Japan after a long period of civil war, had tried to conquer China. To that end, in 1592, a Japanese invasion force crossed the sea into Korea and occupied much of the country. Today it may seem overconfident of Hideyoshi to think he could conquer a country as vast as China, but some three centuries earlier the Mongol leader Kublai Khan had shown that it was possible. From 1279 to 1368, the Mongols ruled China.

But Hideyoshi was less successful than Kublai Khan. In response to the Japanese invasion of Korea, China sent troops to work with the Korean army to drive back the Japanese. After several years of fierce fighting on Korean soil without a clear winner, Hideyoshi died in 1598 and the Japanese troops withdrew from Korea. The outcome of this first Sino-Japanese War was that Korea remained a client state of China. Japan subsequently largely closed itself off from the rest of Asia diplomatically and economically and played no active role in regional geopolitics.

North of the Chinese Empire was the Russian Empire. In the previous centuries, the Russians had extended their dominion further and further east, eventually making most of Siberia and (temporarily) even Alaska part of the tsar's empire. In Siberia, Russia bordered on the empire of the Manchus. By means of the treaties of Nerchinsk (1689) and of Kyakhta (1727), the two empires established their mutual border. Russia was not a relevant geopolitical player in East Asia, but continued to expand its influence in the western part of Central Asia, while the Qing dynasty conquered the eastern part (present-day Xinjiang) in the eighteenth century and added to its empire. Sino-Russian relations remained stable for the time being.

In the meantime, the English East India Company (EIC) ruled large parts of India. This company was a giant trading company with its own army and a mandate to manage British geopolitical interests in Asia. The British government had given the company a monopoly on trade with Asia, and the company maintained diplomatic relations with Asian states on behalf of Britain. From the late eighteenth century, the British government played an increasing role in the administration of India, but formally, India was governed by the EIC until 1858.

Europeans had a colonial presence also in parts of Southeast Asia. On behalf of Great Britain, the EIC administered Singapore as a naval and trading base. The Netherlands was dominant in the Indonesian archipelago, with Batavia (present-day Jakarta) on Java as its most important settlement. Initially, the Dutch East India Company (VOC) had occupied and colonized parts of the archipelago, but in 1796, the Dutch state took over this role. Furthermore, the Philippines was under Spanish colonial rule, with Manila as the administrative centre. Finally, on China's southern coast, there was Macau, a city at the mouth of the Pearl River. Macau was under Portuguese rule but was on Chinese territory and could only exist with the permission and support of the Chinese government. This enclave had existed since Ming times and was tolerated by the Qing dynasty as a way to trade with European merchants. Guangzhou later took over this role, and Macau then became the place where foreign traders stayed outside of the trading season (when they were not allowed to be in Guangzhou).

The most important geopolitical confrontation between Chinese and Western Europeans before the Opium War had taken place in the seventeenth century. At the time, the Dutch East India Company was a powerful military, diplomatic and economic player in the Indian Ocean and Western Pacific region. The VOC, like the EIC a gigantic trading company with a geopolitical mandate, controlled Taiwan (which was not yet part of the Chinese empire at that time) for several decades and carried out military attacks on Chinese coastal areas at various times during the seventeenth century. Those attacks were not directed against the Ming or Qing, but against Portuguese Macau and the forces of Zheng Chenggong (also known as Koxinga), a Chinese warlord who was engaged in a war against the newly established Qing dynasty. However, the VOC never succeeded in conquering Macau and was driven out of Taiwan in 1661 by Koxinga, who died shortly afterwards. The Dutch subsequently gave military support to the Qing government in its fight against Koxinga's successors, but this temporary alliance did not lead to lasting cooperation between China and the VOC. In 1683, without decisive support from the VOC, Taiwan was conquered and annexed by the Qing Empire. This ended the power of Koxinga's successors and immediately wiped out the possibility of the VOC regaining control of the island. The short period of Dutch geopolitical relevance to China was over.

From the late seventeenth century, relations between the Qing Empire and Western Europe were limited and focused entirely on trade. Sometimes the Qing emperor authorized the European trading companies to send envoys to the capital Beijing. The procedure followed was the same as for tribute missions from the Asian client states. As a required part of the ceremonial formalities surrounding a tribute mission, when the foreign envoys met the emperor, they performed the *kowtow*. This involved getting on both knees from a standing position several times and touching the ground with one's forehead. The *kowtow* was a traditional gesture to show respect and submission. In other words, the Qing dynasty also treated the Western European countries, on behalf of which the companies acted, as vassal states. The Western European states could communicate with the Qing government only if they accepted this hierarchy in the relationship. The British in particular had great difficulty with this condition.

## The new world order

In the sphere of national security, the Qing emperors focused their attention exclusively on internal stability and border conflicts with neighbouring peoples. What happened elsewhere in the world was regarded by the Qing as irrelevant. The empire had existed for so long, and was so vast and so limited in its dependence on the outside world, that the Chinese government ignored two developments that would be fundamental to China's future.

One development that the Qing dynasty missed was the accelerating process of globalization, that is, the increasing integration between different parts of the world in terms of transportation and trade. Long before the establishment of the Qing dynasty, China was part of an international trading system. Caravan routes and coastal trade had created a trade network that spanned large parts of Asia, Europe and Africa. The origins of this network, the famous Silk Road, go back thousands of years. A new phase in the globalization process started around the sixteenth century when Western European countries set up direct shipping links between all continents. As a result of the European colonization of parts of North and South America, a global trading system emerged for the first time. In the old system, the goods sometimes travelled great distances, but the traders usually stayed in their own region. In the new system, European traders visited all parts of the world that could be reached by water. The importance of caravan routes over land declined, and the main trade routes now ran over the sea.

Trade between China and Europe was also no longer based on the old Silk Road, but was now in the hands of the Western European trading companies, with the EIC and the VOC leading the way. Chinese producers and traders benefitted from the emergence of direct shipping links by exporting porcelain and tea for sale in Europe. China itself imported large quantities of silver from the Spanish colonies in Central and South America. Thus, the Chinese economy became an essential link in the new global economy. However, the Chinese government was not interested in an active role at the international level. In addition, subjects of the Chinese Empire were forbidden to settle abroad. Despite that ban, Chinese merchants played a major role in East and Southeast Asian trade. But the supply of silver to Asia and the sale of Chinese products in Europe was dominated by Europeans.

The emergence of a global trading system in which Western European countries and traders played a central role led to a second development that completely eluded the Qing government. That was the birth of global geopolitics. For the first time, states engaged in power politics that involved conditions in Europe, Asia, Africa, the Pacific, and North and South America. The protagonists were Western European states that colonized other parts of the world, although they were not yet strong enough to dominate East Asian countries such as Japan and China. In the nineteenth century, however, a new category of great powers emerged: modern industrialized states with colonial ambitions. In the second half of the century, they would dominate global geopolitics. At the time of the Opium War, Great Britain was the first and so far only state in this new category. France, Germany, the United States, Japan and Russia would follow.

When Lord Palmerston learned in 1839 that the Chinese authorities in Guangzhou had temporarily trapped British traders in their factories to force them to surrender their opium, he saw this incident as an opportunity to start a war against China to solve some long-standing problems. Because China exported tea and porcelain to Britain on a large scale but imported few British products, the trade balance on the British side was strongly negative. However, there was a great demand for opium from British India in China. It was clear that unrestricted export of Indian opium to the Chinese market was in the British interest.[7] Unfortunately for Britain, opium was banned in China, and Palmerston did not want to go as far as explicitly demand the legalization of the opium trade in China, given the fierce criticism of the opium trade from the opposition in the British Parliament. What he saw now was an opportunity to make it easier for British merchants to get their wares into the Chinese market, be it opium or something else.

Apparently Palmerston, who had been Secretary at War earlier in his career, thought that a strike force of a few dozen warships, a similar number of transport ships and a few thousand ground troops was enough to defeat China. As it turned out, he was right. But still: the Qing empire had about 430 million inhabitants, or one third of the world's population. At the time, China's economy was the largest in the world, accounting for about a third of the global economy. In addition, Palmerston's estimates had often turned out to be risky and not always correct. In 1839, a British and British Indian force had invaded Afghanistan. Without much effort they took the capital Kabul and installed a new ruler there. After some time, however, it became apparent that it was not possible to stabilize Afghanistan and keep it permanently under control. A guerrilla war ensued, and in early 1842 the British garrison in Kabul decided to withdraw from the country, taking with them a large group of British, Indian and pro-British Afghan civilians. The evacuation became one of the greatest disasters in British military history. By far the largest part of the British garrison of 4,500 military personnel plus the 12,000 civilians who were evacuated were killed by Afghan fighters on their way back to British India. Only one British officer and a handful of British Indian soldiers reached India.

But at the time of the Opium War, the British invasion of Afghanistan still seemed a success, and British self-confidence was high. In 1840, Britain was geopolitically in a very strong position. In Continental Europe, the British had helped create a regional balance of power by which Russia, Prussia, Austria and France guarded European stability and their own interests. In North America, territory was divided between the United States and British Canada. In Latin America and in parts of the Middle East and Africa, Britain was very influential. India was largely a British colony; Australia was also a colony. No other country came close to the power of Great Britain.

# Initial response

After the British attack on Dinghai, it took some time for the Qing government to realize that it was at war with Britain. It was not until 20 July 1840, two weeks after the fall of Dinghai, that the emperor received word that the city had been taken over by British troops.[8] This long intervening time was a result of the great distance between Dinghai and the capital Beijing and the limited speed of courier services. The emperor now knew that China was being attacked by distant Britain, but he did not yet know why. On 17 August, Charles Elliot, who had meanwhile arrived at Tianjin off the coast of northern China, finally succeeded in finding a Chinese official who was willing to receive Palmerston's letter and forward it to the emperor. On 19 August 1840, the Emperor of China read what Palmerston had written six months earlier. Unfortunately, the Chinese translation of the letter did not accurately reflect what Palmerston had meant by it. As a result, the emperor had the impression that the British had come just to complain about the incident in Guangzhou, a situation that appeared manageable.

The emperor's initial reaction was that he was prepared to accommodate the British. Order in the empire had to be restored and the easiest way seemed to be to punish Lin Zexu, the senior official who had seized the opium in Guangzhou, as a gesture that the British complaint was being taken seriously. The British warships would then surely leave and peace would return. However, Palmerston was not at all interested in a punishment for Lin, nor was he willing to negotiate. His strategy focused on blocking China's seaports to force China to accept his demands. As it turned out, the Chinese government hardly noticed that there was a blockade. China's economy was based on agriculture and domestic trade; foreign trade did not play a major role.

After the occupation of Dinghai and the imposition of the blockades, not much happened for a while due to these misunderstandings. Palmerston grew impatient and replaced Charles Elliot, who had extensive experience in China but who, in Palmerston's view, was lagging too much, with the more energetic Henry Pottinger. At the age of twenty, the latter had become famous in Britain for an adventurous exploration he had made alone through Balochistan (now part of Pakistan) and Persia (now Iran). Dressed as a Muslim pilgrim, Pottinger had survived his journey through deserts and hostile territories and then made a career in the colonial administration of British India.

Pottinger shifted British strategy from a trade blockade to attacking and capturing Chinese cities. All along the southern coast of China and deep inland via the Yangtze River, the British conquered one city after another, including Guangzhou, Xiamen and Shanghai. The island of Hong Kong was also occupied. The pattern was always the same: with a combination of shelling from their ships and landings of ground troops, the British forces quickly and crushingly defeated the Chinese defences. The army of the Qing Empire was unable to cope with the modern technology and advanced level of organization of the British army. Hundreds of people were killed on the Chinese side in these battles, while the British usually suffered only a few fatalities.

When the former Chinese capital of Nanjing (then known as Nanking) was also threatened to be attacked, the Qing empire gave up its resistance. In 1842, on a British warship on the Yangtze, both sides signed the Treaty of Nanjing, which included all of Palmerston's demands. The Qing dynasty gave in because it was clear that the British attacks could not be stopped by fighting back or negotiating. Sooner or later the British would also reach the cities in the north and possibly even occupy the capital Beijing. Order had to be restored to the realm, and that could only be done by accepting

Palmerston's demands. Moreover, the emperor and his top officials saw only very limited significance in Palmerston's demands. They thought they were giving away much less than they actually were. The cunning Pottinger realized this and, after peace had already been made, succeeded in getting China to sign an 'additional' treaty in 1843 that went well beyond what Palmerston had envisioned in terms of British trade and military privileges in China.

The British government had every reason to be pleased. From then on, British traders had much wider access to the Chinese market, and Hong Kong became a British colony with Pottinger as its first governor. Britain's costs of the war were reimbursed by China. To the Qing Empire, the damage was great and included:

- Destroyed coastal defences and naval vessels, bombed cities and an unknown number of Chinese military and civilian deaths.
- High costs of warfare, including moving troops between provinces and building forts along the coast and the obligation to pay all the costs of the war on the British side.
- The loss of Hong Kong Island, which is close to Guangzhou and Macau.
- Serious undermining of the legitimacy of the Qing dynasty, which proved unable to prevent war or defend the empire.
- Loss of sovereignty because the British could now live in various coastal cities, British subjects being untouchable by Chinese law, the British navy having the right to station warships in several ports and restrictions on China's ability to set its own import tariffs. The old system by which the Chinese government had kept a grip on foreigners in Guangzhou was no longer there.

The last two components in particular would prove to have a major impact in the long term. In addition, Pottinger had opened the door to even more future problems for China. He had managed to arrange that if the Qing Empire gave rights to other foreign powers for any reason in the future, Great Britain would automatically receive these rights as well. This is called the 'most favoured nation' principle.

Immediately after the Opium War, the United States and France demanded similar treaties from China under the threat of violence. The Qing government agreed. These two countries were also guaranteed that they automatically received all the rights that any other country received from China.

The work of the Opium War expert Mao Haijian shows that two things in particular went wrong for the Qing dynasty. The most fundamental problem was that the Chinese self-image did not match reality. The Qing Empire viewed itself as the centre of the world and its emperor as universal ruler. Britain was not seen as the dynamic and aggressive new world power that it was, but as a rebellious little country on the far periphery of the Chinese world order. The emperor and his top officials treated the Opium War as a domestic law enforcement problem. They did not delve into the motives and power of the British, and even after the end of the war, they did not see the full extent of what had happened.

Although the Qing Empire was defeated militarily, the Chinese negotiators in 1842 and 1843 gave away much more than was strictly necessary because they did not fully understand what was at stake. In the years that followed, the Qing government viewed the Opium War as an unfortunate incident that had better be forgotten as soon as possible. Convinced that China was still the centre of the world, and that sooner or later this was an inescapable insight for the rest of the world as well, no attempt was made to learn from what had happened. The emperor and his officials went about their business.

Their outdated worldview was the cause of the second major problem. The Qing Empire did not have the resources to survive in the new world order, in which all regions were economically linked and great powers aggressively intervened in weaker countries to defend their interests. What was lacking in China was first and foremost a modern army capable of defending its borders against the British attack. A modern army could only be built on the basis of advanced technology and industry. Both were absent from Qing dynasty China. The Qing Empire also had no knowledge of the outside world and no resources to act actively outside its own region. The government had no diplomatic missions abroad, no foreign intelligence and no powerful navy with which to take the fight to Britain itself or its colonial territories in Asia, or at least off the Chinese coast.

All this, in combination with domestic processes such as rapid population growth, rebellions and the decreasing effectiveness of Qing rule, contributed to the disasters that would befall China in the century following the Opium War. Incidentally, the Chinese population, compared to the administrative elite, was even less aware of what was going on. The vast majority of the Chinese lived in the countryside and had no contact with the rest of the gigantic empire apart from the nearest villages and towns. Except for the cities directly affected by the British attacks, and temporarily for the emperor and a number of senior officials and military personnel, the war did not make a great impression on China. The sense of national unity and the realization that China was due for a 'rejuvenation', which Xi Jinping spoke of in his museum speech, were completely absent in China's initial response to the Opium War. And yet this was the beginning of a process that would lead to China's emergence as a global power.

FIGURE 1 *Aisin Gioro Minning, the Daoguang Emperor (photo by Pictures from History/Universal Images Group via Getty Images).*

FIGURE 2  *Lord Viscount Palmerston, from* The Illustrated London News, *1850 (photo by The Print Collector/Heritage Images via Getty Images).*

FIGURE 3 *Signing of the Treaty of Nanjing on 29 August 1842, aboard HMS Cornwallis anchored at Nanjing, to mark the end of the First Opium War, by John Platt, 1846* (photo by Pictures from History/Universal Images Group via Getty Images).

# 2

# New realities (1842–1912)

In early October 1896, a political activist from China arrived in London. His name was Sun Yat-sen. He would play an important role in his country's history, but in 1896, he was still only a marginal figure. Sun was born in South China, in a village not far from the Portuguese colony of Macau. As a teenager, he had lived with an older brother in Hawaii for a few years to attend school and then studied medicine at the University of Hong Kong. As a result of this background, he spoke good English and was internationally oriented. Sun had even converted to Christianity. He had also become increasingly interested in Chinese politics, and he wanted to contribute to the modernization of China's administration. However, he had no chance of joining the proud civil service that had been the backbone of the Chinese empire for thousands of years. Whoever wanted to become a civil servant in China had to study the classic Confucian texts for many years and pass a tough examination system. The sage Confucius, who lived around 500 BCE, laid the conceptual foundation for what later became the central government civil service. A modern Western education like Sun's was of no value in the eyes of the imperial officials.

After a failed attempt to contribute to modernization as an advisor to the government, Sun took a different tack.[1] He was now convinced that the system could not be changed from within. He founded the Society for the Revival of China (in Chinese *Xingzhonghui*), with the aim of overthrowing the Qing dynasty. In 1895, Sun's organization attempted an armed uprising in the city of Guangzhou, but that ended in failure. Many members of the society were arrested by the government, yet Sun was able to flee abroad. After a long journey through Macau, Hong Kong, Japan, Hawaii and the United States, he ended up in London at the age of twenty-nine. On the way, he had his Manchu queue cut off and started wearing Western clothes.

In the first few days after his arrival in London, Sun Yat-sen often visited his former medical school teacher from Hong Kong, the Scottish physician James Cantlie, and his wife. According to Sun, who later wrote a book about his time in London, during one of those visits he learned that the Chinese legation (a diplomatic office similar to what today is called an embassy) was in the same part of the city. Cantlie's wife especially warned Sun to stay away from the Chinese legation building. 'Don't you go near it; they'll catch you and ship you off to China,' she said. All three laughed heartily at this thought.

A few days later, Sun was on his way to church when he was accosted on the street by some compatriots. Before he realized what was happening, he was pushed into a building. Once inside, he saw that he was in the Chinese legation. At least that was how Sun later described it in his book. According to the Chinese government, Sun had come to the place on his own accord. Whatever the way he got there, he was not allowed to leave the legation. Sun had travelled halfway around the world and had now fallen into the hands of the Chinese government.

While imprisoned in the legation, he learned that he would be smuggled out of the country and taken back to China by ship. There he would be interrogated and, as the leader of a banned organization, probably executed. However, Sun Yat-sen managed to convince one of his guards, an Englishman who worked at the legation, to help him. Through the guard, Sun was able to send a note about his condition to James Cantlie. The latter immediately took action. He went to the police and the Foreign Office. When that did not immediately produce results, he approached the media, after which the story was widely reported in the British newspapers. The Chinese legation was now under police surveillance and surrounded by journalists. It was no longer possible for the legation staff to get Sun out of the country unnoticed. Under intense political and public pressure, they finally released Sun Yat-sen after several weeks of imprisonment. Due to the great media attention for his kidnapping, he had become famous overnight, especially in England and, to a lesser extent, also internationally. The fame served him well. Sun Yat-sen remained in England for a while and then travelled on to other countries, making new plans for a revolution in his homeland.

The fact that the Qing dynasty almost succeeded in eliminating a political opponent who had fled to distant Europe shows that an important change had taken place since the Opium War. While China used to be mostly inward-looking, it was now more active towards the outside world. The Qing government had established a legation not only in London, but also in cities such as Paris, Washington, Tokyo, Moscow and Berlin. For the first time, permanent representatives of the Chinese government were present abroad to look after the interests of their country. They could observe what was happening in the world and report on it to the government in Beijing. However, it took another Opium War before this turnaround came about.

## The Second Opium War

As noted in the previous chapter, the Qing government had learned little from its defeat by Britain. It regarded the Opium War as a one-off event that had better be forgotten as soon as possible. The Chinese empire was vast and ancient, and tensions with the British seemed only a temporary and limited problem. But Britain was not satisfied with the way things turned out after the Opium War. Unlike China, the British government regarded foreign trade as very important. Trade barriers to non-opium imports continued to exist, and especially in Guangzhou, the Chinese government made it difficult for foreigners to settle in the city. In 1856, Lord Palmerston, now Prime Minister of Great Britain, took advantage of a minor incident to start a new war against China. A new war meant a new chance to impose demands on China. And since the bill for the war would once again be presented to the Chinese government, the threshold to attack China once more was low.

The incident revolved around the *Arrow*, a small British-flagged vessel registered in Hong Kong. The Qing government was convinced that it was being used by Chinese pirates to attack other ships. The Qing authorities boarded the ship and arrested the Chinese crew. The British acting consul in Guangzhou, Harry Parkes, demanded the release of the crew, an apology and a promise from the regional governor general that this would never happen again. It didn't matter to Parkes whether or not the crew members actually were pirates. What mattered to him was that China should respect the principle that ships flying the British flag were untouchable by the Chinese government.

Parkes knew China well. Having lost his parents at a young age, he had moved to Macau in 1841, at the age of thirteen, to live with an aunt and uncle. At that time, the First Opium War was underway. Parkes had the opportunity to join Henry Pottinger's entourage as an assistant as Pottinger led the raids on Chinese ports. The young Parkes was thus present at the signing of the treaty of Nanjing, which ended the First Opium War. His experience in China convinced him that strong action was the only way to get something done from the Chinese government.[2] In practice, this meant setting hard requirements, threatening military intervention and actually taking armed action if not all requirements were met. In 1856, in the incident of the arrested ship's crew, this is exactly what Parkes did. British pressure prompted the regional governor general, Ye Mingchen, to release the crew. However, Governor General Ye refused to apologize. Dissatisfied that Ye did not do everything he demanded, Parkes advised the British Navy to shell the city of Guangzhou, which they did.

In London, Palmerston learned of the heightened tensions in Guangzhou. He thought this was a good reason to send another attack fleet to China. If firm action was not taken the safety of all British citizens in China would be at risk, was how he explained his decision in the British Parliament. The idea was that if the Chinese government showed no respect for the British flag and nationality, there was a danger that local officials would do nothing to protect British lives in anti-foreign incidents. Because British companies and individuals now settled in several places in China, it became increasingly difficult for the British navy to provide everyone with protection. But

Palmerston's main reason for starting another war was that he wanted better access to the Chinese market for British products. This time it was not opium, which was still being smuggled into the country on a large scale from India, but industrial products from Great Britain.

A difference from the First Opium War was that this time Palmerston coordinated with other great powers. Russia and the United States supported the British decision to attack China again. After all, they would also benefit from better access to the Chinese market and more privileges for foreigners in the country. France went one step further and also sent troops to China. The French government wanted to play a bigger role in China, alongside its old rival Britain. And France had its own reason to declare war on China, namely the execution of Auguste Chapdelaine. This French missionary had gone into the interior of China to convert people to Christianity, although it was illegal according to Chinese law. A local magistrate arrested him and subsequently had him put to death because Chapdelaine allegedly incited the local population to rebellion.

A combined British and French force attacked the Qing Empire in late 1857. First Guangzhou was taken. The recalcitrant governor general Ye, who had refused to apologize, was captured under Parkes's personal supervision and taken to British India. The British probably wanted to set an example for Chinese administrators in other coastal regions: anyone who harms British interests as a senior Qing official runs the risk of being caught personally. Ye was imprisoned in a fort near Kolkata (then known as Calcutta), where he died of illness a year later.

Unlike during the First Opium War, the Europeans did not direct their attack on the southern Chinese coast and the Yangtze, but on northern China. The northern port city of Tianjin was captured, and from there the foreigners advanced on Beijing. Once again, the Chinese coastal defences proved unable to withstand European military power. But an important factor this time around was that the Qing dynasty already had its hands full with several major uprisings in the empire, the largest of which was the Taiping Rebellion.

Years earlier, a Chinese student in Guangzhou named Hong Xiuquan had been given some information about Christianity from an American missionary. Based on visions he experienced, Hong then became convinced that he was Jesus's younger brother. He founded a religious movement inspired by Christianity. The movement caught on in southern China and quickly grew in size, gaining followers in the tens of thousands. When the Qing government tried to suppress the movement, Hong went into open rebellion. He proclaimed the Heavenly Kingdom of the Taiping (meaning 'Great Peace') and ordered his followers to conquer all of China and drive out the Manchus. Surprisingly quickly, the Taiping succeeded in occupying a large part of Chinese territory. In doing so, many Han Chinese joined the rebel army. The Taiping Rebellion degenerated into a civil war of staggering intensity and scope. Only after Hong Xiuquan died in 1864 did the Qing dynasty succeed in defeating the Taiping. The domestic strife caused by the Taiping Rebellion claimed the lives of at least 20 million people, possibly several times that number.

When British and French troops reached Beijing in 1860, the Taiping Rebellion and several other uprisings were still in full swing in other parts of China. The Imperial army that was supposed to defend the capital was decisively defeated by the Europeans. The Xianfeng Emperor, the son of the now deceased Daoguang Emperor, fled to a palace far outside the capital. The foreign troops left the city alone but did plunder the imperial Summer Palace, a large domain with several gardens and many beautiful buildings just outside Beijing, where the emperor liked to stay. Many imperial possessions were taken by the British and French soldiers. A large number of Chinese art treasures that are now in foreign museums and private collections originate from the Summer Palace. After the palace complex was looted, the British commander, Lord Elgin, ordered to burn down the buildings of the Summer Palace.[3] He did this as a show of force, to show that the British and their French allies could target the personal interests of the Chinese emperor, but also as a retaliatory measure. During the war, China had seriously mistreated a group of approximately thirty European and Indian prisoners. Harry Parkes, who had accompanied the attack force from Guangzhou, was also part of this group that had fallen into the hands of Chinese troops near Tianjin. However, due to his relatively high position, he was treated less badly and released earlier than the other prisoners. Many of them did not survive captivity.

As a result of the Second Opium War, the Qing government was forced to sign new treaties with Britain and France. The number of cities where Europeans were allowed to trade and settle was expanded considerably. For example, Tianjin and various cities along the Yangtze were also opened up. The territory of the British colony of Hong Kong was enlarged: Great Britain now also obtained the Kowloon Peninsula opposite the island of Hong Kong. Catholic and Protestant missionaries were given the right to travel inland in China to spread the Christian faith. Legations were opened in Beijing so that the great powers could communicate directly with the central government of China through their envoys. Through the principle of most favoured nation, the United States and Russia also received all these rights.

## Hidden resistance

After the two Opium Wars, Britain was the strongest military power in East Asia. The British navy could shell coastal and riverside cities and land troops whenever it deemed necessary, and China had proved incapable of protecting its own capital. However, the British government had no intention of placing China under British rule. The colonization of India, initially by the East India

Company and later by the British state, was a costly undertaking, as it required the permanent establishment of troops and colonial administrators. A major revolt of British-Indian soldiers in 1857 had also shown that the foundations under British rule were less solid than had been thought. The government in London was not in the mood to take on additional major colonial responsibilities. And they weren't necessary. China had a well-developed central government headed by the emperor. It was easier and cheaper if China continued to govern itself, as long as it was done in accordance with British interests. In China, British policy therefore focused on limiting China's sovereignty for market access, but at the same time, the Qing dynasty had to be strong enough to continue to govern the country. The British government had therefore even given some military support to the Qing dynasty in its fight against the Taiping.

More and more European countries, including smaller colonial powers such as Spain, Austria-Hungary, the Netherlands and Belgium as well as new states such as Germany and Italy, concluded treaties with China. These countries also received the rights that China had previously given to Britain and others. Whenever a country succeeded in obtaining a new privilege through negotiations or military threats, this right automatically also applied to all other powers that had a treaty with China. The treaties between China and the major and minor powers were known as the 'unequal treaties'. The problem for the Chinese government was that they undermined its legitimacy and the country's sovereignty, that the rights in the treaties were often not reciprocal and that China did not sign them voluntarily.[4] Not only China, but also other countries, such as Siam and Japan, were forced by the great powers to conclude such treaties.

The number of Western traders and companies in China increased. Hong Kong, Shanghai and Tianjin were particularly popular as locations for foreign companies. Hong Kong, as a British colony, was open and safe for foreigners. It quickly became a hub for trade between South China and the rest of the world. Shanghai is close to where the Yangtze flows into the sea. That river, the longest in China, runs east from the Himalayas and divides China into northern and southern halves. As China's foreign trade grew, Shanghai became the main logistics hub for Central and Eastern China. Tianjin, located on the coast not far from Beijing, became the international trade centre for northern China. In the cities where foreign companies settled, new neighbourhoods were created, where more and more foreigners came to live. They were protected by foreign warships and marines and were not subject to China's legal authority. This clashed with the Chinese worldview, in which the emperor was the ruler of all people on earth. The Chinese government therefore wanted to limit the foreign presence as much as possible and looked for ways to do so without ending up in armed conflict again.

A pioneer in this field was Liu Yunke, who was governor general of the coastal provinces of Fujian and Zhejiang.[5] He was responsible for Fuzhou, one of the port cities where foreigners were allowed to live and trade. Shortly after the First Opium War, Liu made it as difficult as possible for foreigners to trade in Fuzhou. But he did so in such a way that the British and other foreigners had no concrete reason to intervene militarily. Behind the scenes, he gave instructions to Chinese traders to do business with foreigners only sparingly. He also set up checkpoints outside the city, out of sight of foreigners, to block the supply of tea for export. This approach worked exactly as Liu intended. Under his rule, foreign trade in Fuzhou failed to take off, while it was unclear to the British what exactly caused this. Gradually, and especially after the Second Opium War, more Chinese officials adopted a similar policy of invisible obstruction. The aim was to limit foreign influence without risking another military defeat.

Initially, the Qing government saw only two possible ways to deal with the troublesome Westerners. The same two that the Empire always applied to domestic insurgents and foreign aggressors: fight them by military means or give them what they wanted. Which of the two was used depended on how strong the government was and what worked best. The goal was the same: to restore order in a way that strengthened the state, and thereby the legitimacy of the dynasty. Liu's policies marked the beginning of a third way in relations with the Western powers. In public he seemed to accept the presence of the Westerners, but in reality he was working against them. Officials such as Liu who took this approach ran the risk that Westerners would still see reason for military action, such as shelling by foreign warships. On the other hand, they also risked being seen as traitors by their Chinese colleagues. Public acceptance of the unequal treaties was not consistent with upholding the doctrine of the emperor's universal rule.

## Participating in the international system

New developments led more and more officials in the Qing government to recognize that reducing foreign influence was a matter of the long term and required China itself to become more active in the outside world. An important new development was the large-scale migration of Chinese people abroad. Officially, it was forbidden to leave China. But in practice, there had been a lot of trade from China to Southeast Asia for centuries. This had already led to the emergence of overseas Chinese communities in places such as Batavia and Manila. But after the First Opium War, it became much easier for Chinese to travel abroad. Western companies specialized in recruiting Chinese contract workers settled in the opened ports. The latter typically entered into an agreement to work abroad for a period of about five years. The recruitment agencies advanced the travel costs and arranged the transport. Western ships transported these contract labourers in large numbers to their overseas destinations. During this period, slavery was abolished in the European colonies and in countries such as the United

States. As a result, there was a great demand for labour. The supply of unskilled Chinese workers filled this need.

Hundreds of thousands of Chinese workers ended up on plantations and in mines in places such as the British and Dutch colonies in Southeast Asia, Cuba, Peru, Surinam and Australia. In the United States, many Chinese went to work as railroad workers, and Chinatowns sprang up in San Francisco and New York. A large proportion of these migrant workers went back to China after the contract expired, but many others continued to live abroad. In addition to the contract workers, there were also many Chinese who went abroad on their own initiative to look for work or to start their own small business. Sun Yat-sen's older brother was such a person, having successfully set up his own business in Hawaii.

Before the Opium Wars, the Chinese government paid little attention to Chinese living abroad. But now there were reasons to keep track of what these people were doing. The overseas Chinese made an increasingly important contribution to the Chinese economy by sending home money they earned abroad. In addition, migrant workers were often treated badly. Work on plantations and mines was hard, and many Chinese workers were exploited by their employers. In some places, such as the United States, they were seen as unwanted competitors because they were willing to work for lower wages. Stories of mistreatment and discrimination abroad reached China, leading to popular expectations that the Qing government would take steps to protect Chinese people abroad. Not only did the government have to uphold the image of the emperor as the universal ruler, but many Chinese living in the coastal areas saw that Western countries were very active in protecting their own citizens in China. Finally, there was also the concern of the Chinese government that some Chinese abroad were opponents of the Qing dynasty. People like Sun Yat-sen, who had fled the country, could make plans abroad to spark an uprising in China one day.

It became increasingly clear to the Chinese government that it was necessary to open legations (for official communication with foreign governments) and consulates (for contact with its own nationals) abroad. In 1876, China's first legation was therefore opened in London. Soon official representations were also established in other capitals of influential countries and in places with Chinese overseas communities. The driving force behind this process was Li Hongzhang. This top official had made a career as a strategist during the civil war with the Taiping. Although China had no formal foreign minister, in practice he served in that role from 1870 until his death in 1901. Li was a classically trained Confucian official who was open to innovation to make China stronger. He was prepared to go much further than many of his colleagues. At the same time, he favoured gradualism and, where possible, preserving existing traditions. He saw nothing in alternative approaches outside the traditional system. It was Li who rejected the young Sun Yat-sen's offer to become a government adviser, after which Sun would become a revolutionary.

Like Liu Yunke, Li Hongzhang realized that China was weak militarily and looked for alternative ways to reduce foreign influence in China. The country that had acted from a position of strength for so long now had to learn to become proficient in the defensive strategies of a weak country. The first reaction of pride and strong resistance had not worked; now the time had come for shrewdness and ingenuity: 'After the lions came the foxes,' as the German historian Jürgen Osterhammel put it.[6] But even though they were both foxes, Li Hongzhang went a big step further than Liu Yunke. While Liu openly accepted the system imposed by the Westerners but secretly sabotaged it, Li saw opportunities to use that same system to China's advantage. Liu tried to resist on a local level and immediately. Li looked at the long term.

In his view, restoring China's strength required a longer path, in which knowledge of the outside world and the use of modern diplomatic instruments played an important role. Li was always willing to talk to the foreigners, which meant that they were less likely to have a reason for military intervention. This was important as there were more and more local officials who applied the strategy of covert resistance. As a result, foreign diplomats in Beijing repeatedly complained about difficult access to the Chinese market, despite the treaties they had concluded with China. Under Li Hongzhang's leadership, diplomacy became a means for China to make the great powers feel they were about to make progress when, in fact, it often was a way to play for time. But Li had to act with caution, not just towards the great powers who were always ready to send their gunboats into action if talks failed. Modern diplomatic relations, in which legations played a central role, were based on the principle that countries are formally equal. That principle deviated from the Chinese view that the Qing empire was fundamentally different from, and more important than, all other states. That is why the opposition within the Chinese government to this innovative trend was still very strong for the time being.

## Maritime customs

Some administrative innovations were initiated not by the Chinese government, but by the great powers. Chief among these was the establishment in 1854 of the Imperial Maritime Customs Service. This was mainly a British project, aimed at levying import duties on foreign goods in Shanghai and other ports. Britain as a great trading nation had an interest in China's customs policy being consistent and not corrupt. The customs service was not integrated into the Qing bureaucracy, as it did not fit in at all, but was set up according to a Western model and functioned largely autonomously. Although the organization formally came under the Qing government, there were no Chinese or Manchus in leadership positions. The management was largely British, but many other Western nationalities were also represented. The customs service grew into an extensive organization that formed the basis for a modern administrative apparatus within the traditional Qing dynasty.

More than anyone else, the Northern Irishman Robert Hart was responsible for the important role that this organization played in the relationship between China and the Western powers. At the age of nineteen he had gone to China to work in the British consular service. For a time he worked in Guangzhou under Harry Parkes. When a local customs branch was set up in Guangzhou, Hart resigned as a British civil servant to work for the customs service. He quickly made his career, and in 1863, he was appointed head of the service. He would hold this position for 48 years. Under his leadership, the Imperial Maritime Customs Service grew into an organization with tens of thousands of employees with offices in all parts of China. It not only collected import duties, but also modernized ports and waterways, combatted smuggling and set up a postal service.

Robert Hart became very influential, acting as a bridge between the traditional imperial bureaucracy and the modern world order. He advised the Qing government on administrative modernization and strategic issues. Hart believed his work served both China's and Great Britain's interests, and in crisis situations he often acted as a mediator between the two countries. He also played an important financial role. As China's foreign trade grew rapidly and the customs service functioned highly efficiently, the amount of money it collected at the ports also grew fast. Customs became responsible for a significant portion of the central government's revenue. Hart's customs service symbolized both unwanted foreign influence in China and its growing dependence on the global economy.

## The Boxer crisis and new geopolitical relations

As time went by, China grew weaker instead of stronger. Acts of covert resistance to foreign influence and the establishing of legations abroad did not change that process. In 1884 another war broke out, this time between France and China, over the northern part of Vietnam. France won and two thousand years of Chinese political influence in Vietnam came to an end. Ten years later, war with Japan ensued. Like three hundred years earlier in Hideyoshi's time, the battle with Japan was over Korea. The Chinese defeat against France was not a big surprise, because France was one of the main European powers. But the outcome of the Second Sino-Japanese War (1894–5) came as a total surprise to many. China was crushingly defeated by Japan. The Qing Empire had now lost its two main vassal states, Vietnam and Korea. But even worse was that not only were the Western powers clearly stronger militarily, but even neighbouring Japan. China's reputation as the region's leading power was destroyed.

Japan had largely kept its borders closed since the seventeenth century, but had seen what had happened to China in the Opium Wars. Rather than also risk such military defeats by opposing the Western powers, the country had chosen to radically change course. The Westerners were given access to Japanese ports and rights similar to those they had in China. At the same time, Japan embarked on a process of rapid political and economic modernization, importing Western technology and expertise on a large scale.

China had also started importing military and other technology from the West after the Second Opium War. Li Hongzhang was involved in the establishment of several modern enterprises based on Western technology. That was part of his long-term approach to making China strong. The most famous of these new companies was a shipping company: the China Merchants Steam Navigation Company, founded in 1872. The companies that Li founded, including arms factories, shipyards, textile factories, a mining company and a telegraph company, had a commercial objective but were under government supervision. This combination was called *guandu shangban* ('commercial management with government supervision'). The concept was not invented by Li Hongzhang, but he was the first to use it as a tool to reduce foreign influence.[7] The aim was to transfer the modernizing function that foreign companies had in the Chinese economy to Chinese companies that were indirectly controlled by the state. For example, China Merchants was designed to restrict through competition the space foreign companies had to move in China's coastal waters and, especially, on China's rivers. According to the unequal treaties, the Qing government could not prohibit foreign shipping in Chinese waters.

The innovations that Li Hongzhang and several other senior officials were striving for focused on preserving the existing administrative and social relations. The government was increasingly open to modern technology and diplomacy, but the Qing dynasty was unwilling to reform politically. The Japanese government adopted a very different strategy. It aimed at acceptance by the great powers as one of their own. Japan reformed its entire political and economic system. Following the example of the West, the government stimulated industrialization and the emergence of large private companies. The aggressive imperialism of the Europeans was also copied. Indeed, by defeating China and forcing unequal treaties on the Qing Empire, Japan won the recognition of the Western countries as a new great power.

Japan quickly turned from a victim of modern imperialism to an enthusiastic participant. Not only did Korea now come under Japanese political influence, but China also had to cede the island of Taiwan to Japan. It seemed that China might soon be completely partitioned between the great powers. For decades, Britain had kept the competition between them in check, and had ensured that the Chinese market was equally accessible to all. But the rise of new powers like Japan, Germany and the United States meant that the British lost their leading role in China. After the Japanese annexation of Taiwan, other countries came forward with demands for exclusive military bases and spheres of influence in different parts of China. The fact that the British, who did not want colonial possessions but market access, also joined in was a sign that the British geopolitical leadership role in the Far East had come to an end.

All this made a big impression on many people in China. In 1898, in the aftermath of the defeat by Japan, a group of progressives within the Chinese government attempted to initiate a programme of reform. In imitation of Japan, they wanted to make the country stronger in this way. They received support in doing so from the emperor, Aisin Gioro Zaitian (known formally as the Guangxu Emperor). Unfortunately for the reformers, the emperor was at that time in a power struggle with his aunt, the mother of the former emperor. This aunt, Empress Dowager Cixi, was a highly powerful political figure in China at the time.

Cixi had become a concubine to the Xianfeng Emperor in 1852 at the age of seventeen. Chinese emperors had concubines in addition to their first wife, the empress. These lived together with thousands of female servants and eunuchs in the Forbidden City, the large palace complex in Beijing. Because her son was five when he became emperor, and her nephew was three when he became emperor next, Cixi had been regent for a long time. In 1898, when the now adult Guangxu Emperor wanted to rule more independently of his aunt, Cixi decided to intervene. Many civil servants opposed the reforms or thought they were moving too fast. Li Hongzhang thought so too and therefore kept a low profile when the Guangxu Emperor was launching his reforms. Empress Dowager Cixi sided with the conservatives within the government and had the emperor placed under house arrest. With that his political role was finished, and Cixi was the undisputed ruler of China. The reforms were reversed.

Around the same time, an anti-foreign movement emerged in rural China. Its members practiced a traditional form of martial arts and were therefore called Boxers by the Westerners. The Boxer movement arose in part from rural tensions between Chinese Christians and non-Christians. Western missionaries had been very active in converting Chinese since the Second Opium War, supporting the new converts in local conflicts. The missionaries, in turn, were supported diplomatically and militarily by their own governments. The Boxers at first only attacked and killed Chinese Christians, but later also foreigners. The movement grew rapidly, and in January 1900, large groups of Boxers went to Beijing to attack the symbol of foreign influence, the legations.

The conservatives within the government saw this as an opportunity to free China from foreign presence and restore the situation before the First Opium War. Militarily, China was too weak to defend its own borders, but which foreign power could resist the overwhelming numbers of the Chinese people? In the wars that China had fought and lost since 1840, the common people had not played an active role. But now a popular movement had sprung up out of frustration at foreign influence. China was the largest country in the world by population. Not modern weapons, but the large reservoir of people was now seen by conservative Manchu leaders as the trump card in the balance of power with the great powers. Administrative reforms and adaptation to the modern world order were not necessary. According to the conservative strategy, all the government had to do was support the Boxers and encourage the rest of the country to revolt against the Westerners and the Japanese.

Once again, Cixi sided with the conservatives and gave them a chance to realize this plan. On 21 June 1900, the Qing government simultaneously declared war against eleven countries: both the major powers (Britain, Japan, Russia, Germany, France and the United States) and some European countries that were less influential in East Asia but that had unequal treaties with China nonetheless (Spain, Italy, Belgium, the Netherlands and Austria-Hungary). The legations of these countries in Beijing were ordered to close, and all Westerners and Japanese were ordered to leave the city. Cixi guaranteed that they would be allowed to travel unharmed to the nearest port city, Tianjin, to embark there and return to their own countries. There were already many Boxers in and around Beijing, and the imperial army also seemed ready to attack the foreigners. Possibly thinking of the dramatic outcome of the British evacuation attempt from Kabul in 1842, the foreigners decided to entrench themselves in their legations in the hope that an international relief force would soon arrive.

Most of Beijing's eleven foreign legations were in close proximity to each other. Intermediate buildings were occupied and streets were hastily barricaded to create a closed and defensible whole. The somewhat more remote legation buildings, such as those of the Netherlands, Belgium and Austria-Hungary, were evacuated. Because the foreigners felt unsafe without the proximity of their warships, soldiers were stationed in the city to guard the legations. In total, several hundred foreign soldiers of various nationalities were there to protect some 500 foreigners plus 3,000 Chinese Christians. At another location in the city, there was a cathedral containing another 3,000 Chinese Christians, which was defended by 43 French and Italian soldiers. On 20 June, the siege of the legations and the cathedral by the Boxers and Chinese troops began. Despite constant shelling and the heat of the summer, the foreigners held out. A feared large-scale assault failed to materialize, but the terrain held by the defenders became increasingly smaller and their supplies were exhausted. Weeks passed, and more and more of the besieged were wounded or killed. The head of customs, Robert Hart, was also in the legations. Although he was in Chinese service, as a foreigner he was also in danger. On 17 July 1900, British media reported that he had been killed in battle.

In several other places in northern China, foreigners and large numbers of Christians were killed by the Boxers or by local authorities. But the governors of the provinces in central and southern China decided to stand aside. They probably knew what would happen next: the great powers would surely send troops to China to relieve the besieged legations and teach China another hard lesson. The cities on the coast and along the Yangtze were especially vulnerable to foreign attacks. Li Hongzhang, then governor general of Guangzhou and other coastal cities in the south, spread the false message that the declaration of war against the eleven foreign powers was not genuine. He did this to have an excuse, however transparent, for disobeying the central government. The Boxer movement itself was confined to northern China. In the rest of the country, the Boxers were fought by the local government and Westerners were left alone.

What the provincial administrators had foreseen indeed happened. Eight of the eleven countries with legations in Beijing sent troops to China. The eight countries decided that this should be a joint operation. That was all the more necessary because they did not trust each other. Each great power feared that the others would use the opportunity to occupy parts of China or to force new concessions from the Qing dynasty that would not be in everyone's best interests. Gradually, troops from Japan, Russia, Great Britain, France, the United States, Germany, Austria-Hungary and Italy arrived in Tianjin and prepared to advance from there to Beijing. They were the very countries that would face each other not much later in the First World War. Some of the troops had to come all the way from Europe. The German government succeeded in obtaining (more or less) consent from the other countries that a German officer, Alfred Graf von Waldersee, was in overall command of the multinational intervention force. When the German troops left for China, Kaiser Wilhelm II held his infamous 'Huns Speech'. He urged his soldiers to show no mercy in China and not to take prisoners. He is said to have spoken these words: 'As a thousand years ago the Huns under their king Atilla established a reputation which still impresses today in traditions and stories, so the reputation of Germany in China must be established by you for the next thousand years, so that no Chinese will ever again dare to look at a German in disrespect.'[8]

The need to wait (because of mutual distrust) for most foreign forces to arrive in China meant that the besieged in Beijing had to be patient a little longer. But eventually the attack was launched, and after a short campaign, on 14 August 1900, the multinational force reached Beijing and the legations were relieved. Once again China proved to be too weak militarily to defend itself against a foreign invasion. Two days later, the survivors in the cathedral were also liberated. The majority of the besieged had survived the adventure. This included Robert Hart. The British media turned out to have been premature with his obituary.

The Boxer crisis was over. Cixi fled the city disguised as a peasant woman, taking her imprisoned nephew with her. The foreign troops occupied Beijing and other parts of northern China, but not the provinces that had kept aloof. They established their military headquarters in the Forbidden City. All Boxers that could be found were rounded up and executed. Many ordinary citizens were also killed, and Beijing was thoroughly looted. Many art treasures once again disappeared abroad. The military occupation, including terror against the civilian population and looting, lasted for a year. An influential Chinese official and military commander, Yuan Shikai, who had stood aside during the siege, collaborated with the foreign forces in capturing and executing alleged Boxers. Many tens of thousands of Chinese probably died during the occupation of northern China. Meanwhile, negotiations were underway about what China should do to end the occupation. On the Chinese side, the negotiations were led by the experienced Li Hongzhang. The same envoys who had endured the siege in Beijing negotiated on behalf of the foreign powers. They were not in a forgiving mood. It was only after Li agreed on behalf of the Qing government to massive compensation, the execution of leading conservative officials and various other demands from the great powers that these withdrew their troops. The exhausted Li Hongzhang died soon after.

## The end of the Qing

After the disastrous year of 1900, it was clear to everyone in the Qing government that China's status from before the Opium Wars could not be restored without far-reaching adjustments. The government led by Empress Dowager Cixi now started a reform process. The ancient Confucian examination system for civil servants was abolished and modern universities based on the Western model were founded. Cixi moved back into the Forbidden City and now took a friendlier attitude to foreigners. The envoys and their wives were invited to tea and were surprised to receive a kind and warm welcome from the Empress Dowager. But all this came too late for the survival of the Qing dynasty.

The occupation of the Forbidden City and the sack of Beijing were a humiliation for China and for the dynasty. The final blow to the Qing dynasty's last bit of legitimacy came in the aftermath of the Boxer crisis. In China, Russia tended to be somewhat less visible as an imperialist power compared to the British and the French. During the Second Opium War, when the Qing dynasty had its hands full with the Taiping Rebellion and the conflict with Britain and France, Russia had threatened to attack China. To avert this threat, China had ceded Southeast Siberia to Russia. The Russians then built a new city there, with a naval port, which they called Vladivostok ('Ruler of the East'). During the Boxer crisis in 1900, Russia saw an opportunity to once again take advantage of the chaos and further expand its influence. While everyone's attention was focused on relieving the Beijing legations, a large Russian force invaded Manchuria. This was the country of origin of the Qing dynasty, bordering Russia and Korea. After the other great powers withdrew their troops from northern China in 1901 and the dust of the Boxer crisis had settled, the Russian occupation force was still in Manchuria. China was now too weakened to do anything about it. The Japanese government, however, saw this as a threat to its position in

Korea. In 1904, Japan therefore launched a surprise attack on the Russian troops in Manchuria. The result was a fierce war in which Russia suffered major military defeats.

The different ways in which Britain and the United States responded to the war were telling. The British were no longer the power broker they once were and were mainly concerned with maintaining the status quo. In 1902, they formed an alliance with Japan, hoping that their new ally would preserve the regional order in a way that suited British economic and geopolitical interests. The most important of these were maintaining access to the Chinese market and preventing Russia from becoming too powerful in Asia. The fact that Japan turned out to be stronger than Russia was therefore a welcome outcome for the British government. But the United States, as an emerging power, looked further ahead and – as it turned out – had a sharper view of regional dynamics. The US government was particularly concerned that Japan would eventually become too dominant and that this country would then want to keep the Chinese market to itself. That is why US President Theodore Roosevelt initiated peace negotiations between the two warring parties during the Russo-Japanese War. He wanted to prevent the war from going on so long that Russia would be too weakened.

The negotiations resulted in a peace treaty that stipulated that Russia would withdraw from the southern part of Manchuria. Japan got what it wanted, but at the same time Russia remained strong enough to one day threaten Japanese interests in China and Korea once more. The balance between the great powers thus also seemed to be secured in the longer term. Theodore Roosevelt had achieved what he had wanted and even was the first American to receive the Nobel Peace Prize in 1906 for his role as a mediator. Still, the Russo-Japanese War was a step towards further international destabilization. Japan had seen what it could achieve with military means, and it was only a matter of time before it would use them again. For Russia, defeat by an Asian country was a major blow to the prestige of Tsar Nicholas II's reign. The Russo-Japanese War was a conflict of great geopolitical significance that was fought on Qing territory, in the region of origin of the imperial family no less. But except as a battlefield, China played no part in this conflict.

The end of the Qing dynasty came not long after. Cixi died in 1908. Her nephew, the Guangxu Emperor (while still under house arrest) had been poisoned the day before. Whether this was done at Cixi's behest or by someone else who had an interest in the emperor not reigning again is not known. On her deathbed, Cixi named a two-year-old nephew of the Guangxu Emperor as his successor. Only a few years later, the nephew, Aisin Gioro Puyi, would abdicate at the age of six. A revolution had broken out in China. The insurgents proclaimed a republic on 1 January 1912. The old system no longer stood in the way of China's adaptation to the modern world order. For the first time, China was headed by a president rather than an emperor. The name of the new president was Sun Yat-sen.

FIGURE 4 *Chinese officials pulling down the British flag on the* Arrow *on 8 October 1856 (photo by Culture Club/Getty Images).*

FIGURE 5  *Li Hongzhang during a visit to England, 1896 (photo by Hulton Archive/Getty Images).*

**FIGURE 6** *Sir Robert Hart, Inspector General of Chinese Customs, in his den in Beijing, from* The Illustrated London News, *1891 (photo by De Agostini Editorial/ Gerry Images).*

FIGURE 7 *Official portrait of Empress Dowager Cixi by court photographer Yu Xunling,* circa 1895 *(photo by Pictures from History/Universal Images Group via Getty Images).*

FIGURE 8 *US troops in the Forbidden City, Beijing 1900 (photo by Hulton Archive/Getty Images).*

# 3

# Entering the world stage (1912–25)

On 17 February 1917, a French steamship sailed in the Mediterranean Sea, near Malta. The *Athos* was on its way to Marseilles. The passengers included about 950 Chinese men who had signed up to work in France for several years. Because of the First World War there was a great shortage of workers in that country. Many French men were in military service, and Chinese labourers were hired to work in French ports and factories. They were also used to dig trenches and to remove the bodies of fallen soldiers from the battlefield. The *Athos* had sailed to China twice before to pick up Chinese workers. But on this day a German submarine, the U-65, encountered the French ship. Germany was at war with Britain and France, and the U-65 was ordered to sink all ships flying the enemy flag without warning. At 12.27 pm the *Athos* was hit by a German torpedo. Fourteen minutes later the French ship had sunk. Of the nearly 2,000 people on board, 754 died, including 543 Chinese.

After the outbreak of the First World War in August 1914, the Chinese government remained neutral. However, some Chinese diplomats now hoped that the attack on the *Athos* would lead China to declare war on Germany. One of them was Gu Weijun.[1] Five years earlier he had obtained a PhD degree from Columbia University in New York. His dissertation was on the legal privileges of foreigners in China. Gu wanted to know all about international law and how it applied to China. For, he believed, such knowledge was necessary to conduct an effective foreign policy.[2] Although he came from a wealthy family, he had experienced as a child what the unequal treaties meant in practice. As a schoolboy in Shanghai, Gu had once been stopped by a British-Indian police officer for cycling on the sidewalk while, according to Gu, a British boy who was doing the same was left alone. Young Gu ended up at a police station where his bicycle was confiscated and he had to pay a fine.

After his studies in the United States and the fall of the Qing dynasty, Gu returned to China to work for the new government. Gu Weijun was an outstanding representative of the new generation of Chinese diplomats. Like Li Hongzhang, he was a civil servant who understood the importance of knowledge of the outside world and that modern diplomatic relations could be used to China's advantage. The difference with Li was that Gu had no classical Confucian training, but he had studied in the United States. He had built up a good network there and had started using the first name 'Wellington' in his contacts with non-Chinese people. Gu was strongly driven in his career by the ideal of freeing China from foreign domination. This passion went back to the moment when he learned of China's defeat by Japan in 1895, as a seven-year-old. In his later life, as a result of this experience, he wanted to devote his work to restoring China's status and ending the Japanese threat.[3] Gu favoured entering the First World War on the Allied side because he expected that side to win and he wanted China to have a voice in decision-making about the international order after the war.

In reaction to the sinking of the *Athos*, China broke off diplomatic relations with Germany. And, as Gu had hoped, on 14 August 1917, the Chinese government declared war on that country. The United States had done the same shortly before, urging China to follow suit. For both countries, attacks by German submarines on international shipping played a role in the decision to participate in the First World War. One difference, however, was that China itself had become the stage for acts of war between the warring factions. All the great powers had a permanent military presence in the country for decades. At the start of the war, Germany and Austria-Hungary concentrated their troops in China (together about 4,000) and equipment (six warships and an aircraft) in Qingdao, a port city in eastern China where the Germans had established a naval base in 1898. Japan immediately saw an opportunity to increase its influence in China and declared war on Germany and Austria-Hungary. A Japanese invasion force, assisted by a smaller British contingent, captured the German naval base in November 1914. The battle of Qingdao was short-lived but fierce. The great powers ignored China's neutral status in their military operations. China therefore had little to lose if it discarded that status by entering the war.

The Chinese declaration of war on Germany was a milestone, even though China did not participate in combat. For the first time, China was involved in a major geopolitical event outside its own region. As envisioned by Gu, the Allies were victorious and China was subsequently invited to participate in the peace conference in Paris, where the victors would define the new international order. The Chinese contribution to the victory was that the government had made it possible for some 140,000 workers to go to Europe. Their presence allowed many French and British men to be released for military service. The costs for the Chinese labour deployment were paid by the French and British governments. Some two to three thousand Chinese workers did not survive the war, partly as a result of the sometimes very dangerous work close to the front lines.

Gu Weijun was one of five diplomats selected by China to attend the Paris conference, which began in January 1919. Shortly before, his wife had died from the effects of the Spanish flu, a pandemic that is estimated to have killed tens of millions of people worldwide.[4] The pandemic started during the war (probably not in Spain, despite the name), spread around the world and ended quite abruptly after a spike in deaths in the autumn of 1918. Despite the recent loss of his wife, Gu went to Paris and was the most active and outspoken member of the Chinese delegation there. The challenge he faced was enormous, as China's international standing had not improved since the fall of the Qing dynasty.

## Worse than a colony

The new republic had started in 1912 as a Western-style democracy. China got a parliament, with political parties and elections. But it soon became apparent that the real power lay with the military, and especially with Yuan Shikai, the military leader who had assisted the foreign invasion force in suppressing the Boxer movement in 1900. Although the republic was proclaimed on 1 January 1912, with Sun Yat-sen at its head, the Qing dynasty was not yet completely defeated. Civil war loomed. Yuan took advantage of the situation by arranging an appointment with the leaders of the republic. If Yuan could get the imperial family to abdicate power, he would be rewarded with the presidency. He did what he promised. Aisin Gioro Puyi, the last emperor of China, describes in his autobiography his recollection of an encounter between his aunt, the Empress Dowager Longyu, and a fat old man kneeling in front of her.[5] That was around his sixth birthday. He later understood that that man was Yuan Shikai, who had come to tell the court that the emperor's abdication was unavoidable. It was apparently a very emotional conversation, because Puyi remembered that not only his aunt but also Yuan was in tears. The latter reminded the Empress Dowager of the fate of the French King Louis XVI, who was arrested and beheaded during the French Revolution. Yuan gave guarantees that the emperor would be safe after his abdication, that he and his court would be allowed to continue to live in the Forbidden City and that he would receive a fixed annual income. After Longyu announced her nephew's abdication on 12 February, Sun Yat-sen also abdicated and Yuan Shikai became the new president. Sun, who had lived abroad for a long time and did not have a strong power base in China, had been president for only a month and a half.

Yuan did not share Sun Yat-sen's democratic and republican ideals. Soon he sidelined the parliament and began to rule like a dictator. After a failed attempt to found a new dynasty with himself as emperor, he died in 1916. China remained a republic, but the parliamentary system no longer functioned. There was also no clear successor to Yuan as the new strongman. The only remaining political force was the army, but it broke up into regional units. At the head of these were officers who began to fight each other more and more openly. They turned into warlords who each ruled their own part of China. Some of them controlled several provinces, others only part of a single province. There was still a central government in Beijing, but in practice, it was subordinate to whichever warlord ruled the northern part of the country. Due to shifting coalitions and increasing armed struggle between the warlords, Beijing kept falling into different hands in the years from 1916 onwards. Against this backdrop of political instability at home, diplomats like Gu Weijun sought to represent China's interests on the world stage.

Meanwhile, the country was still tied to the unequal treaties. When China changed from an empire to a republic, the foreign powers demanded that the new government continue to respect the treaties. Based on the treaties, they had built up a sizeable presence. Foreign gunboats patrolled the coast and the Yangtze. Gunboats were built for coastal and inland navigation and ideal for small-scale military actions such as shelling and ground attacks by marines. The number of foreigners in China continued to grow, and most of them were immune from Chinese jurisdiction. Instead, the laws of their own countries applied. The coastal cities where they lived, mostly in enclaves where the Chinese government had no authority, had special facilities for foreigners such as hotels, churches and schools. Catholic and Protestant missionary organizations from Europe and the United States were active throughout the country to spread Christianity.

Unequal treaties, military interventions and the presence of foreigners not covered by domestic law were not unique to China. In geopolitical terms, there were roughly three categories of countries in the early twentieth century: (1) economically and militarily advanced states, (2) other independent states and (3) colonized territories. The first group consisted of the major powers plus the smaller Western European states. China, together with various other states in Asia and Latin America, was in group two. These states were formally independent, but in practice, they were exposed to far-reaching economic and political influence from the group one states. The third group was politically subjected to, or integrated into, states from the first two groups and played no autonomous role in international relations. The means of power used by the great powers in China were typical of the relationship between groups one and two. What was special about China, however, was that the country was the collective target of *all* states in the first group. No country in the world shares this experience with China. Sun Yat-sen, who had moved to southern Guangzhou after his brief presidency, felt China was in a worse state than if it had been a colony of a single country. A colony had a ruler who usually felt a certain degree of responsibility, Sun believed. But China was exploited by everyone, while no one felt responsible for the fate of the Chinese people.[6]

Foreign influence in China was more than the sum of the activities of the individual powers. There were also institutions in China that were collectively controlled by foreigners. The most important of these was the Beijing Diplomatic Body. On the eve of the First World War, its members were the envoys of the eleven countries that had signed treaties with China. They oversaw a group of international banks tasked with arranging compensation for the Boxer crisis. The compensation that China had to pay also included the costs for the military actions against China and the occupation by foreign troops. The amount was so high (including interest about US$40 billion in today's dollars) in relation to the limited revenues of the central government that China was given thirty-nine years to pay it all.[7]

The duties collected by the customs service, still managed by foreigners, were the main source of income for the Chinese central government. But much of that revenue had already been used to pay off various railway loans that China had taken out (often under pressure from the great powers) and the compensation that China had to pay Japan after the Sino-Japanese war of 1894–5. The central government therefore decided to put pressure on the provinces to contribute to the repayment of the Boxer debt. To strengthen their grip on China's finances, the great powers placed the customs revenues under the supervision of the Diplomatic Body. The Chinese government could not access the money until the compensation payments (which were administered by a consortium of foreign banks) were on schedule and the Diplomatic Body agreed. The Chinese government no longer had any influence over the customs service, although it was nominally still a part of China's bureaucracy. In the early decades of the twentieth century, China's external debt, arising from railroad loans and the Boxer debt, was an important tool for great powers to put pressure on the Chinese government.

The Diplomatic Body not only had financial powers but also held the majority of seats on the Legation District Board. That district was rebuilt after the siege of 1900 (at the expense of China), after which Chinese were not allowed to live there. The area was walled and the entrance gates were guarded by foreign soldiers. Henceforth, foreign troops were permanently stationed in Beijing and along the route from Beijing to the coast. A new kind of forbidden city had thus been created in the middle of the Chinese capital, close to the original Forbidden City where the deposed Qing emperor still lived.

However, most foreigners did not reside in Beijing but in Shanghai. Many international companies had their regional headquarters there. The city consisted of three parts. The most important part was the International Settlement, where many shops, offices and factories were located. This sprawling international quarter formed the heart of the city, had its own police force and was governed by a municipal council elected by foreign landowners, mainly the big companies. The nine members of the City Council were of British (five persons), American (two persons) and Japanese (two persons) nationality. However, they did not represent the countries they came from, but the companies they worked for. In addition, there was a separate French Concession, which was administered by a French consul, while another part of the city was under Chinese rule. The vast majority of Shanghai's residents, including of the International Settlement and the French Concession, were Chinese. Shanghai grew into the largest city in China and the most cosmopolitan trading city in Asia.

## The attractiveness of the Chinese market

As important as the role of foreign diplomats, military personnel and missionaries was, the business community constituted the core of the foreign presence in China. The main prize for most of the great powers was the Chinese market. Foreign governments provided certain preconditions by forcing access for foreigners and foreign products, but it was up to the companies to do something useful with it. China exerted a strong attraction on international companies from Europe, the United States and Japan. These came in all shapes and sizes. Trading firms, banks and industrial multinationals were especially influential because they often formed the centre of networks that many other (foreign and Chinese) companies were part of.

The trading firms exported Chinese products and imported foreign goods. After the Opium Wars, they were the first wave of foreign investors in China. British companies such as Jardine Matheson and Swire, their German and American competitors and the Japanese conglomerates Mitsui, Mitsubishi, Sumitomo and Okura were not only active in trade but, often through subsidiaries, also in other activities, such as transport and industrial production. Many trading firms acted as agents for large foreign companies that did not (yet) have a presence in China.

After the trading houses, the banks followed at the end of the nineteenth century. The most important were (the predecessors of) HSBC, Standard Chartered, Citibank, MUFG Bank, Deutsche Bank, ABN AMRO and Crédit Agricole. They financed China's international trade and at times were co-founders and shareholders of various other foreign companies in China, such as shipping companies that handled traffic between China and the rest of the world. The banks worked closely with the trading firms and were part of the same networks. Since China did not have a central bank, the foreign banks issued their own banknotes and set the exchange rates between Chinese and foreign currencies. In addition, the banks helped finance railway construction and port construction by extending loans and issuing bonds on foreign capital markets. This modern infrastructure was designed and built by foreign construction companies, using Chinese workers through subcontractors. Much equipment, such as locomotives and wagons, was imported from abroad. The construction of railways, in addition to the reparations for the war against Japan and the Boxer crisis, created a huge foreign debt for the Chinese government.

In the first decades of the twentieth century, the third major group of foreign companies arrived: industrial multinationals from the West. They had grown large in Europe and North America and were now looking for new markets. China, with its huge population and rapidly modernizing major cities, offered growth opportunities that did not exist anywhere else for certain products. For more and more large companies, going to China was not a strategic option, but a strategic necessity. The petroleum industry, for example, had grown big by selling lamp oil in the United States and Europe, but there, oil lamps were rapidly being replaced by electric lighting. In Western countries, oil companies started to focus on the sale of petrol, anticipating the rise of the car. They were looking for another destination for lamp oil, and China was ideal for that. The Chinese market was large and developing rapidly, but it was far from reaching the level of the Western world. Major American and European oil companies used the profits they made in China to charge lower petrol prices in Western markets. In this way, they pushed smaller competitors out of the market. Those who wanted to stay in the race on the petrol market in any part of the world could not ignore China. China also became a strategically important market for a number of products other than oil.

Like the trading firms and banks, most industrial companies, such as Siemens, AEG, Philips, General Electric and ITT, settled in the major coastal cities. Not only did many foreigners live there, but a considerable Chinese middle class gradually emerged that had a need for Western products. Sometimes foreign companies built their own factories to produce for the local market. For example, General Electric established a light bulb factory and Unilever a soap factory in Shanghai.

However, there were also industrial multinationals with even greater ambitions. Of the approximately 450 million Chinese, the vast majority did not live in the now relatively modern coastal cities, but in rural towns or villages deep inland. Notably British American Tobacco (BAT), Imperial Chemical Industries (ICI, later merged into AkzoNobel and other companies), IG Farben (now BASF and Bayer, among others), Unilever, Shell, Standard Oil (now ExxonMobil) and Texaco (now part of Chevron) built a presence in large parts of China. These companies often used their own means of transport, such as trucks and barges, to transport their supplies inland to regional warehouses located throughout China. Chinese merchants, acting as agents for the foreign companies, managed the warehouses and stocked shops in cities and towns, which sold the items to Chinese consumers. Besides the missionaries with their churches and schools, the products (cigarettes, fertilizers, soap and lamp oil) and advertisements of these companies were the most visible expression of foreign influence for many Chinese people.

The large industrial companies active in China mainly came from Great Britain, Japan, the United States, Germany and the Netherlands.[8] They had a certain degree of legal certainty as a result of their extraterritorial rights, and the foreign enclaves in the big cities offered security and all kinds of amenities that made it comfortable to live there. Efficient customs, low import tariffs, the presence of international banks and the construction of modern ports and railways all contributed to more international trade. And through trade, also Western companies that were not themselves present in China acquired interests in the Chinese market.

Still, doing business in China remained a major challenge. Outside the enclaves, the foreign companies had to deal with often corrupt and unpredictable local Chinese governments. Whether and to what extent these actively tried to counter foreign influence was difficult to fathom. Apart from the major rivers and the newly constructed railway lines, there was very little transport infrastructure inland. Although there was a uniform import tariff for foreign products, Chinese governments imposed various local transit taxes for domestic trade. So there was a big difference between the cities on the coast and along the Yangtze, which were easily accessible for foreign products, and the rest of China, where the costs of transport were high.

But even in the coastal cities, foreign companies sometimes struggled. Chinese entrepreneurs soon began to manufacture the same products that the foreigners traded. Thus, from the beginning of the twentieth century, modern Chinese companies were created that started making things such as textiles, soap and cigarettes for the domestic market. Western and Japanese companies faced stiff Chinese competition. Sometimes this was based on counterfeiting foreign products or on support from the Chinese government. But above all, Chinese companies often benefitted from low production costs, local networks and good knowledge of the market.

## The emergence of Chinese boycotts

As foreign companies became more successful in developing and conquering the Chinese market, they and their governments found that there was also a downside. They became increasingly dependent on that market while, at the same time, Chinese consumers developed greater political awareness. In 1905, Chinese traders and consumers in parts of southern China staged a boycott in protest of the mistreatment of Chinese immigrants in the United States. For them, an important symbol of anti-Chinese sentiments in the United States was the Chinese Exclusion Act: a law dating from 1882 that restricted the immigration of Chinese workers. At a time when large numbers of Europeans were emigrating to the United States, the Chinese were the first ethnic group to be targeted by US anti-immigration legislation. Chinese who had arrived earlier were able to stay but were discriminated against in various areas by the US government. The Chinese boycott against the United States, which lasted almost a year, had begun after an appeal by Chinese organizations in US Chinatowns.

Chinese diplomats had long warned the US government that the anti-immigration law would harm US trade interests. However, they kept a low profile during the boycott. In 1905 Liang Cheng, China's ambassador to the United States, advised the Chinese government to give the green light to merchant organizations to participate in the boycott. Liang had stayed in the United States for several years from the age of twelve (and shown to have a talent for baseball) as a participant in one of the first college programmes for Chinese students in America. As ambassador, he felt a boycott was an effective way to pressure the United States to repeal the immigration law, but it had to be done in a way that would not enable the American authorities to hold the Chinese government accountable. Liang was convinced that if the interests of US companies were affected, they would lobby for a more pro-Chinese policy from the US government. Once the boycott had begun, Liang implicitly supported the activists in speeches. But he made sure not to do this too openly.[9]

Although the 1905 boycott did not change US immigration law, the Chinese government had now learned that access to the Chinese market could be a tool for exerting pressure on the great powers. Crucially, this was done, as Liang Cheng had advised, in a way that did not reveal the government's role. If the boycott seemed like a spontaneous action by citizens and entrepreneurs, it was difficult for foreign governments to take countermeasures. Liang, like Li Hongzhang before, followed in the footsteps of Liu Yunke, who behind the scenes had created obstacles for British merchants in Fuzhou after the First Opium War. Liu and Li had recognized that reducing foreign influence in China was a matter of patience. Liang Cheng understood that the great powers had become increasingly dependent on the Chinese market. Open attempts by the Chinese government to hinder trade would undoubtedly have led to military interventions against China. But a consumer boycott was a different story, as it could not easily be suppressed by foreign military action.

It was also important that the Chinese population in the major port cities had now discovered that it was possible to take political action by no longer buying certain products. A boycott could arise with covert support from the government. But as the Chinese government quickly learned, it was also possible for a boycott to ensue without any government involvement. This happened in 1908. In that year, the Chinese navy seized the cargo of a Japanese freighter, the *Daini Tatsu Maru*. That cargo consisted of guns and ammunition, which the ship's crew had tried to land in Macau. The Chinese authorities suspected that the weapons were intended for revolutionaries who were preparing an uprising against the Qing dynasty. Because the *Daini Tatsu Maru* sailed under the Japanese flag, the government of Japan responded according to the approach developed by Harry Parkes half a century earlier. Japan demanded damages and an apology for disrespecting the Japanese flag and threatened military action. The central government in Beijing yielded to this pressure and apologized as requested. However, unlike at the time of the Opium Wars, the local population now had a strong opinion about such incidents. Dissatisfied with what they saw as Japanese aggression and the weak attitude of their own government, traders and residents of several southern Chinese cities proceeded to boycott Japanese goods. In Hong Kong, there were even riots and attacks on shops selling Japanese products. Under pressure from Japan, the central government in Beijing banned the boycott, but to little effect. The boycott eventually ended because Chinese traders could not sustain the decline in turnover for too long.

A new trend had emerged. Whenever the Chinese public was outraged by the actions of the great powers, this led to boycotts. In 1915 and 1919, there were anti-Japanese boycotts, both related to the occupation of Qingdao and other manifestations of growing Japanese influence. Many more would follow in the 1920s and 1930s, often against Japan, but other foreign powers could also be targets. Such actions were temporary and usually had no material effect on the foreigners' influence. But they ensured that larger parts of the population became aware of the international position of their country. This was the beginning of nationalism as a mass movement in China.

## Paris 1919

The 1919 peace conference was not China's first time participating in an international conference. In the period 1909–14, the country took part in four international meetings. The first of these was held in Shanghai and the next three in The Hague in the Netherlands. These meetings were an American initiative and aimed against abuse of narcotics, especially opium. The main outcome of this was the International Opium Convention of 1912, the first international treaty against drug trafficking. China, where opium use had become a major social problem, was one of the signatories. By participating in international conferences, China hoped to show that it was a full member of the international community and that there was no moral justification for maintaining the unequal treaties. The main negotiator on the Chinese side was Liang Cheng, who had previously played a role in the boycott of 1905 as ambassador to Washington. After the signing of the Opium Treaty, Liang, a loyal servant of the Qing dynasty that now no longer existed, retired.

China was thus not entirely inexperienced in international conferences during the Paris peace negotiations. The country was a co-victor in a war against two European powers (Germany and Austria-Hungary), but at the same time weaker than ever due to internal political divisions. During the war, Japan had expanded its power in China at the expense of the other great powers which had been absorbed in the struggle in Europe. In addition, a revolution had broken out in Russia in 1917, which ended the rule of the tsar. Japan focused its attention mainly on China, but did send warships to the Mediterranean to protect Allied supply lines against German submarines. On the basis of this, and the capture of the German naval base in Qingdao, Japan could claim to have contributed to the armed struggle. Japan's geopolitical interests, however, were not in Europe but in Asia. In 1915, Japan had pressured Yuan Shikai's government to recognize the expansion of Japanese influence in eastern and northeastern (Manchuria) China.

In Paris, the Chinese delegation quickly discovered that all the countries that had won the war were not equals. This was reflected in the allocation of seats at the conference table. The Americans, Italians and Japanese each had five seats, the French had seven, and Great Britain (including the British colonies) had fourteen. China got two seats, as many as Siam, Romania, Greece, Poland and Portugal but less than Serbia and Belgium (with three seats each). More importantly, a group of four countries, namely Britain, France, Italy and the United States, made all important decisions independently of the rest. The new revolutionary Russian government, which had previously made a separate peace with Germany, was not welcome at the conference.

The diplomat Gu Weijun and his colleagues wanted to gain support in Paris for their efforts to end the unequal treaties and special rights foreigners had in China. Their most concrete goal was to restore Chinese authority over Qingdao and the surrounding region, where Germany had a dominant influence before the war. The Chinese delegation proceeded energetically and did so in a way that was completely new to China. The Chinese hired Western advisers, set up a media office in Paris and organized dinner parties to which they invited diplomats from the major powers. At the conference, the eloquent speaker Gu explained the Chinese position in fluent English. He used arguments that appealed to a Western audience, and that were based on international law. Behind the scenes, he lobbied US President Woodrow Wilson, whom he knew from his time as a student in the United States. Gu also served on a special committee set up at the conference to create a new international organization aimed at preventing future wars. This new organization, the League of Nations, was an idea of President Wilson and would indeed be founded in 1920, with China as one of the original members. At the Paris Peace Conference, China took its first steps on the stage of world politics. It was clear that the country had learned to adapt to Western diplomacy.

Still the efforts of the Chinese delegation came to nothing. The Treaty of Versailles, with which the victors imposed their demands on Germany after months of negotiating, stated that the former German possessions and privileges in and around Qingdao were henceforth Japan's. What China did gain was that the treaty stated that Germany was no longer entitled to compensation for the Boxer crisis of 1900. In addition, Germany had to return a number of astronomical instruments that German troops had taken during the sack of Beijing that same year. But the system of unequal treaties remained unchanged.

The performance of the Chinese delegation at the peace conference was not flawless. Because the political situation in China itself was chaotic, there was a constant lack of clarity about the division of tasks within the delegation. Moreover, the media campaign backfired. The Chinese media office in Paris had been so energetic in attacking Japan's reputation that it aroused more annoyance than sympathy from the other countries.[10] It also didn't help that it turned out that at the start of the war, Japan had concluded a secret agreement with Yuan Shikai stating that Qingdao was Japan's. According to Gu, that agreement was not valid because it was concluded under duress. But the most important factor was that while China was now playing the game by the formal rules, it was doing so from a position of weakness. The great powers had already made agreements with each other during the war about the post-war distribution of influence, and moreover at the Paris negotiations geopolitical power was decisive. Japan was much stronger militarily than China (and the leading power in East Asia) and was therefore able to force the Western powers to decide in favour of its claim on Qingdao. The British saw Japan as a serious partner in maintaining regional order in East Asia and had therefore allied with that country since 1902. China, with its political instability, was seen as troublesome rather than as a partner.

The members of the Chinese delegation faced a dilemma. Should they sign the Treaty of Versailles, despite the fact that it assigned Qingdao to Japan? Not signing meant that China would formally remain at war with Germany, and that it distanced itself from the rest of the victors, just when it had been accepted as a participant (albeit a minor one) at a major international conference for the first time. In Beijing on 4 May 1919, students took to the streets to demand that the treaty would not be signed. The demonstrators moved to Tiananmen Square in central Beijing. Riots broke out and the home of a minister who was known to be pro-Japanese was set on fire. Gu feared that if he signed the treaty, he would be attacked by radical students when he returned to China. He tried to find a compromise by proposing that he would sign if he could include in the text that he objected to the handing over of Qingdao to Japan. However, the other allied countries did not allow this, and the Chinese delegation decided not to sign. China was the only country on the Allied side not to sign the Treaty of Versailles. It wasn't until several years later that China and Germany came to a separate peace agreement. Disappointed with the outcome of the negotiations, but engaged to a daughter from a wealthy family of overseas Chinese whom he had met in Paris, Gu left the city to start a new job as ambassador to London.

After the negotiations in Paris were concluded, another member of the Chinese delegation made a tour of Europe. His name was Liang Qichao. He had been the minister of Finance for a short time, but was also a historian and philosopher who was known for his many journalistic publications on political issues.¹¹ His ideas about China's future were influential and were partly shaped by a few trips abroad. After an earlier visit to the United States, Liang had already concluded that Western democracy is not for the Chinese people. He had visited San Francisco's Chinatown and was amazed at what he had seen there. There, he observed, the Chinese lived isolated from the rest of the city and behaved culturally as if they were still in China, be it less orderly. According to Liang, they made no use of the freedoms of American society at all and had no idea of the rights and responsibilities they had as citizens. At a different level, the same applied to the Chinese in China itself, according to Liang. According to him, they were not yet ready for democracy in the coming decades because they lacked national consciousness. What China needed was strong leadership and a curtailment of individual freedoms.¹²

Like Gu Weijun, Liang Qichao was disappointed with the Treaty of Versailles. But what shocked him most about his tour of Europe was the bad shape in which the continent was. The First World War had led to widespread misery and destruction and now Europeans seemed to have no idea how to proceed. Not only was Western democracy not a suitable model for China, Liang believed, but also China should not try to imitate the West in general. This gave him a new insight. The fact that China was lagging behind the West could also be an advantage. China could learn from the mistakes of Western countries and avoid them itself. Moreover, the West could also learn something from China, with its long history, he thought.¹³ Back in China, Liang Qichao passed on his insights to his compatriots through articles and lectures.

## Agents from Moscow

Meanwhile, there were new developments in Russia that would have a major impact on China. As a result of the 1917 revolution, the Communist Party led by Lenin (whose real name was Vladimir Ulyanov) had come to power there. In 1919, an organization was founded in Moscow with the aim of coordinating the activities of communist parties around the world. The chairman of this organization, the Comintern, was Grigory Zinoviev, one of the leaders of the Communist Party of the Soviet Union. In the background, however, Lenin was the dominant figure. All communist parties represented in the Comintern were expected to follow the instructions of this organization. This gave Lenin an instrument to exert great influence internationally.

Lenin sent Comintern agents to several countries that did not yet have a communist party in order to set one up. Because the Comintern was formally an international organization, non-Russians were also among these agents. In 1920, for example, the Dutch communist Henk Sneevliet was asked by Lenin to go to China. He had a lot of experience useful for this job, because in 1914 he had helped to set up the Partai Komunis Indonesia (PKI) in the Dutch East Indies. Sneevliet travelled from Europe by ship to Shanghai where he arrived in June 1921. He came at the right time because more and more people in China were open to new political ideas. The way the country was treated by the great powers had led to a growing awareness of international political relations. The student protest of 4 May 1919 on Tiananmen Square was followed by demonstrations, boycotts and strikes in various Chinese cities. The protests were directed against foreign influence, but also against the warlords who, in the eyes of activists, were holding back China's modernization.

These protests were organized by activists who were not part of the Chinese government. One of them was Mao Zedong. Born in 1893, he grew up near Changsha, the capital of Hunan province in China's interior. His father was a successful farmer and grain merchant. At fourteen he had married against his will to a girl four years his senior who had been chosen by his father. The marriage ended two years later when his wife died of dysentery. Mao then was a soldier for a short time, after which he went to study in Changsha. Once graduated, he worked for a while as an assistant librarian at Peking University. He also spent a short time in Shanghai. From 1920, Mao was back in Changsha, where he had a job as a primary school principal. In his spare time he worked for a bookstore and a study group he had set up himself and wrote magazine articles about social abuses.

Initially, Mao's political activism was aimed at deposing the local warlord and making Hunan province an independent state. Gradually he became interested in the Russian Revolution as an example of a successful uprising against the incumbent regime and then in Communism as a revolutionary ideology. Soon Mao's quest for provincial independence faded into the background, and he joined a group of pro-Communist activists in his hometown. A Comintern agent, Grigori Voitinski, who had come to China a year before Sneevliet, had ensured that communist groups were established in a number of Chinese cities. Mao and his fellow activists in Changsha also created a local communist organization.

Sneevliet's task was to ensure more cohesion between these local clubs. He therefore helped organize the first nationwide gathering of communist organizations in China. On 23 July 1921, representatives of the local organizations met in Shanghai's French Concession. The meeting location was a nondescript building at number 106 rue Wantz. Besides Sneevliet and a fellow Comintern agent, Vladimir Neumann, there were thirteen Chinese communists. Mao Zedong was one of them. The Chinese Communist Party (CCP) was founded at this meeting. The building that housed the CCP's founding meeting still stands in what is now a busy shopping and entertainment district of Shanghai.

The Chinese Communist Party had an international orientation from the beginning, not only because of the link with the Comintern but also because many Chinese students abroad became members. Especially in France, there were many Chinese students who were attracted to communism. The European section of the CCP was formed there in 1922. Those who joined through their studies in France included many future top officials of the CCP. The two who were to become the most famous were Zhou Enlai and Deng Xiaoping. Both had sailed to France in 1920 (Zhou on the *Porthos*, the sister ship of the ill-fated *Athos*). There they gained their first experience in organizing political activities.

Zhou Enlai came from an impoverished family of officials in eastern China. Before going to France, he had studied in Tokyo for two years. There he had become interested in politics, but it was only in Europe that he became involved with a group of Chinese communist activists. A little later, Deng Xiaoping joined the same group. Deng, short in stature (he was four feet, eleven inches tall) and six years younger than Zhou, was from the Western Chinese province of Sichuan where his father was a prosperous landowner. A network of young Chinese who believed that communism was the right ideology to take their country to a better future thus came into being in France. A hotel on rue Godefroy in Paris, where Zhou stayed for two years and where Deng often visited, became the hub of this network.[14] After several years in Europe, these students returned to China. Some, including Deng, first went to Moscow for a few years to continue their studies there.

Sneevliet's work was not finished with the establishment of the Communist Party of China. He knew that despite the rapid increase in members and branches, the party would still be too small and weak to influence the political situation in China for the time being. Sneevliet was still looking for a partner in China for the Comintern. The dominant players were the warlords, but they were not very interested in communism and revolution. Then his eyes fell on Sun Yat-sen. The latter had become a marginal figure in Chinese politics after his presidency, but he was still active. He had retired to Guangzhou, where he had founded a political party, the Kuomintang (Nationalist Party). Moreover, with the support of some local warlords, he had formed an alternative government for China. Although his government was not recognized by the foreign powers, Sun still had hopes for a second chance to lead his country to a brighter future.

## Blueprint for China's modernization

Sun Yat-sen believed that China's troubled relationship with the great powers could only lead to two possible outcomes. One was that China would weaken even further and eventually disappear as a civilization. The other was that China would once again become so strong that it would regain its historic status of great power. So the resurrection of China as a powerful state was a matter of necessity: it was all or nothing for Chinese civilization. The only way to do that was to stir up the nascent Chinese nationalism and make it the dominant force in Chinese society.[15] It was necessary for the Chinese people to become involved in the great goal of saving the country.

In 1920 he published *The International Development of China*.[16] This book, previously published in Chinese, was a blueprint for the modernization of his country. The English version was dedicated to James Cantlie and his wife.[17] In his book, Sun predicted that rivalry between the great powers over access to the Chinese market would lead to a war even bigger and more terrible than the First World War. To prevent this, he proposed a programme for China's economic development. That programme consisted of the construction of railways, roads, canals, ports, cities and factories. Innovations in agriculture and mining were also included. The book described exactly where the new ports and railway lines should be built. Sun was particularly ambitious in his plan: in his vision, China should build several large seaports in a short time with the same size as the port of New York.

He also proposed the colonization of Xinjiang, Tibet, Mongolia and Manchuria. By this he meant that these very large but sparsely populated areas, which the Republic of China had inherited from the Qing Empire, had to be populated by Han Chinese so that they could be economically developed. He was inspired by the internal colonization that had taken place in countries such as the United States, Australia and Argentina. The new rail lines would connect China's deep interior with coastal ports. He also wanted to build a rail connection with other countries. That railway was to connect Beijing with countries in Asia and Africa and go all the way to Cape Town in South Africa.[18]

Sun Yat-sen wanted to finance these grandiose plans with foreign capital. In economic terms, China would become a second United States: a developed, large market that would play a central role in the global economy. It would benefit everyone. Foreign investors would make a profit and the Chinese population would become more prosperous. Although he strongly opposed the system of foreign privileges in Chinese port cities, Sun did not want to drive away foreign investors. From a source of instability, China would turn into a source of prosperity for the whole world. China would thus eventually become 'the keystone in the arch' of the newly established League of Nations. He called the future era in which there would be no more wars, and to which China could make an important contribution, the era of Great Harmony. This term comes from the Confucian tradition and originally referred to an ideal society that would have existed in a distant past.

At the end of his book, Sun pointed to the increased tensions between labour and capital in industrialized countries. China should choose a different path: 'It is my idea to make capitalism create socialism in China so that these two economic forces of human evolution will work side by side in future civilization.' Important economic functions would be in the hands of state-owned companies, but there would also be room for private companies.

Although Sun was not a communist, Henk Sneevliet saw him as a useful ally. With support from the Soviet Union, Sun Yat-sen and his Kuomintang could fight the warlords and push back against the influence of the Western powers. In this way they would clear the way for the Communist Party, which could take over power at a later stage. For his part, Sun was also interested in cooperation with the Comintern, as he needed weapons to reunite China under his leadership. Japan and the Western powers had no intention of supplying those weapons. Sneevliet advised Sun to create a military branch of the Kuomintang and urged the Kuomintang and the CCP to form an alliance.

After several years in China, Sneevliet was replaced by another Comintern agent, Mikhail Borodin, who was born in what today is Belarus and had lived in the United States for a while. Borodin continued Sneevliet's work and convinced Sun to integrate the members of the CCP into the Kuomintang in exchange for military support from the Soviet Union. An important requirement from Sun was that the cooperation with the CCP should not be based on equality. The Comintern therefore ordered the Chinese communists to join the Kuomintang, but without abolishing the CCP. Mao Zedong, Zhou Enlai, Deng Xiaoping and the other communists were now members of both the CCP and the Kuomintang. Zhou (before returning to China from France) even became co-founder of the European section of the Kuomintang. Their accession gave the Kuomintang a stronger left-wing and revolutionary character, but liberal and conservative ideological movements were also represented in the party.

The Kuomintang was originally founded as a Western-style political party, designed to garner votes and thus compete with other parties. This did not correspond to the political reality in China, where elections played no role at all and parliament was sidelined. Inspired by the events in Russia, Sun decided that the Kuomintang should become a very different kind of organization. It should no longer be *a* party, but *the* party. Sun felt that the Western model was not suitable for China. The Chinese people had been familiar for thousands of years with the idea that the state was ruled by an emperor who acted in the interests of everyone and on the basis of the Heavenly Mandate. In Western democracies, political parties each had their own supporters. They represented the interests of those constituencies, Sun thought, and not the general interest of the state. He wanted the Kuomintang to be an umbrella organization for all national interests and become the national party of the country. And so China didn't need more than one party. Sun saw the Kuomintang as the reincarnation of the former emperors.[19] The Party, once in power, would rule the state as emperors used to. Like Liang Qichao, Sun Yat-sen felt that a democratic political system did not suit China. The state had to be able to exercise its power without restrictions. China would be strong if it were freed from the influence of other countries. The Chinese people had to sacrifice personal freedom to ensure the freedom of China as a whole.[20]

With Borodin's help, the Kuomintang was reformed on the model of the Communist Party of the Soviet Union: a well-organized and tightly run party above the state with representation at all levels of the government bureaucracy. Sun followed the example of Russia, not because he strove for a communist revolution, but because, in his view, this example fit in particularly well with the Chinese political tradition. Incidentally, Borodin also helped to further build up the CCP, which, too, was organized after the Leninist example.

## Sun Yat-sen's death

Sun had plans for what he wanted to do when he was in power, and he had a political party with which to run the country in due course. But also he was still in Guangzhou, far from the capital. To change this, the Kuomintang founded a military academy in that city in 1924, with the support of the Soviet Union. Its purpose was to form a professional armed force with which the party could engage in armed struggle with the warlords. Sun appointed one of his associates, Chiang Kai-shek, as commander of both the newly formed army and the military academy.[21] Chiang had joined Sun Yat-sen shortly after the 1911 revolution and had proved himself extremely loyal. He was someone Sun could confidently leave in command of the party's military wing.

Born in 1887, Chiang Kai-shek came from a family of salt merchants in Xikou, a town south of Shanghai. Chiang, whose father died when he was nine years old, was, like many of his contemporaries, very impressed by China's weakness in relation to the great powers. He wanted to contribute to a powerful China and thought that a military career was the best way to do so. After Russia's crushing defeat against Japan in 1905, Chiang decided to get his military training in Japan. At that time there were many young Chinese who were studying at a university or doing military training in Japan. Through compatriots he met there, Chiang came into contact with Sun Yat-sen's revolutionary movement, which at that time maintained close contacts with Japan.

Back in China, as a follower of Sun, Chiang was not a standout figure. He lived a spartan lifestyle and started every day by meditating for half an hour. Loyalty to his superiors and to his country were values he considered particularly important. As a commander, Chiang was the superior of the communist Zhou Enlai, who had returned from France and who taught political affairs at the Kuomintang military academy. All its students were members of the Kuomintang. Zhou had in common with Chiang that he also valued loyalty. The two men worked together for now.

Sun finally had everything he needed to become leader of the country again. The Kuomintang army was quickly built up with Soviet aid and was getting ready to advance from Guangzhou into the parts of China ruled by the warlords. But Sun was also ill with cancer and severely weakened as a result. He died in March 1925 at the age of 58, before the military campaign had started. The Kuomintang was now solid enough as an organization to survive Sun's death. As military commander, Chiang Kai-shek used his position to seize power in the party. Under his leadership, preparations to conquer the rest of the country from Guangzhou continued.

FIGURE 9 *Sun Yat-sen and his wife Song Qingling (photo by Bettmann/Gerry Images).*

FIGURE 10  *President Yuan Shikai surrounded by his staff, 1912 (photo by Photo12/UIG/Getty Images).*

FIGURE 11 *The German surrender to Japan at Qingdao, 1914 (photo by Universal Images Group/Getty Images).*

FIGURE 12 *A British soldier sharing a cigarette with a Chinese labourer in France during the First World War, circa 1916 (photo by Paul Thompson/FPG/ Hulton Archive/Getty Images).*

FIGURE 13 *Gu Weijun (also known as Wellington Koo) and his wife Oei Huilan (photo by Walter Gircke, Ullstein Bild/Gerry Images).*

# 4

# Emancipation (1925–43)

Since the Kuomintang had as its aim to reduce foreign influence in China, the Western powers and international business did not want it to drive out the warlords and form a new national government. Shortly after Sun Yat-sen's death, a top Shell executive, A. S. Debenham, sent a letter to the British Foreign Office. He thought it was time to teach the Kuomintang a lesson. What triggered his letter was that the local government of Guangzhou, led by the Kuomintang, had imposed a special tax on imported lamp oil. The Kuomintang needed extra income to build an army, and lamp oil was one of China's most traded foreign products. In response to this tariff, Shell, Texaco and Standard Oil had stopped distributing lamp oil through Guangzhou. But Shell wanted to send a stronger signal and, moreover, to resume the lucrative oil trade as soon as possible. Debenham therefore suggested that Britain intervene militarily.

The concerns of the oil multinational went beyond just the tax. The company was part Dutch and part British but presented itself in China (and to the government in London) as an all-British company and, therefore, as a British interest. Debenham proposed that British troops occupy the Kuomintang arms depot. Other possibilities he put forward were a blockade of the rail link between Hong Kong and Guangzhou or taking over local customs offices to put economic pressure on the Kuomintang. He pointed out that the lack of a central government in China was a major problem. In the past, under the emperors and under President Yuan Shikai, the foreign powers could put pressure on China by threatening to cut off the central government's access to funding. In the current situation, however, there was no other solution than to put direct pressure on those who did not comply with international treaties, in this case the Kuomintang. If action was not taken now, foreign influence in China would ebb away. Shell's lobbying campaign seemed to have an effect. It is likely that the US oil companies, in coordination with Shell, simultaneously submitted a similar plan to the government in Washington. In any case, there was support within the British government for the idea of sending a combined British-American fleet to

Guangzhou to threaten a military attack if the Kuomintang did not comply with certain demands.[1]

The proposed military intervention never materialized. A few weeks after Debenham made his proposal, the foreign establishment in China was forced onto the defensive. The Kuomintang organized anti-foreign demonstrations and strikes in various places. The purpose of this was to mobilize the population and thus facilitate the takeover of power by the Kuomintang. During a protest at a Japanese factory in Shanghai, a Japanese supervisor shot and killed a Chinese activist. This led to a chain reaction through new anti-Japanese demonstrations. In the international district of Shanghai, a group of Chinese students on their way to such a demonstration was arrested. On 30 May 1925, a student demonstration took place in Shanghai in protest against this arrest. The International Settlement police intervened and arrested some of the leaders of this protest. A large group of demonstrators then went to the police station where the just arrested student leaders were imprisoned. At 3:37 in the afternoon, Edward Everson, the police station commander, warned the crowd not to approach. Inspector Everson, who was married to a Chinese, gave his warning in Chinese, but no one heard him because of the noise. Ten seconds later, he ordered the officers present to shoot at the demonstrators, killing eleven. A British-Japanese-American commission of inquiry would later conclude that the shooting was justified. But to appease the matter, Everson was forced to resign after nineteen years of service.

Like Everson, many leading police officers in the international district police force were British nationals, and Britain was also the most visible foreign power in Shanghai. In response to the events, there was now a boycott of British products. First in Shanghai, but then to an even greater extent in Hong Kong and Guangzhou. Large-scale anti-British strikes also broke out in those cities and would last for more than a year. On 23 June, a large anti-foreign demonstration in Guangzhou spiralled out of control. British and French troops fired on the demonstrators, killing fifty-two. There were incidents also elsewhere in China: eight demonstrators were shot dead in the foreign section of Hankou (in present-day Wuhan) in Central China. Military action against the Kuomintang, as had been proposed by Shell, was now out of the question. This would only add fuel to the fire and would make the position of British companies and citizens even more difficult.

This atmosphere of anti-foreign protests and high political emotions was exactly what the Kuomintang needed. The warlords were only interested in maintaining their power, while the Kuomintang could claim to be committed to a better future for China. The political awareness of Chinese citizens in more and more cities undermined the position of the warlords and made the Kuomintang more popular. In 1926, the military campaign to reunify China began under the leadership of Chiang Kai-shek. In the following years, the Kuomintang managed to expand the area under its control and establish alliances with many of the warlords.

## China reunited

During the campaign, Chiang established himself as the undisputed leader of the Kuomintang. In 1927, he married Song Meiling, the youngest daughter of wealthy businessman Song Jiashu. His other two daughters, Song Ailing and Song Qingling, had played a role in Sun Yat-sen's life. Ailing, the eldest, had worked for Sun for a while as his secretary. Sun wanted to marry her,[2] but was still married to another woman at the time. Song Jiashu (a Christian like Sun) therefore disapproved of the marriage, and shortly afterwards Ailing married another Chinese Christian (and allegedly a descendant of Confucius in the seventy-fifth generation), the economist Kong Xiangxi. Qingling now took over her sister's job as Sun's secretary. Sun also fell in love with her, and again her father was against the marriage. He tried to keep Qingling away from Sun and even locked her in her room. However, she escaped by climbing out of the window and in 1915 married Sun Yat-sen (by now divorced), twenty-six years her senior. The two remained together until his death. Chiang Kai-shek had previously proposed to Meiling, Song's only unmarried daughter, but she was not interested in him. It wasn't until Sun was dead and Chiang was the new leader of the Kuomintang that she changed her mind. His marriage to Song Meiling symbolized Chiang's bond with Sun Yat-sen and increased his legitimacy as his successor.

Chiang Kai-shek also took steps of a different nature to cement his position of power. The role of the communists within the Kuomintang had been particularly helpful in strengthening the party against the warlords. The Communists' membership induced the Soviet Union to provide financial and military support, and they were also very skilled at mobilizing segments of the population such as students and workers. The problem, however, was that the CCP members formed an important power factor within the Kuomintang. Moreover, they were so radical in their anti-foreign activities that cooperation with the West or Japan probably was impossible. But the strategy that Sun bequeathed to the Kuomintang was aimed at modernizing China through foreign investment.

In April 1927, there were large-scale acts of violence in Hankou by Chinese citizens against Japanese residents of that city. So far the Kuomintang had turned against the warlords not foreigners, but this seemed to be the beginning of violent actions against the foreign enclaves in China. Chiang wanted to get rid of the communists, whom he saw as a threat to his own position, and to allow the Kuomintang to follow a less-radical course. Shortly after the events in Hankou, Chiang began an anti-communist purge of his party. Many communists were arrested and executed. Those who managed to escape fled to the Chinese countryside, from where the CCP continued to fight against the Kuomintang. The Soviet Union ended its cooperation with the Kuomintang, and Borodin and the other Comintern agents left the country.

Chiang had caused the death of a large number of communists through his attack on the CCP, but he had also made a personal sacrifice. At the time of the purge, his eldest son (born of Chiang's first marriage) was studying in Moscow. This son, Chiang Ching-kuo, had been a fellow student of the communist Deng Xiaoping there. After the break of the Kuomintang with the CCP, the Soviet Union did not allow the younger Chiang to return to China. Chiang Kai-shek then refused to negotiate his return. He felt that his personal interests were subordinate to the higher political goal of the Kuomintang: to reunite China and make it a strong country, with a central role for the party.

In 1928, for the first time in twelve years, China again had a central government that administered a large part of the country. The Kuomintang decided that henceforth not Beijing, but Nanjing, on the Yangtze River, would be the capital. Western companies initially had great concerns about the new regime. Even though there were no communists left in the Kuomintang, the party was founded to make China strong again and to push back foreign influence. Shell, which had urged the British government to put pressure on the Kuomintang, discovered that its rival Standard Oil soon proved willing to cooperate with Chiang Kai-shek's government. Shell's management was deeply disappointed in the British government, which was apparently unable to intervene militarily in China for British economic interests. The era of far-reaching Western influence in China was over. It was time for the multinationals to change course.

The director of the new central bank set up by the Kuomintang, Song Ziwen, approached Shell to discuss cooperation. At the end of 1927, both parties came to an agreement. Shell would pay the Kuomintang taxes on its extensive trade in oil products in China. In addition, Shell would provide an advance on future tax payments, which amounted to important extra income for the new government at a time when it hardly had any revenue. In exchange for this financial support, Shell would only have to pay taxes at a central level at a standard rate, and the Kuomintang would ensure that all kinds of irregular local taxes would be abolished. The Kuomintang entered into a similar agreement with Standard Oil.[3] Western multinationals began to see the benefits of the new regime. There would be more stability in China and there was again a clear interlocutor. Unlike under the Qing dynasty with its conservative, inward-looking bureaucracy, companies could do business directly with the Kuomintang. The intervention of foreign diplomats was no longer necessary. Central banker Song Ziwen, who was also Minister of Finance from 1928, was an example of a Kuomintang official who was accessible to foreign companies. Song was a brother of the Song sisters and thus brother-in-law of Chiang Kai-shek. He had studied at Harvard and Columbia University and had worked for a US bank in New York for a while.

From 1928, Party and state were integrated, as Sun Yat-sen had wanted. The Party did not rule remotely, through a parliament, but directly, as in the

Soviet Union. All political power was concentrated in one organization: both the government and the army were controlled by the Kuomintang. Individuals in senior government positions were members of the Party. China's new flag symbolized party–state integration. The country had only had a national flag since the nineteenth century. The Second Opium War had broken out as a result of an incident involving a ship flying the British flag. After the Second Opium War, the Qing dynasty decided that Chinese naval ships should henceforth fly a yellow flag with a dragon and a pearl on it. In 1888, the government established that this naval flag would also be the national flag of China. After the fall of the dynasty, a new flag was needed for the republic, because the colour yellow and the dragon were symbols of imperial power. From 1912, the Republic of China opted for a flag with five horizontal bands in different colours. These stood for the five main ethnic groups of the Qing dynasty. From top to bottom: red (Han Chinese), yellow (Manchus), blue (Mongols), white (Central Asian Muslims), and black (Tibetans). In 1928, this five-colour flag was replaced by a flag in which the emblem of the Kuomintang (a white sun against a blue background) was central. The Party and not the cooperation between the five main ethnic groups would be the most important pillar of the Republic.

China's reunification process was not yet complete. Much of the country was controlled by warlords who had joined the Kuomintang. After 1928, there were still several military clashes between the central government and recalcitrant warlords. In areas where hardly any Han Chinese lived, such as Tibet, Xinjiang and Mongolia, warlords were also active or local rulers tried to break away from the Republic of China partially or completely. Meanwhile, the Communist Party no longer had a significant presence in large cities. Mao Zedong saw an opportunity in this, as he wanted to seek the support of peasants rather than try to regain influence in the cities. The vast majority of the Chinese population lived in rural areas, but the problem was that the peasant population lived isolated in small villages and did not feel politically involved. It was not resistance to exploitation by foreigners in the distant coastal cities, but to exploitation by local large landowners that appealed to the peasants. The CCP's propaganda therefore focused more on the promise of land reform: the land of rich peasants would be distributed among the poor peasants.

But for now, the Communists were on the defensive, and Mao and other CCP leaders such as Zhou Enlai and Deng Xiaoping, who had returned from abroad, gained experience in waging guerrilla warfare and mobilizing the rural population. One day the Communist Party would rule China, but that was still a long way off. Many early communists did not survive the long period of struggle with the Kuomintang. One of the communist guerrilla leaders was Yang Kaihui, Mao Zedong's second wife. In 1930 she fell into the hands of a warlord who had joined the Kuomintang. She refused to renounce the CCP, after which the warlord had her executed.

Although the Kuomintang failed to completely destroy the CCP, China could now get back to work on reducing foreign influence. The main thing was that there was again a central government that maintained contacts with the outside world on behalf of China. Chiang Kai-shek and his government sought cooperation with the West, but at the same time, they intended to end the inequality in China's relationship with foreign countries. Although China was still no match for the great powers militarily, the country was now in a stronger position than under the Qing Dynasty. A milestone was 1931, when China regained the right to set the tariffs on imported goods. The ability to do this had been lost by the Chinese government because of the Opium Wars. From now on, China also decided for itself what happened to the customs revenues. The Diplomatic Body in Beijing thus lost its influential role in China's public finances.

Although these measures were unfavourable to the great powers, the Kuomintang government was able to implement them thanks to the rise of nationalism as a broad popular movement in China. In the nineteenth century, the Chinese population had hardly been a factor in relations with the great powers. Now, however, the foreign powers always had to reckon with the risk of strikes and boycotts motivated by strong nationalistic feelings. For access to the Chinese market and the physical safety of foreign persons and assets, the great powers depended more than ever on the cooperation of the Chinese government. The Kuomintang could dampen anti-foreign feelings among the population, but it could also fuel them. On this point, the views of the Western powers and Japan grew further and further apart. While the Europeans and Americans felt that military interventions had become less effective and only strengthened resistance against foreigners, Japan was increasingly inclined to send troops to China with the aim of protecting its nationals and interests. A 1928 clash between Kuomintang troops and Japanese soldiers in the eastern Chinese city of Jinan had convinced both sides that the other was a dangerous adversary.

## Participating in the international community

Many Chinese leaders had received international training and were very well aware of what was happening in the world. The country had adopted Western diplomatic practices and henceforth participated in international conferences and organizations. In 1922, despite their country's political divisions, Chinese diplomats had won a diplomatic victory at a conference in Washington. There, a stable balance of power in East Asia was sought between the great powers. The military alliance that had existed between Britain and Japan since 1902 had ended. Instead, the British, American and Japanese governments agreed to maintain a fixed ratio in terms of the size of their navies. In terms of tonnage, the split would be 5:5:3 in terms of British, American and Japanese battleships and carriers, respectively, regardless of where they were stationed. France, which no longer played a leading role as a maritime power, had to settle for a smaller share (equal to that of Italy). Defeated Germany and the Soviet Union did not participate in the conference.

With the 5:5:3 formula, the United States and Britain, who had their navies spread over several oceans, recognized that Japan was the dominant military power in East Asia because the Japanese fleet was only active in that one region. But as long as the British and American military forces in East Asia worked together, they would counterbalance Japanese military might. This was an important reason for Britain, as a declining power, in the 1920s and 1930s to increasingly collaborate with the United States, which as a rising power was a geopolitical rival just like Japan. The government in London saw Japan as a bigger threat than the United States. An important reason for this was the Anglo-American consensus that the Chinese market should never be monopolized by a single power. Under the influence of a powerful America, China would probably still be open to British (and most other foreign) companies, while a dominant Japan was expected to be considerably more protectionist. Thus, any future Japanese rule in China would harm both British and American economic interests. The governments in London and Washington began to see that it would not be to their advantage if Japanese influence in China increased further. Korea had already been annexed by Japan in 1910. One concession Japan had to make at the Washington conference under British and American pressure was that it returned Qingdao to China.

Chinese diplomats not only participated in one-off conferences such as those in Paris and Washington, but also in meetings of the League of Nations. That organization was based in Geneva and made it possible for governments to manage the stability of the international order on an ongoing basis. Although the League of Nations was an idea of US President Wilson, the United States was missing in Geneva. The US Congress was not in favour of an active American role in the League of Nations and blocked US accession to the organization. Germany and the Soviet Union were also not members. Power within the League of Nations was largely in the hands of four countries that held permanent seats on the Executive Council: Great Britain, France, Italy and Japan. China did not play a major role in the League of Nations, but its membership was a sign that the country now was an active part of an international community of states.

The Chinese government maintained diplomatic relations with more and more countries. For this it used its own legations abroad and the foreign legations in the Chinese capital. When the Kuomintang moved the capital, and the seat of government, to Nanjing in 1928, this created a dilemma for the great powers. In Beijing the legation quarter was under foreign rule, while in Nanjing there was no foreign enclave at all. Several years earlier, the deposed Qing emperor had already moved to Tianjin, leaving the Forbidden City. Beijing was henceforth no more than a provincial capital. However, the powers did not want to give up their privileges in Beijing and decided to keep their old legations. In order to be able to do their job, they opened sub-legations in Nanjing, and from then on, the envoys travelled back and forth between the two cities (which were almost a thousand kilometres apart). It was not until the mid-1930s that the British government decided to move its legation (which would from then on be called an 'embassy', a more modern term carrying greater prestige) to Nanjing. But there was no question of the foreigners in Nanjing getting their own quarter. China increasingly became an equal of Western and other modern states in this regard. As China's international role became more dynamic, its own representations abroad played a greater role and that of the foreign legations inside China declined.

## Crisis in Manchuria

In the late 1920s, it became increasingly clear that Japan, now the largest economic and military power in East Asia, was seeking a high degree of exclusive influence in China. This provoked resistance from both the Chinese population and the other great powers. Moderate Japanese politicians wanted to act with caution and keep the door open for international cooperation. Within the Japanese military, however, there were officers who felt it was time for a significantly more assertive foreign policy. The influence of the West in the region was waning, while China and the Soviet Union were gaining strength. In the eyes of radical, often young, officers, circumstances were favourable for Japan to shape the regional order in a way that suited Japanese interests. Later it might become more difficult to do this. The most radical officers were not in Japan itself, but in China. Like other powers, Japan had troops stationed in China, but in much greater numbers. The centre of gravity of the Japanese military presence was in Manchuria. After it had expelled Russia from Manchuria in 1905, Japan left a few thousand troops behind in the region. Their task was to protect the South Manchurian Railway and the port of Dalian, which was in Japanese hands. The rest of Manchuria was under the rule of a Chinese warlord, Zhang Zuolin.

In 1928, as Chiang Kai-shek's Kuomintang forces were about to capture Beijing and were approaching Manchuria, some Japanese officers decided it was time to act. One of them, Colonel Kenji Doihara, acting without his own superiors' knowledge, ordered the elimination of Zhang Zuolin. Doihara, who had extensive experience in China and was fluent in Chinese, worked for Japanese military intelligence. His intention was to create a crisis that would lead the Japanese government to order the military to occupy all of Manchuria before the Kuomintang could do so. On 4 June 1928, on Doihara's instructions, Japanese soldiers detonated a railway viaduct just as the train Zhang Zuolin was traveling on passed underneath it. He did not survive the attack, but the intended crisis did not materialize. Moreover, his son Zhang Xueliang succeeded him as warlord and regional strongman. Zhang junior understood the purpose of the attack and avoided a confrontation with Japan. He did not openly accuse Japan of his father's murder. The Japanese government did not invade Manchuria, but Doihara was also not punished for his actions. Several months later, when tensions eased, Zhang Xueliang announced that he and his army were joining the Kuomintang.

The younger Zhang was much more than his father a nationalist who wanted to make China a strong country. He supported Chiang Kai-shek's government and viewed both Japan and the Soviet Union as major threats. As a warlord, Zhang was often involved in military affairs, but he also had a busy social life and was addicted to opium. For some time he had an affair with Edda Ciano, a daughter of the Italian dictator Benito Mussolini. She was in China as the wife of Galeazzo Count Ciano, who was consul in Shanghai. In 1929, Zhang turned his attention to the northern portion of the Manchurian railway system, which was not under Japanese control. A legacy from Russia's imperial era was that railways in northern Manchuria were jointly run by China and the Soviet Union. Zhang, in accordance with the Kuomintang government's policy, sought to push back Russian influence. Joseph Stalin (born Ioseb Besarionis dze Jughashvili, in what is now Georgia), who had succeeded the now deceased Lenin as Soviet leader, rose to the challenge and sent troops into northern Manchuria. Fighting broke out, and it soon became apparent that Zhang's forces were no match for the Soviet army. Zhang Xueliang and Chiang Kai-shek had to give in to Stalin's demand, and the railways remained under joint control by China and the Soviet Union.

Kenji Doihara and other radical Japanese officers in southern Manchuria had observed these events with great concern. Apparently, Zhang Xueliang and the Kuomintang were unable to resist the Soviet Union. In their eyes there was a good chance that sooner or later the Russians would expand their influence in Manchuria. This would lead to a repeat of the Russo-Japanese War, and it was uncertain who would win this time. In addition, in Japanese eyes, Zhang began to exhibit increasingly dangerous behaviour. In 1930, he ordered the construction of a new seaport at Huludao, on the coast of southern Manchuria. This port, which was being built by a European contractor,[4] was a possible competitor to the port of Dalian, Japan's main commercial and military base in Manchuria. The likelihood of anti-Japanese boycotts remained high, and once the new port was completed, trade flows might no longer be routed through Dalian, reducing Japan's influence in the region.

Doihara and a few fellow officers sprang into action. At 10.20 in the evening on 18 September 1931, they detonated a charge of dynamite on the tracks of the South Manchurian Railway. The explosion caused hardly any damage: only a few minutes after the explosion a train passed without any problems. But unlike in 1928, what Doihara had hoped for now did happen. The matter escalated. Local Japanese forces blamed China for the attack and attacked Zhang Xueliang's soldiers. The Japanese military command saw an opportunity in the crisis that had now arisen and proceeded to a large-scale military invasion of Manchuria. Both Zhang Xueliang and Chiang Kai-shek believed that China was not yet ready for war with Japan. Zhang's Chinese troops retreated to other parts of the country, and all of Manchuria was occupied by the Japanese army. Fierce fighting did break out in Shanghai, where many Japanese troops were also stationed, but hostilities there ended after more than a month.

China, as a militarily weak actor, appealed to the League of Nations. The League's task was, after all, to counter armed aggression between states. Gu Weijin, who had argued in Paris in 1919 for the Japanese return of Qingdao, again played an active role in representing China's interests as a diplomat. He travelled to Geneva, where he energetically and eloquently promoted Chinese interests. The Japanese government argued that it had no aggressive intentions and had acted in self-defence. To emphasize this, the Japanese military formed a new government in the occupied territory, which then proclaimed the independent Empire of Manchuria (otherwise known as Manchukuo). The ruler of the new state was none other than Aisin Gioro Puyi, formerly the last emperor of China. Puyi had lived for some time as a commoner in the Japanese concession of Tianjin and, at the invitation of the Japanese, had gone to Manchuria, the land of his ancestors, to start a new career as a ruler. However, he soon discovered that he had very little influence and was in fact a prisoner of the Japanese military, which held the real power in Manchuria.

The League of Nations appointed a commission to investigate what was really going on. When this commission concluded that Japan was indeed the aggressor, that the Japanese troops should pull back and that Manchukuo should not be recognized as an independent state but was part of China, Japan withdrew its membership of the League of Nations. China had won a diplomatic and moral victory, and there were hardly any countries in the world that recognized Manchukuo. The United States, still not a member of the League of Nations, also declared that it would not recognize Manchukuo because the new state was the result of Japanese aggression. But otherwise nothing changed about the fact that Japan now occupied a large part of China. The League of Nations had no military means, and the Western powers were averse to another war after the First World War. No economic sanctions were imposed either. After the stock market crash of 1929, the world economy had entered a major depression and countries such as Great Britain and the United States had little appetite for a trade war with Japan. The Soviet Union also kept quiet. Stalin avoided conflict by selling the Soviet share of Manchuria's railways to the Japanese.

In Japan, the population responded enthusiastically to the occupation of Manchuria, contributing to the emergence of a highly militarized society. On 15 May 1932, Japanese Prime Minister Tsuyoshi Inukai, an opponent of an aggressive China strategy, was assassinated by a group of Japanese junior naval officers. Charlie Chaplin, the film star, was in Japan at the time and was scheduled to be received by Inukai on the same day the assassination took place. The attackers knew this and planned to kill Chaplin as well, hoping that this would lead to a crisis between Japan and the United States. However, the actor decided to deviate from the schedule set by his hosts and attended a sumo wrestling match with Inukai's son. He thereby escaped the attack. After the death of the prime minister, the army took over power in Japan, leaving no room for moderate politicians. Western companies were largely driven out in Manchuria, as large Japanese companies now came to dominate that market with the support of the Japanese military.

## Modernization plans for China

Under Chiang's leadership, the Kuomintang tried to realize Sun Yat-sen's plans. The party controlled the state and the army and pushed for a greater role for the government in the economy and society. Chinese public opinion was increasingly nationalistic and against foreign influence in China. At the same time, the Kuomintang sought cooperation with the West. Investments by Western companies were necessary to modernize the Chinese economy, and only Europe and the United States could provide a geopolitical counterweight to Japan and the Soviet Union as long as China itself was not strong enough. The foreign policy of the Kuomintang government was therefore moderate: China wanted good relations with Europe and the United States. Its leaders preferred to avoid a war with Japan for the time being.

Chiang Kai-shek was surrounded by people of Western education and a pro-Western worldview, including his wife Song Meiling, her sister Song Ailing and brother Song Ziwen (who would later serve as foreign minister and prime minister), Kong Xiangxi (the husband of Song Ailing and Song Ziwen's successor as Central Bank Director and Finance Minister) and Gu Weijun (the diplomat, who had served as interim president after Sun Yat-sen's death and then prime minister for a short time, and for a long time served as ambassador). That a Western education did not necessarily lead to a pro-Western view of the world was shown in the case of Song Qingling, Meiling's other sister and widow of Sun Yat-sen. Like her sisters and brother, she had studied in the United States, but she had now become a strong supporter of communism. From her hometown of Shanghai, she provided financial support to the CCP when it waged a guerrilla war against the Kuomintang.

Chiang was raised as a Buddhist, but after marrying Song Meiling, he converted to Christianity. His wife played a major role in the 'New Life' movement. It was launched by the Kuomintang with the aim of giving Chinese society a new moral and ideological foundation. This publicity campaign was aimed at the prevailing culture of corruption and hedonism

(Chiang himself had a mostly austere lifestyle) and at promoting modern standards of hygiene. The New Life movement was inspired by traditional Confucian values as well as Christianity, rejecting both communism and liberalism. As an ideology, however, the ideas of the movement were not coherent and the strong emphasis on hygiene and good manners did not match the problems of poverty and lack of security that the majority of the population faced on a daily basis. It also didn't help that the far right wing within the Kuomintang had set up a network of thugs, the fascism-inspired blue shirts, who tried to promote the New Life movement through brute force. The movement never became very popular with the Chinese population.

The European powers had emerged from the First World War weakened. Although France was among the victors, it no longer played a significant geopolitical role in China. However, Germany, having lost all its assets and privileges in China, managed to become an influential player once more. German industrial firms continued to be major investors in China after the war. After the split between the Kuomintang and the CCP, and the departure of Borodin, mainly German advisers took the place of the Comintern agents.[5] The regime of Adolf Hitler, who came to power in 1933, intensified cooperation with China. Nazi Germany saw China as a valuable source of raw materials. As part of this strategic cooperation, the Chinese army was trained and armed by Germany.

China also wanted to modernize in the technological field with support from abroad. In 1932, the Chinese government approached Telefunken, a joint venture of the German conglomerates Siemens and AEG, asking it to contribute to the construction of a factory in Shanghai for vacuum tubes, the main components of radio equipment at the time. As precursors to transistors and semiconductors, vacuum (or electron) tubes were highly advanced technology in the 1930s. The Chinese government offered the German company two options. One was that Telefunken would sell the requested technology to China and provide technicians and raw materials for the new factory. The other option was that the plant would become a Sino-German joint venture between Telefunken and a Chinese state-owned company. The negotiations were complex and eventually came to nothing as the long-anticipated war between Japan and China broke out a few years later. In the meantime, China tried to gain access to vacuum tube technology not only at Telefunken but also at its Dutch competitor Philips and (most likely) RCA of the United States. Indicative of the changing relationship was that Philips was considering agreeing to a minority interest in a joint venture for the production of radio equipment, under Chinese management, with a state-owned company. Philips would train Chinese technicians and provide all the technology needed for the new factory. The reason why Philips was willing to hand over so much, even though the company had little faith in Chinese management capabilities, was that it expected the participation of the Chinese government would lead to the plant becoming a monopoly.

Moreover, China now being strongly nationalistic, there was always the danger of anti-foreign activities by unwilling local officials, consumer boycotts and strikes. For large foreign companies, the central government was therefore an indispensable partner and patron. But the cooperation plans of the government and Philips were never realized because of the Sino-Japanese war.[6]

## Hostage in Xi'an

Chiang Kai-shek not only wanted to strengthen China militarily and economically, but also to defeat the communist resistance before confronting Japan. But pressure from the Chinese population to reduce Japanese influence as quickly as possible increased. There were calls to seek cooperation with the Chinese communists and with the Soviet Union in order to stand stronger against Japan. One proponent of this approach was the warlord Zhang Xueliang, who now was off his opium addiction and determined to work for a stronger China. He urged Chiang for a coalition with the CCP. When the latter refused, Zhang made a plan to force him to cooperate with the communists. Mao Zedong, who had meanwhile risen to become supreme leader of the CCP, had already expressed his openness to such cooperation. In December 1936, at the invitation of Zhang Xueliang, Chiang flew from the capital Nanjing to Zhang's military headquarters in the northern Chinese city of Xi'an. There, Chiang Kai-shek and his bodyguards were captured by Zhang's soldiers. He did not want to let Chiang go until he reached an agreement with the CCP.

Mao sent Zhou Enlai, Chiang's former subordinate at the Kuomintang military academy, to Xi'an to negotiate with the Kuomintang leader. Zhou promised that the CCP would place its troops under the supreme command of the Kuomintang on the condition that they would fight Japan together from then on. Chiang Kai-shek, after being imprisoned for several weeks, agreed to Zhou Enlai's proposal. It is likely that he was influenced by the fact that Germany had signed an anti-Comintern pact with Japan shortly before. According to that agreement, both countries would work together to counter the influence of the Comintern. It was a signal that they both viewed communism and the Soviet Union as major threats. The German-Japanese rapprochement meant that German military aid to China might come under pressure in the future. Cooperating with the CCP opened up an opportunity for Chiang Kai-shek to receive military support from the Soviet Union.

It is striking that all those involved in the Xi'an agreement kept their promises. Zhang Xueliang put Chiang on a plane back to Nanjing and also boarded the plane himself. After arriving in the Chinese capital, Zhang surrendered to the central government. He probably wanted to show that he had not committed his betrayal out of self-interest or lack of loyalty, but out of the belief that his action was necessary for the country. Zhang lost his position as regional leader of northern China and was placed under permanent house arrest. Only half a century later, when he was already in his nineties, would he be able to travel freely again. He would eventually die at the age of 100 in his then hometown of Honolulu, Hawaii.

Chiang Kai-shek ordered an end to the fight against the CCP after his return to Nanjing. Mao then arranged for the CCP's military forces to become part of the Chinese National Army and thus formally under the command of Chiang and the Kuomintang. Stalin, who, because of the anti-Comintern pact between Japan and Germany, thought it wise to seek rapprochement with the Kuomintang government, agreed to arms transfers to China. He also gave permission for Chiang Kai-shek's son to return to his homeland. The son, Chiang Ching-kuo, had lived in the Soviet Union for twelve years and was now married to a Belarusian woman, Faina Vachrava. They had met at the machine factory in Yekaterinburg (then known as Sverdlovsk) where they both worked. Chiang junior and his wife moved to China.

Sino-German relations had become uncertain. Economically, Germany was very interested in China, but geopolitically, a partnership with Japan seemed more useful as a counterbalance to the Soviet Union. Despite the arms deliveries to China and the training of the Chinese army by Germany, the German government believed that Japan was militarily stronger. In June 1937, Kong Xiangxi visited Germany in his capacity as Chinese finance minister. In Germany, Kong spoke with several Nazi leaders, including Hitler. The latter offered to mediate if there was a dispute between China and Japan but gave no guarantees that the German military support would be permanent. Indeed, it would soon become apparent that Germany was not a stable partner for China.

## China and the Second World War

Late in the evening of 7 July 1937, for reasons that remain unclear, a firefight broke out between Chinese and Japanese troops in the Beijing area: the infamous 'Marco Polo Bridge Incident' (named after a nearby ancient bridge that figured in Marco Polo's travel account). The scale of hostilities expanded rapidly. Within weeks, Japanese troops managed to capture Beijing and the neighbouring port city of Tianjin. The centre of gravity of the battle then moved to the Shanghai area. What began as an accidental local-level confrontation turned into all-out war, with no declaration of war being issued. Both sides believed that the war would end in their own favour. Attempts at de-escalation were made but not vigorously pursued. As during the Sino-Japanese War of 1894–5, Japan soon proved to be militarily superior. Chiang Kai-shek unsuccessfully deployed his best German-trained troops to defend Shanghai. The Chinese part of Shanghai fell into Japanese hands, after which Japanese troops also captured the capital Nanjing. Soon, in addition to Manchuria, large parts of northern and eastern China were now also occupied. In taking Nanjing, the Japanese troops committed large-scale acts of violence, probably to discourage further resistance to the Japanese advance. Many, probably several hundreds of thousands, of Chinese prisoners of war and civilians were murdered in what is known as the Nanjing Massacre (or also the Rape of Nanjing, in reference to the probably tens of thousands of women who were raped by Japanese soldiers).

In the West, media attention was mainly focused on the fact that American and British ships on the Yangtze near Nanjing were attacked by the Japanese military. Standard Oil and Shell tankers, accompanied by United States and British gunboats, were moving oil from Nanjing storage facilities of the two petroleum companies. Their goal was to keep the oil safe from destruction or seizure. The tankers also carried a large number of evacuees from Nanjing, mainly employees of the companies and their families, but also foreign journalists. The Shell tanker *Tien Kwang* alone had about 250 refugees on board.[7] On 11 and 12 December 1937, the ships were attacked several times by Japanese aircraft, ships and guns stationed on the riverbank. Three Standard Oil tankers and the American gunboat *Panay* were sunk. Several Shell ships and a British gunboat were damaged. Some Westerners, including *La Stampa* correspondent Sandro Sandri and two Standard Oil captains, and an unknown number of Chinese were killed in the attacks. Because the vessels had flags and deck paintings to make their nationalities visible from all directions, no one in the United States or Britain believed the later Japanese statement that it was a mistake.

Due to the involvement of several reporters – apart from Sandri also *Corriere della Sera* correspondent Luigi Barzini and Norman Soong of *The New York Times* were present – the incident, was reported in the Western press. Photographs and film footage of the events were widely circulated. Against this background, a minor incident a month later also received significant attention in the United States. The American consul in Nanjing, John Moore Allison, was punched in the face by a Japanese soldier. Public opinion in the United States was strongly anti-Japanese after these events. But perhaps most striking from a Japanese and Chinese perspective was the lack of a strong response from the British and American governments. Japan apologized and paid damages and the matter was settled. There were no credible guarantees that the Japanese military would not do something similar again. This was a big difference from how eighty years earlier the incident with the ship *Arrow* was sufficient reason for the British government to start the Second Opium War. For China, the moral of the story was clear: also in the modern world, power relations, not principles or rules, are decisive.

To the great frustration of the Japanese army, China continued to fight, despite the military defeats and unlike in 1895 when it quickly gave in. There was no turning back for the Kuomintang. A peace treaty with Japan would mean the end of its political legitimacy. After all, the party's primary raison d'être was to liberate China from foreign domination. Just as the attempt of the Japanese warlord Hideyoshi to conquer China in the sixteenth century had ended in an impasse, the Japanese advance came to a standstill. The difference was that Hideyoshi got no further than Korea, while the Japanese army had now conquered a large part of China. In the years after 1939, the military situation in China remained largely the same. Japan had occupied many coastal areas and most of the major cities, while the Chinese government continued to fight from the temporary capital of Chongqing, located deep in the country's interior. China was not strong enough to defeat or drive out the Japanese armies, while Japan was not strong enough to conquer all of China or to permanently pacify the occupied territories. The CCP waged an intensive guerrilla war against the Japanese forces in the countryside.

Large numbers of soldiers died in this Third Sino-Japanese War, especially on the Chinese side. But the vast majority of casualties were among the Chinese civilian population. The Chinese people had suffered considerably in recent decades not only because of the widespread fighting of the 1920s and 1930s, but also because of looting and murder by soldiers and criminal gangs. As the government had stopped performing all kinds of vital functions since the fall of the Qing dynasty, the country repeatedly suffered from major famines and floods. Moreover, in the fight against Japan, Chiang decided to have the dikes of the Yellow River pierced. He wanted the flooded land to hamper the Japanese advance in northern China.[8] However, the collateral damage was dramatic: according to an official estimate by the Kuomintang themselves, 800,000 Chinese civilians drowned. Thousands of villages were destroyed and millions of people had to flee to other parts of the country.

In 1938, Germany definitively sided with Japan and ended all military aid to China. Yet it was Hitler who, inadvertently, made the push that would ultimately save China from its predicament. His decision to invade Poland in September 1939 led to another major war in Europe between Germany on the one hand and Great Britain and France on the other. The long-term effect of this was in China's favour. Japan initially saw the European war as an opportunity to put further pressure on China. For the Chinese government, the port of Haiphong in the north of Vietnam, part of French Indochina, was the most important supply channel for the import of fuel and weapons. The Chinese ports were either in Japanese hands or (like Hong Kong and Shanghai) were largely cut off from the hinterland because they were in China's occupied coastal zone. Haiphong was connected by rail to cities in the unoccupied southwest of China.

After France's surrender to Germany in 1940, Japanese troops invaded northern Indochina and forced the French colonial government to end trade relations with China. Chiang Kai-shek now had to route his supply line via Rangoon (now Yangon) in the British colony of Burma. In the spring of 1941, Japan and the Soviet Union agreed that they would not attack each other and would remain neutral in the conflicts in which they were involved. In the late 1930s, the two countries had fought a brief border war with each other. Japan had lost and chose to avoid, at least for now, a possible new conflict with the Soviet Union. As a result of the 1941 neutrality pact with Japan, Stalin cut off military aid to China. The agreement with Japan came just in time for Stalin, as in June 1941 Germany invaded the Soviet Union. Japan then occupied southern Indochina, which provided a convenient base for the Japanese military to attack other parts of Southeast Asia if necessary.

The United States considered all these developments particularly threatening to its interests in Asia. These interests included maintaining access to the Chinese market and raw materials in Southeast Asia, protecting the Philippines (an American colony) and preventing any major power from becoming dominant in the region. The situation in Europe left the British, French and Russians unable or unwilling to hold back the Japanese advance. The best long-term counterbalance to Japan was China, but that country was now increasingly isolated. The US government decided to resort to heavy economic pressure on Japan to force it to withdraw from Indochina and China. The United States, together with Great Britain and the Dutch government in exile (based in London after the German occupation of the Netherlands), imposed an oil embargo against Japan and started supporting China with loans and military supplies that reached the country via the Burma route. At the same time, the United States stationed long-range bombers in the Philippines as a deterrent against any Japanese attack plans.

The threat of an acute crisis into which Japan's armed forces and economy would plunge once their oil supplies were exhausted prompted Japan to attack the weakly defended colonial possessions of the Netherlands and Britain in Southeast Asia. Moreover, the Japanese army wanted to occupy Burma in order to block that supply route to China as well. Convinced that it was inevitable that the United States would declare war on Japan once it moved against the British and Dutch presence in Southeast Asia, the Japanese military command decided to attack the Philippines and the US naval base at Pearl Harbor in Hawaii. Thus, on 8 December 1941 (in Europe and the United States it was 7 December, due to the time difference with Asia), the war between Japan and the Western powers began. In the following months, Japan occupied almost all of Southeast Asia plus many islands in the Pacific Ocean. The International Settlement of Shanghai and the British colonies of Hong Kong and Singapore, the latter being the main British military base in the Far East, were also captured.

In Europe, Hitler reacted enthusiastically to the news of the Japanese attack on the British, American and Dutch colonial territories in Asia. A few days after Pearl Harbor he declared war on the United States, probably in response to the material support the Americans had been giving to Britain for some time. From then on, German submarines could act without restraint to cut off British supplies from the United States. The two great regional conflicts in Asia and Europe were now even more closely intertwined and together formed the Second World War. For now, the Soviet Union and

Japan were not at war with each other. It was not until August 1945 that Stalin would declare war on Japan.

In 1942, Japan was more powerful than ever, as it now controlled much of Asia. The still unoccupied part of China was largely cut off from the outside world because Burma was now also largely in the hands of Japan. But at the same time, the attack on Pearl Harbor was the beginning of the end for Japan as a leading geopolitical actor and for China the beginning of its salvation. The crucial factor was the United States, a rising world power since the late nineteenth century, with an economic and military potential far greater than that of Japan. But it took time for the United States to fully focus on the fight with Japan. The US government agreed to the British proposal to concentrate the Allied war effort on Germany first. US President Franklin Roosevelt (a distant cousin of Theodore Roosevelt) decided to greatly increase aid to China with the aim of occupying a large part of the Japanese armed forces and exhausting Japan as much as possible. At the same time, the United States began capturing several of the Pacific islands to put Japan on the defensive.

Because China's supply routes through Indochina and Burma were cut off, the US military set up an airlift. From British India, American planes flew over the Himalayas to supply China with fuel and weapons. Although the route was extremely dangerous, not only due to the Japanese air force, but even more so because of severe turbulence, ice formation on the aircraft and lack of experienced pilots, it was possible to get large amounts of goods to China in this way. In addition, the United States stationed its own fighter planes in China and sent military advisers. Joseph Stilwell was appointed as Chiang Kai-shek's Chief of Staff. Unfortunately, General Stilwell, although he spoke Chinese, turned out not to be a happy choice. The nickname by which Chiang was known internationally was 'the generalissimo', but Stilwell invariably referred to him in his diary as 'the peanut'. In direct dealings with the Chinese leader (and others), the American was hardly more subtle. In addition, he and Chiang had different ideas about the strategy to be followed against Japan. But despite such frictions, something fundamental had changed since Pearl Harbor. China was no longer alone.

## Chiang's big moment in Cairo

The year 1943 brought the greatest improvement in China's geopolitical position since the Opium Wars. In that year it became increasingly apparent that Germany and Japan would not win the war, even though it was not clear how much longer they would last. Chiang Kai-shek understood that it was only a matter of time before the Japanese occupation of China ended. And what would happen next? Cooperation with the CCP was aimed at combatting the common Japanese enemy. If the latter would no longer be there, China's internal power struggle would erupt again. Many of the best troops of the Kuomintang, the units trained and armed by Germany, were lost in the early stages of the war. Chiang grew more cautious now; there was no point in further losing large numbers of troops in the fight against Japan. Those would later be badly needed to fight the CCP.

At the same time, the war effort had to be sustained because this greatly improved China's negotiating position vis-à-vis the Western powers. These needed China to keep up the pressure on Japan and to ensure that a large part of its land and air forces could not be deployed elsewhere in Asia. Chinese diplomats saw their chance and demanded that the unequal treaties be abolished now, because they did not fit with an alliance on an equal basis. Sensitive to this Chinese pressure, the United States and Britain announced in October 1942 that they would end the unequal treaties. In January 1943, China therefore concluded new treaties with the two Western Allies.[9] A few months later, the new 'equal' treaties came into force and British and American colonial privileges in China came to an end. Smaller Western powers soon followed suit. At that time it was a gesture without many practical consequences, because large parts of China were under Japanese occupation. Still, it was a very important gesture. It gave recognition to China as a full participant in the international system. And after the war, foreigners in China would no longer have legal privileges, military bases or enclaves of their own.

Around this time, Chiang Kai-shek published a book, written in Chinese and intended for a domestic audience.[10] In it he indicated that the fight against Japan and the end of the unequal treaties were parts of the larger process of 'national recovery'. That process, he said, had begun with the First Opium War and was driven by the desire of the Chinese people to make the country strong and to make amends for the national humiliation that had resulted from the interference of the great powers. Ultimately, what mattered in the process of national recovery was the survival of the Chinese nation. The condition for this was to regain all the territories that China had lost since the First Opium War. The restoration of China's status as a great power, including the undoing of national humiliation, was necessary for the liberation of all of Asia from colonial oppression, according to Chiang. A post-colonial Asia would subsequently form the basis for the independence of territories in other parts of the world, which was necessary for global stability and peace. Thus, Chiang presented the building of a strong China not only as a national interest (to prevent the demise of Chinese civilization) but also in the interest of the rest of the world (to achieve international stability and an end to oppression).

The view expressed by Chiang in his book was closely aligned with that of Sun Yat-sen. The core of his argument was the same, but he put different emphasis on a few important points. Where Sun had been concerned with the political awakening of the Chinese people, Chiang now claimed that a sense of national humiliation had gripped the people since the First Opium War. Chiang also went further in his outlook on China's future international role as a great power. Like Sun, Chiang argued that a strong China would make a necessary contribution to global order, but he also anticipated possible concerns that China might one day pose a threat to other countries. 'China is opposed to the existence of imperialism in this world and she herself will under no circumstances follow in the footsteps of the imperialists and repeat the mistakes they have made,' Chiang wrote.[11]

Although Chiang was highly critical of both Japan and the West in his book, China was accepted as one of the four most important countries on the Allied side not long after its publication. On 30 October 1943, Britain, the Soviet Union, the United States and China signed a joint declaration (known as the 'Four Power Declaration') that they would fight the war against Germany and Japan in concert.[12] In addition, they announced that they would set up a new organization to monitor international peace and security with a view to the post-war world. This organization would become the successor to the League of Nations and was eventually named the United Nations. Both the idea of implicitly giving China the status of major power (by accepting it as a member of the group of leading allied countries) and the plan for the UN came from Franklin Roosevelt. For the post–Second World War era, he envisioned a new world order anchored in the UN and led by the 'Big Four', the four major allied powers who would be formally equals.

Roosevelt's view was probably that the United States, Britain and the Soviet Union would balance each other out in Europe, while the United States, China and the Soviet Union would do the same in East Asia. The colonial powers Britain and France would have to withdraw from Asia and Africa. The United States and the Soviet Union would then be left as the only trans-regional powers, with the weight and geographic reach of US power being superior. In practice, the United States would actually be the leader because it would be permanently able to play the three other great powers off against each other. Although Churchill and Stalin saw no point in giving China the status of major power (also because in their eyes China was not even a great regional power at the time), Roosevelt got what he wanted. In less than a year, China's formal status had changed from colony-of-everyone to member of a grouping of leading powers and co-founder of a major new international organization.

For the first time, a Chinese leader was invited to participate in a summit with other world leaders. This took place from 22 to 26 November 1943 in Cairo. The participants were Chiang, Roosevelt and British Prime Minister Winston Churchill. Stalin refused to meet Chiang in person. The Soviet leader wanted to prevent Chiang and the Kuomintang from gaining legitimacy at the expense of the CCP through such an encounter. After the Japanese defeat, legitimacy would likely be a crucial factor in the power struggle between the two Chinese parties. It was agreed that Churchill and Roosevelt would first talk to Chiang in Cairo and then go to Tehran to speak to Stalin.

Accompanied by his wife, Chiang Kai-shek travelled to Egypt. The conference took place at the Mena House Hotel, located on the outskirts of

Cairo near the Great Pyramid of Cheops. Song Meiling was present at many of the talks between the three leaders. Because she had studied in the United States, she (unlike her husband) spoke fluent English. As China's first lady, the charismatic Song (Chiang himself was far from charismatic) had already been playing an active role in what is now known as public diplomacy. By giving interviews and speeches, she contributed to a pro-Chinese (and anti-Japanese) sentiment in the public opinion of the United States as early as the 1930s. She continued to do this during the war. In February 1943 she had given a speech to the US House of Representatives asking for more support for the fight against Japan. She also spoke about the need to prepare for the post-war world. In doing so, she contributed to the idea that a new international order had to be formed and that China and the United States had a role to play in this.[13]

Chiang, Churchill and Roosevelt spoke in Cairo about the strategy to be followed in the fight against Japan. But the most important part of the talks was about what the regional order in East Asia would look like after the war. The three leaders agreed that Japan should evacuate all occupied territories after the war, that it should return 'all territories stolen from China' and that Korea would become an independent country again. Combined with the end of the unequal treaties, this meant that China was given the opportunity to replace Japan as the most important regional power in East Asia.

In Cairo, it was clear to Chiang that President Roosevelt and Prime Minister Churchill were not on the same page when it came to what the world should look like after the war. Churchill was determined to restore the British colonial empire, but Roosevelt strongly believed that colonialism did not fit the modern world. The United States itself was born out of an anti-colonial struggle (against Great Britain), and Roosevelt saw his country as the champion of global anti-colonialism. What was at play below the surface was that the United States had taken over the former British role of the most influential great power in the world. During the war, America gave massive financial and material support to China, the Soviet Union and especially Britain. The British needed the Americans more than the other way around.

The gradual decline of British influence in the world had already begun at the end of the nineteenth century. This process was related to the rapid economic and military development of several other powers, including the United States, as well as the rise of anti-colonial nationalism in countries such as South Africa, India and China. This transition phase of roughly half a century was now poised to result in a global American leadership. With Germany and Japan posing acute threats, and its long-standing geopolitical rival Russia (now as the Soviet Union) as a potential long-term threat, Britain was forced to accept this new American leadership. Churchill knew that having a colonial empire would be a crucial factor in the balance of power between his country and the United States. Roosevelt knew this too, and this probably motivated him even more to push for worldwide decolonization.

On 25 November 1943, the day the United States celebrated Thanksgiving, there was a photo session in the garden of the residence of the US ambassador to Egypt. Chiang Kai-shek, Song Meiling, Franklin Roosevelt and Winston Churchill were photographed together, sitting side by side on lawn chairs. The photos would be visible proof to the world that henceforth China was a prominent member of the allied powers. Later that same day, the Chinese couple had a conversation with Roosevelt and his son Elliott, who accompanied the trip as his father's attaché. No one else was present at the meeting. The US president confided in Chiang that Churchill's attitude was his biggest problem at the time. According to Roosevelt, the British leader wanted to prevent China from becoming a great power. He and Chiang both believed that in the coming world order, the British would have to give up their colonial empire.

One concern about China that Roosevelt brought up was the relationship between the Kuomintang and the CCP. He wanted Chiang to continue cooperating with the CCP after the war. Chiang promised to form a government with the communists. In return, he wanted the United States to ensure that the Soviet Union and Britain would not make any claims that conflicted with Chinese sovereignty. The Russians should stay out of Manchuria after the war, and the British should give Hong Kong back. Apparently, Roosevelt did not object to these terms. He also promised to arm and train the Chinese military.[14] The two also spoke about the future of French Indochina. When Roosevelt, who believed that the French should not return there as colonial rulers, asked Chiang 'if he wanted Indochina,' Chiang replied that he was not interested ('Under no circumstances!').[15] The Chinese leader said that Indochina should be placed under UN supervision and prepared for independence and that Korea should become independent immediately after the war.[16] These statements by Chiang did not mean that he believed that Indochina (with Vietnam as the largest part) and Korea would henceforth fall outside China's geopolitical sphere of influence, but that China made no territorial claims to these colonized territories.

Chiang and Roosevelt found each other in their anti-colonialism and in the idea that the world order after the war should look very different from what it had been before. For Chiang, the United States was a necessary counterweight to a hostile Japan and to the unreliable Soviet Union and Britain. He was, at least for the time being, only interested in driving foreign influence out of China and strengthening his domestic position. Chiang had no interest in taking over European colonial responsibilities in other parts of Asia. His new status as Allied co-leader was helpful, but his focus was entirely on China, not on geopolitical issues in other parts of the world.

Roosevelt on the other hand did concentrate on forming new geopolitical relations far beyond the borders of his own country. He had organized the conference in Cairo with the specific aim of making Chiang feel that he was being taken seriously as a strategic partner. But what he failed to tell the Chinese leader was that he doubted Chiang's ability to sustain the fight against Japan. After the conference, Roosevelt discussed with General Stilwell that they might need to consider finding another person or group within China as a US partner in the long run. Roosevelt also believed that the British should give up Hong Kong, but he had not told Chiang that he wanted the city to be given the status of an international free port.[17]

The Cairo conference was special in several respects. It was China's first time to attend an international summit. It was the first and last time Chiang met with Churchill and Roosevelt. The meeting of these three leaders symbolized the start of China's evolution towards becoming a major power at the global level. On 1 December, the United States, Great Britain and China issued a joint statement. In it they called themselves 'the three great allies'. The statement stated that they would fight Japan together until the Japanese surrendered unconditionally. Japan had to give up all areas it had occupied by force and return all areas 'stolen from China', including Taiwan and Manchuria. After Cairo, Roosevelt and Churchill travelled to Tehran, where they spoke with Stalin and where the Soviet leader promised to declare war on Japan once Germany was defeated.

Not long after, on 24 December 1943, President Roosevelt delivered a Christmas address to the American people. In it he explained that after the end of the war there would be four legitimate great powers: the United States, Great Britain, the Soviet Union and China.[18] He also announced his plan to establish the United Nations under the leadership of these four countries. Chiang Kai-shek for his part considered the Cairo conference the greatest success in the history of China's foreign policy.[19] The long-awaited moment of China's resurrection as a great power seemed within reach. After the conference, he and Song Meiling spent some time relaxing and touring the pyramids of Giza. Then they flew back to China. But shortly after arriving, Chiang noted in his diary that, despite the recent success, he felt uneasy.[20] He was anxious and worried, but he didn't know why exactly.

FIGURE 14 *Aisin Gioro Puyi, former emperor of China, with his wife Wanrong, Tianjin* circa *1925 (photo by Pictures from History/Universal Images Group via Getty Images).*

FIGURE 15 *Zhang Xueliang (left) and Chiang Kai-Shek, 1930s (photo by Hulton Archive/Getty Images).*

FIGURE 16 *Chiang Kai Shek, Franklin Roosevelt, Winston Churchill and Song Meiling, Cairo 25 November 1943 (photo by Daily Mirror/Mirrorpix/Mirrorpix via Getty Images).*

# 5

# From big four to big three (1943–79)

On 1 October 1949, a large crowd gathered in Beijing's Tiananmen Square. People looked in the direction of the building after which the square is named, the *Tian'anmen* ('Gate of Heavenly Peace'), a gatehouse behind which lay the entrance to the Forbidden City. On top of that building stood Mao Zedong along with some other leaders of the Chinese Communist Party. At 3:00 in the afternoon he gave a short speech to the people in the square. Mao declared that China would henceforth be called the 'People's Republic of China', that Beijing was once again the nation's capital and that the CCP had formed a national government.

Mao and his male colleagues wore a special costume, which was neither traditional Chinese nor Western. This costume would become internationally known as 'Mao suit' and be seen as a symbol of communist China, because from now on all men in China would wear it. However, the costume was not introduced by Mao or the CCP, but by Sun Yat-sen. He thought that China should have its own style in clothing. For the Chinese, Sun's costume was an expression not of communism but of nationalism, and thus of the struggle against the imperialism of the great powers. In addition to Sun himself, Chiang Kai-shek and other nationalists had also worn the costume.

Since 1935, Mao Zedong had been the undisputed leader of the Communist Party and of the People's Liberation Army, as the CCP's armed forces were now known. He now also became the president of the new government. Zhou Enlai became prime minister and Sun Yat-sen's widow, Song Qingling, became one of the six vice presidents. After Mao spoke, China's new flag, red with five yellow stars, was raised for the first time. The design for the flag had been chosen just days earlier after much discussion among the CCP leaders. A salute of twenty-one gun shots sounded during the flag ceremony. This was followed by a victory parade: some 16,000 soldiers from the People's Liberation Army marched across Tiananmen Square.

What Chiang Kai-shek had long feared had come true. The Communists had seized power in China.

After Cairo, things had initially gone according to plan for Chiang. At the end of April 1945, the founding assembly of the United Nations was held in San Francisco. Chiang's brother-in-law Song Ziwen was present on behalf of China. At subsequent UN meetings, veteran diplomat Gu Weijun acted as China's representative. As Roosevelt had wanted, China was given special status as one of the permanent members of the UN Security Council, as were the United States, the Soviet Union, Britain and France. The latter country was the fifth and last to be added to this group, at Churchill's insistence. The British prime minister believed that otherwise anti-colonial sentiments would prevail too much in the Security Council, the most powerful body of the UN.

As the driving force behind the creation of the United Nations, Franklin Roosevelt was the founder of a new international order. He himself did not experience the start of the UN. Roosevelt died on 12 April 1945, at the age of sixty-three. At the time, he was at his vacation home in Warm Springs, in the southern United States, preparing for the founding meeting of the UN. Roosevelt had been largely paralyzed in the legs for more than twenty years and was unable to stand or walk without aid. He often went to Warm Springs, which took its name from the natural hot springs the president liked to swim in. Just over two weeks after Roosevelt's death, as Soviet troops were about to take Berlin, Hitler committed suicide. A few days later, Germany capitulated and the war in Europe came to an end. The Asian part of the Second World War continued for a few more months. The United States was the stronger actor and was preparing to invade Japan. After the destruction of many Japanese cities by bombing, the use of nuclear weapons (6 and 9 August 1945) and the entrance of the Soviet Union in the war against Japan (9 August), the latter surrendered on 15 August 1945.

As soon as the common enemy Japan had disappeared from the scene, the struggle between the Kuomintang and the Communist Party flared up again in China. However, the balance of power had changed. Before 1937, the Kuomintang was the stronger of the two in all respects. This party was then considerably weakened by a number of major military defeats against Japan, the loss of the economically most important cities and the Japanese blockade of the interior of China. From the end of 1941, Chiang Kai-shek expected the United States to defeat Japan and wanted to save his troops. The CCP had less to lose and used the opportunity to gain ground. By conducting a guerrilla war against Japan, the communists were able to establish their influence over a large part of the Chinese countryside. There they could recruit new fighters and party members. Moreover, this created the public perception that the CCP was more committed than the Kuomintang in the fight against Japan. After the Second World War, the CCP was seen by many Chinese as an energetic and decisive organization that was able to bring about renewal and China's long-awaited recovery. This had once been the very image of the Kuomintang, but that party had now lost much of its lustre.

Both sides had a strong nationalist orientation and thus focused on changing the relationship between China and the foreign powers. But the Communist Party also wanted to radically revise social relations within China. This appealed to many Chinese, especially in rural areas. Land belonging to rich farmers would be redistributed to poor farmers. The CCP succeeded in mobilizing large parts of the rural population against Chiang Kai-shek's troops and then conquered the cities from the countryside. Chiang continued to fight even after the establishment of the People's Republic. But in order to have something to fall back on, he had already ordered in 1948 to put the island of Taiwan in a state of defence. Taiwan was returned to China by Japan in 1945 after fifty years of colonial rule. On 10 December 1949, when Chengdu fell to the Communists as the last major Chinese city to do so, Chiang concluded that the military situation in China was hopeless for the Kuomintang and took a plane to Taiwan.

## Change of dynasty

Not only Chiang but also many others fled mainland China. In addition to politicians, entrepreneurs, academics and civil servants, some 2 million Kuomintang military personnel crossed over to Taiwan. Ministries, universities and the entire collection of the museum of Beijing's Forbidden City were transferred to the Taiwanese capital Taipei. Many of the refugees took their relatives with them. Chiang brought his wife Song Meiling. Chiang Ching-kuo followed his father to Taiwan with his Belarusian wife. Others fled China for the United States. Song Ailing went to live in the United States with her husband Kong Xiangxi. Her brother Song Ziwen also moved to America. Gu Weijun, now China's ambassador to Washington, was already in the United States.

Song Qingling, unlike her sisters, stayed in China. She was not a member of the CCP and had limited political influence despite her position as vice president, but she would continue to work for the Communist Party until her death in 1981. The fact that she was Sun Yat-sen's widow symbolized the bond between Sun, now widely regarded as the father of the nation, and the People's Republic. Song Qingling was also a symbol of the (very limited) openness of the political system. She was able to fulfil a highly visible but not very influential role without being a CCP member. Political parties other than the Kuomintang were also allowed to continue to exist in the new China. But at the same time, there was no doubt where the real political power was. The Communist Party dominated the government of China at all levels and in all major aspects.

There was one more person who was of great help to the CCP in legitimizing the new regime. Aisin Gioro Puyi, last ruler of the Great Qing, had become ex-emperor in 1945 for the second time in his life. Japanese-dominated Manchukuo had been conquered by the Soviet Red Army in the closing days of the Second World War. Puyi tried to flee but was caught. Stalin then imprisoned him in the Soviet Union, while making it possible for him to attend the Allied war crimes tribunal in Tokyo after the war. There Puyi acted as a witness; he was not on trial himself. The accused were Japanese soldiers like Kenji Doihara, the Japanese officer who had worked so hard to initiate the Japanese invasion of Manchuria. Doihara had risen to the rank of general and was one of the top figures of the Japanese armed forces. He was sentenced to death and hanged for crimes against humanity.

After his appearance as a witness in Tokyo, Puyi was returned to the Soviet Union. Stalin initially did not want to extradite him to China, to the relief of the ex-emperor, who feared that he would receive the death penalty for collaborating with Japan. But after Chiang Kai-shek fled to Taiwan, Stalin decided to hand over Puyi to the Chinese government. This was part of the cooperation between the Soviet Union and communist China. In 1950, Puyi was sent by train to Manchuria, where he was arrested by Chinese authorities. To his surprise, he was not sentenced to death. Mao and other communist leaders thought he was worth more alive. They wanted the former emperor of China to become a model communist citizen, which would support the notion that the CCP was the legitimate successor to the old imperial dynasty.

Puyi ended up in a prison where he went through a programme to make him see how disgraceful the Japanese occupation of Manchuria had been and that he was partly responsible for it. The programme consisted of presentations by Japanese officers about their actions against the Chinese people, meetings with victims, and self-criticism. After nine years, he was released and allowed to live in Beijing. One of the first things he did there was to visit the Forbidden City, which had been turned into a museum in 1925. Puyi worked successively as a street sweeper, as a staff member of the Beijing Botanical Garden and then in an editorial office. He married a nurse and appeared to be content with his simple life. Particularly helpful to the CCP was that Puyi published an autobiography about his youth and gave media presentations, both of which aimed at presenting a portrayal that suited the Party's interests (namely, that China had been in a bad shape before 1949, while the new communist China had put everything in order). The last emperor spent his years as a citizen of the People's Republic until his death in 1967. The other surviving members of the former imperial family now also lived and worked as simple citizens.

From 1949, like the Kuomintang before it, the Communist Party ruled China. But the CCP had learned from the experience of the Kuomintang. Mao's party was better organized and had a stronger ideological base. Nationalism formed the ideological core, as with the Kuomintang. Mao regarded the confrontation with the imperialist powers since 1840 as the most significant part of China's recent history.[1] But unlike the Kuomintang, the CCP's nationalism was embedded in a comprehensive, Communist ideology. It was adopted from Marx and Lenin and adapted to Chinese conditions by Mao Zedong.

Communism offered a universal legitimacy that transcended China's specific circumstances. After all, the conflict of interest between rich and poor was not unique to China. Thus, the CCP had a coherent narrative that explained why the world was the way it was and why only the CCP could be China's legitimate leader. Incidentally, it was not only foreigners such as Marx and Lenin in whom Mao found inspiration. He also found the ideas of Chinese thinkers such as Liang Qichao, who was so shocked by the miserable state of Europe after the First World War, very relevant. To emphasize that the Communist Party government was fundamentally different from the Kuomintang administration, the Chinese government used the term 'New China' to refer to post-1949 China.

## Challenges for the new government

As ruler of China, the Communist Party dominated China's government and military. Although since 1949 individual political leaders could be very influential, they tended to rule on behalf of the Party and not on their own behalf. During the last decade of his life, Mao Zedong came close to destroying the Party, but the CCP survived him. Just as emperors used to rule under a heavenly mandate, the Communist Party claimed to be destined to rule China.[2] According to the Party, it was inevitable that sooner or later every country would adopt a socialist system. But also, like the emperors, the CCP's legitimacy was based not only on ideology but also on its ability to maintain order and provide a better life for citizens. From 1949, the new Chinese government faced the task of rebuilding China's economy and restoring stability to the country. At the same time, however, the CCP was faced with major challenges that stood in the way of economic growth and the country's stability.

The most pressing challenge was domestic. The economy had to be rebuilt and the authority of the central government had to be restored throughout the country. To do this, the CCP needed a solid power base. After the Kuomintang had been driven out, there still were influential non-CCP figures everywhere who might or might not be willing to cooperate with the new regime. The Communist Party took a radical approach to becoming the dominant political force at the local level. Poor farmers throughout the country were incited to round up their wealthier fellow villagers. The land of landowning farmers was confiscated and distributed among peasants who had no land of their own. Hundreds of thousands, possibly millions, of people died as a result of this violent redistribution campaign. Some of them were executed, whereas others were driven to commit suicide. Large landowners who failed to escape the country in time and who survived the wave of violence were sent to re-education camps by the communist government. Thus, within a few years, the Chinese rural elite disappeared, a population group that had dominated life outside the cities for thousands of years and from which many of the officials who administered the empire had emerged.

The CCP's approach to the cities was very different. There the Party adopted a moderate attitude and there was no sharp break with the policy of the Kuomintang. Mao Zedong and the other communist leaders had waged a guerrilla war from the countryside for the past twenty years. They had no experience of running cities. The arrival of the Europeans and other foreigners after the Opium Wars had led to major changes in many cities. Modern Chinese and foreign companies were located there. The CCP leaders believed these were crucial to China's economic development. The party leadership therefore followed the course that Sun Yat-sen had set and that the Kuomintang had followed earlier. Everything had to serve the Chinese national interest, and the government was given an active steering role in the economy. But most private companies, Chinese or foreign, were initially largely left alone.

In 1945, the Kuomintang government had confiscated the extensive assets in China of Japanese companies (which had themselves taken over properties of various Chinese and Western companies during the Japanese occupation). The Kuomintang itself had set up several state-owned enterprises. Consequently, there was already an important group of state-owned companies in China before the CCP took over. From 1949, the Communist Party expanded this group by establishing new state-owned enterprises. In China's economy, therefore, both state-controlled and private companies played important roles.

Like Sun Yat-sen and Chiang Kai-shek, the CCP leaders believed that cooperation with the West was indispensable. Japan was temporarily eliminated as a major economy, and the Soviet Union could not offer what the West had to offer economically. Unlike the Soviet Union's state-owned enterprises, many Western companies had a long-standing presence in and close ties to China. Stalin had already shown that, despite his support for the CCP, he was not particularly generous when it came to economic cooperation with China. Soviet troops had liberated Manchuria from Japanese occupation in 1945. It was precisely in that part of China, as a result of Japanese investment, that there was the greatest concentration of modern factories, especially in the strategically important steel industry. Steel was essential for the construction of a modern transport infrastructure, for example for railways and ships. In addition, steel was needed for the production of modern weapons, such as tanks and aircraft. When the Soviet troops returned home after several years, they took a large part of the Manchurian steel industry with them. Factories were dismantled, transported in parts and reassembled in the Soviet Union. The People's Republic of China had to start building a steel industry from scratch.

## America's response to New China

In the United States, Harry Truman had succeeded Roosevelt as the thirty-third president of the United States. As a youth, he had gone to work for a railroad company after graduating from high school. Later he had served as an artillery officer with the American troops in France during the First World War, eventually taking up a career as a politician. As a Democratic senator for Missouri, he was asked by Roosevelt in 1944 to run as vice president in the presidential election. The Roosevelt–Truman duo won, and Truman was sworn in as vice president in January 1944. Less than three months later, Roosevelt died and Truman became the president of the United States, now the leading world power. It was Truman who ordered two atomic bombs to be dropped on Japanese cities in August 1945 and who was America's leader when Germany and Japan surrendered.

In 1949, the Truman administration was faced with the question of how to respond to the communist takeover of China. During the Second World War, Roosevelt had urged Chiang Kai-shek to rule jointly with the CCP. The fact that the CCP was communist was not of decisive importance to him. Much more important was whether this party was able to exercise effective rule and whether it was willing to cooperate with the West. Just as the British government in the late nineteenth century favoured cooperation with the Qing dynasty so long as it was able to maintain order in China and did so in a way that suited British interests, Roosevelt hoped that a combined Kuomintang–CCP government could do the same for US interests. He believed that the Kuomintang would be less effective on its own and that the communists were too strong to be kept out of government. When the conflict between the CCP and Kuomintang broke out again after 1945, the US government tried to mediate between the two sides. But that was not a success and after that the United States felt compelled to choose sides. They chose the Kuomintang. However, large-scale military support from America for Chiang Kai-shek's party was to no avail, and the People's Republic was established in 1949.

In the United States, many people were disappointed with this outcome of the Chinese Civil War. Americans had felt great sympathy for the Chinese population during the Sino-Japanese War. American public opinion was dominated by the perception that the United States had always been committed to China's interests. Many American missionaries had gone to China since the Opium Wars to provide spiritual and material assistance to people there. Tsinghua University was founded in Beijing in 1908 on America's initiative. The funding came from the United States share of reparations imposed on China after the Boxer crisis. The US government had always pursued an 'open-door policy', that is, it had used its diplomatic clout to discourage other powers from dividing China into exclusive spheres of influence. The United States believed that free competition should prevail on the Chinese market and that foreign powers should not interfere in each other's business interests. The American open-door policy and the Japanese pursuit of dominance in China did not match, and this contradiction was an important root cause of the Second World War in Asia. During that war, the United States had given a lot of support to China. Roosevelt had also ensured that China had become a permanent member of the UN Security Council.

It was difficult for the United States to comprehend that China was now a communist state led by the CCP, which maintained close ties with the Soviet Union, America's new main geopolitical rival. What preoccupied policymakers in Washington in 1949 was not China but the Soviet Union. America had emerged from the Second World War as the economically and militarily strongest country in the world, but the Soviet Union surprisingly quickly (as early as 1949) was able to make its own atomic bombs and became a geopolitical player on a level somewhat approaching that of the United States. A successful espionage programme had enabled the Soviet Union to become a nuclear power in a very short time. In addition, strong tensions had arisen in Europe between the United States and the Soviet Union over the division of influence in Germany. These tensions soon spread to the rest of Europe and then to other regions such as the Middle East and Asia. The new geopolitical situation became known as the Cold War. The administration of President Truman viewed controlling, and ultimately winning, the burgeoning geopolitical rivalry with the Soviet Union as its main foreign policy objective.

The American response to the establishment of the People's Republic of China was to impose a trade embargo. The United States and its Western European allies had previously decided not to sell military equipment to the Soviet Union and imposed restrictions on the export of items that might have a military function. These measures also applied to satellite states of the Soviet Union, such as the Eastern European countries and North Korea. Without an embargo against these countries, they would be able to import the prohibited goods on Stalin's instructions and transfer them to the Soviet Union. From 1949 China was also a satellite state of the Soviet Union in America's view.

The government in Washington DC wanted to prevent China and the Soviet Union from collaborating even more closely. Top US officials were convinced that China's economy could not survive without US support. They also believed that the American missions, churches, schools and universities that still existed in China had an enormous appeal to the Chinese people. The trade embargo, which included a limited number of goods, was also intended as a warning to Mao and his colleagues. Instead of further strengthening their cooperation with the Russians, they should opt for America, which had so much to offer economically and ideologically. The United States may have been shocked by the CCP's civil war victory but kept the door to cooperation with the new regime open.

That cooperation, in which the leadership of the CCP was also very much interested, did not materialize. One problem was that the United States offered an all-or-nothing choice, while the CCP wanted to cooperate with both the Soviet Union and the West. Another problem was that war broke out on the Korean peninsula in June 1950, which caused China and the United States to view each other in a completely different way. Immediately after the start of that war, President Truman ordered American warships to take up positions between mainland China and Taiwan. A Chinese invasion of the island was thus made impossible. The United States wanted to prevent the strategically located island of Taiwan from coming under communist rule. The island formed a central link in a chain of islands that also included Japan and the Philippines, two countries with American military bases, and the British colonies in Southeast Asia. From this island chain, the United States and its British allies could, if necessary, close off access to the East and South China Seas in order to establish a blockade against China. The Americans saw the crisis in Korea as an expansion of the Cold War from Europe to Asia. They wanted to put up a dam against what they viewed as Russian influence. But to China's leaders, Truman's naval action was an intervention in China's civil war. Preventing this kind of foreign intervention was precisely one of the aims central to Chinese nationalism, and also to the CCP.

## War in Korea again

When the Korean War broke out, General Douglas MacArthur was the commander of American forces in the Far East. He came from a military family and had spent his childhood in the American Old West, where his father was stationed. MacArthur had retired in 1937 after a successful military career. However, just before the outbreak of war between Japan and the United States, he was called upon by President Roosevelt to re-enlist. During the war, he led the American campaign against Japan in the Pacific and the Philippines. In 1945 MacArthur became commander of the Allied (American–British) occupation force in Japan. Since then he was the de facto ruler of Japan and as such one of the most powerful people in Asia. The general had his staff draft a new constitution for Japan, which is still in force. He also ensured that the Japanese Emperor Hirohito, whose cooperation he needed, was not held responsible for the Second World War in Asia.

In June 1950, MacArthur was given an additional position when the Korean War began. Korea had become divided after the Allied defeat of Japan. In the north the Soviet Union had established a communist government, in the south the United States had installed a pro-Western regime. Immediately after the start of the North Korean attack in June 1950, the UN Security Council authorized the US government to appoint the leader of the UN forces tasked with restoring peace on the Korean peninsula. The US appointed

MacArthur, who was now commander-in-chief of all US forces in the Far East, the US-British occupation forces in Japan and the UN forces in South Korea. The South Korean army was also placed under his command. In addition to the United States, Britain and various other countries also sent troops to Korea under the UN mandate. They, too, came under MacArthur's command. Under his leadership, there was now a great concentration of Western military power in the vicinity of China.

The Security Council functioned exactly as Roosevelt wanted it to, namely as a guardian of American geopolitical interests. Three of the remaining permanent members were US allies heavily dependent on US military and economic support: Great Britain, France and the Kuomintang government that had fled to Taiwan. Although Chiang Kai-shek had lost China, the Chinese seats in the UN and on the Security Council were still held by his government. The representative of the Soviet Union boycotted the Security Council in protest against the UN membership of Taiwan instead of the People's Republic of China and thus could not veto the decision to support South Korea militarily. The United States could now claim that its intervention in the war was not only morally justified because North Korea had started it, but also in accordance with international law and aimed at restoring peace and stability. Moreover, other UN member states were now more likely to feel a moral obligation to actively support the intervention.

After the North Korean army had conquered large parts of South Korea in a short time, MacArthur managed to turn the tide and recapture South Korea's territory. In the autumn of 1950, the question arose whether that meant that it was time to end the war or whether the UN troops should enter North Korea to overthrow the government of North Korean leader Kim Il-sung. Kim was born in Korea when that country was under Japanese rule. When he was young, his family had fled the country to live in Manchuria, where Kim grew up and where he joined the CCP. After the Japanese army occupied Manchuria, Kim was active as a guerrilla leader in the CCP resistance against the Japanese. After years of anti-Japanese struggle in Manchuria, he eventually fled to the Soviet Union, where he enlisted in the Red Army. After the war, with support from Stalin, Kim became leader of the newly established North Korea, although he had lived in China for most of his life. Kim, who was said to barely speak Korean due to his long stay in China, thus had close ties to both the People's Republic of China and the Soviet Union. However, the initiative to attack South Korea came from himself.

President Truman believed that the Korean War should continue until North Korea was conquered and Kim was overthrown. He received support from the Security Council (which was still boycotted by the Soviet Union) for this plan. The UN troops crossed the border into North Korea and took its capital Pyongyang on 19 October 1950. Kim and his troops retreated further and further north, towards the border with China. MacArthur also ordered his UN army, of which some 125,000 American troops formed the main part, to move north. On 21 November, the first American units reached the Yalu, the river that constitutes the border between North Korea and China.

By that time, some UN troops had engaged in combat with enemy fighters who did not appear to be North Korean. Several of them were captured and interrogated. It turned out they were Chinese. MacArthur concluded that Mao had ordered a limited intervention in the Korean War, although it was not clear to him what China hoped to achieve by doing so. The US commander was not impressed by China's military capabilities. China had never won a war on its own against a modern great power. In 1950, the United States was the greatest economic and military power that had ever existed, while China was exhausted after years of civil war and Japanese occupation. Those few units Mao had sent to Korea wouldn't be much of a problem for the UN troops, MacArthur appears to have thought. Moreover, they seemed to be retreating again in the direction of the Chinese border. Determined to destroy the last remnants of North Korean resistance and push the Chinese back across the Yalu, MacArthur ordered a final major offensive that was to start on 24 November 1950, to end the war. There was still a month to go before Christmas, and he would make sure that by then Korea was reunited and the American soldiers were back home.

## Military confrontation between China and America

The US deploying large numbers of troops with UN support after the outbreak of the Korean War immediately set off alarm bells among leaders in Beijing. They had not forgotten that Japanese military interventions in Korea in the sixteenth and nineteenth centuries were related to attempts to conquer China. Even if the Americans did not attack China directly, their military presence along the border between China and North Korea would pose a permanent threat.[3] The Chinese government soon began preparing for a possible military confrontation with the United States. Chinese troops were sent to the border with North Korea and the government launched a media campaign to prepare the Chinese people for conflict with the United States. In that campaign, America was portrayed as an imperialist power and a major threat to China.

By the time the first South Korean army units entered North Korea, China warned that US troops should not do the same. If the US military advanced to the Sino–North Korean border, China would enter the fray. Zhou Enlai and other Chinese leaders issued this warning through public speeches, editorials in Chinese state media and in conversations with diplomats from countries such as India, who maintained relations with both China and the

United States. There were no diplomatic contacts between the United States and the People's Republic, so there was no direct channel of communication between the two governments.

In Beijing in the fall of 1950, an intense debate arose between CCP leaders about whether China should enter the Korean War. Many members of the politburo, the governing body of the Party, showed no interest in participating in the war. Mao, however, was in favour of intervention, despite China's weak position and although he well understood the risk involved in participating in the Korean War. Around this time, Mao informed Stalin that he reckoned that any Chinese intervention could lead to a full-scale war between China and the United States. In that case, the US Navy would likely attack China's coastal areas and US aircraft would launch strikes against Chinese factories and cities, Mao believed. So the war was likely not to be limited to Korea, but could spread to China itself. Mao also expected domestic unrest in such a crisis and that part of the Chinese population, such as the lower middle class, would not support the war. And yet he believed that China should intervene in Korea.

Zhou Enlai shared that view, as did the military commander Peng Dehuai. He believed that doing nothing was more dangerous than intervening. Peng reasoned that if China remained passive, the United States would try to pressure China not only in Korea but also from Vietnam and Burma. The Americans might also rearm Japan and use it against China. In addition, anti-communist groups in China would feel encouraged to actively oppose the CCP's rule. Intervening, however that would turn out, would in any case bring the advantage of having the initiative.[4]

On 7 October 1950, the UN General Assembly decided that Korea should be reunited under a democratic government, which meant that Kim Il-sung's regime was to be removed. That was not acceptable to the CCP's leaders, who decided a day later to send Chinese troops to North Korea. On 19 October, the day Pyongyang was captured by UN troops, the first Chinese soldiers crossed the Yalu. The Chinese intervention force, consisting of some 300,000 troops and led by Peng Dehuai, was initially not noticed by the UN. The lightly packed Chinese marched at night so they could not be seen by American reconnaissance planes. More than a month after Chinese troops entered North Korea, MacArthur still had no idea of the size of the Chinese presence. On 25 November, in extremely cold weather conditions, the Chinese army started its offensive. The American forces and their allies were taken completely by surprise by the scale and ferocity of the Chinese attack. They suffered significant casualties and had to retreat. By Christmas 1950, when the war should have been won according to MacArthur, the UN troops had been driven out of North Korea. Soon after, Chinese troops captured the South Korean capital Seoul.

The military personnel in China's intervention force in Korea were designated as volunteers by the Chinese government, even though they were regular units of the Chinese armed forces. The reason for this was that China wanted to reduce the chance that the United States would think it was aiming for a large-scale war between the two countries. So formally Chinese volunteers were fighting against UN forces, but in reality, this was the first large-scale military confrontation between China and the United States. The Chinese government meanwhile insisted that the United States was the enemy, not the UN or US allies who also had sent troops.

After the Chinese army had conquered North Korea and a small part of South Korea, the front began to stabilize. Seoul soon fell back into UN hands, after which the border between North and South was roughly back to what it had been before the war broke out. China's goal was not to conquer South Korea and reunite Korea, but to restore the status quo and neutralize the American threat. The best way to do this was to show that China was not intimidated, that it could not be defeated on the battlefield and, above all, to discourage the United States by killing many American soldiers.

In the United States, meanwhile, the shock was great. How was it possible that the mighty US military had been pushed back from North Korea? But most of all there was a feeling of indignation. China was seen as ungrateful. After all the Americans had done to support the Chinese people, or so the Americans thought, China had launched a treacherous attack against UN forces that did nothing but restore stability to the Korean Peninsula. Truman and his administration believed that this required a severe response. An extension of the armed struggle outside Korea was not desirable because of the danger of an escalation into the third World War. Indeed, Truman and several US military leaders believed that the Soviet Union would intervene if the local conflict in Korea developed into a general war between the United States and China. Therefore, American bombers did not attack targets on Chinese soil. The United States also considered a blockade of Chinese ports with warships, as Palmerston had once done, too risky. Soviet naval units were present in the southern Manchurian port of Dalian (where they would remain until 1955). A blockade would possibly lead to a clash between Russian and American ships. In addition, Britain strongly objected to a blockade of Chinese ports because it would undoubtedly also apply to Hong Kong.

Instead of entering into a full-scale war with China, the United States used economic and diplomatic weapons. The partial trade embargo against China was now extended. Chinese financial assets in the United States were also frozen. In practice, it became almost impossible to export goods from the United States to China, Hong Kong or Macau. The fact that American business, despite the attractiveness of the Chinese market, accepted this without too much resistance shows how strongly anti-Chinese the mood in the United States had become. The US government succeeded in getting the United Nations to also impose a trade embargo against China.

The US pressured allies to cooperate with the trade embargo. However, that proved difficult, because many countries were very keen to continue trading with China. So was Britain, America's main ally. British companies traditionally had a larger presence in China than their US counterparts. Furthermore, the future of Hong Kong as a British colony depended on the transit trade between China and the outside world. And finally, the British did not share the intense disappointment that the Americans had when it came to China. They had never had much expectation that China would adopt Western values and become a reliable ally. Such idealistic thinking had played no part in Palmerston's conduct during the First Opium War, nor was it part of the view of Churchill, who had resigned in 1945 after losing an election but who would become Prime Minister of Great Britain again in 1951. Other Western European countries also had a pragmatic attitude towards communist China. Despite a sense of intense frustration at this attitude, the government in Washington decided not to pressure the Western Europeans too hard. As a region, Europe was strategically more important than Asia, and the United States needed its European allies in the geopolitical struggle with the Soviet Union.[5]

## The San Francisco treaty

On the diplomatic front, the US government also tried to increase pressure on China. In 1951, at a meeting in San Francisco, Japan signed a peace treaty with the United States and many other countries. The US government had drafted the text of the treaty in coordination with the British government. The Soviet Union and smaller allied countries were merely allowed to attend the ceremony in San Francisco and sign the document. China was completely excluded from the process and was not welcome in San Francisco. So while Roosevelt had announced to the world in 1943 that China was one of the four Allied leaders, eight years later his successor Truman made sure that China was not even invited to the big peace ceremony that ended the Asian part of the Second World War.

On the same day the peace treaty was signed, the United States and Japan signed a defence treaty, which turned Japan into a military ally of the United States. After that the Allied occupation of Japan was lifted. On the one hand, the Americans had given Japan a constitution that stipulated that the country would no longer have a military and that it would never use force to resolve international disputes. But on the other hand, they had now stipulated in the defence treaty that the United States would maintain military bases in Japan and that Japan had an obligation to defend Japanese territory, and therefore also the US bases. To fulfil that obligation without violating the constitution, the Japanese government, with American support, established a self-defence force. Soon Japan had a military again, only no one called it that. The two San Francisco treaties formed the basis of the new order in East Asia, which was dominated by the global Cold War. The United States set the tone, supported by its main allies: Great Britain and now also Japan. From then on, the main geopolitical opponents in Asia were the Soviet Union and China.

There were quite a few problems with the peace treaty. It was not signed by China (which was not invited, because the United States did not want it), Taiwan (also not invited, because the British did not recognize the government of Taiwan), the Soviet Union (which refused to sign because the treaty was designed by the Americans and the British without Soviet involvement) or the two Koreas (since the peace treaty did not recognize that there now were two separate states on the Korean Peninsula that denied each other's right to exist).

In addition, the treaty did not specify who was the new rightful owner of former Japanese possessions such as the islands in the South and East China Seas. As the historian Kimie Hara has shown, the US government deliberately kept this issue vague. Earlier drafts of the treaty stated that Japan should hand over these islands to China, as Roosevelt, Churchill and Chiang Kai-shek had discussed in Cairo. Now, however, the United States saw China as an enemy and it seemed more useful to leave such territorial issues unresolved. China did not get the islands, but neither did other countries in the region. In future disputes, the United States could act as arbiter, thus retaining considerable influence in the region.[6]

## Armistice in Korea

Participation in the Korean War constituted a major effort for China. Partly due to the American trade embargo, China's economic recovery was slowed considerably, and there was no prospect of the conquest of Taiwan and taking a seat on the UN Security Council for the time being. Stalin, who had initially wanted to stay out of the war, had deployed fighter jets to help defend North Korean airspace. The Soviet Union also supplied arms to China, for which it needed to pay. This showed that, as far as Stalin was concerned, the conflict in Korea was primarily an issue for China and the North Koreans themselves to deal with, rather than for the Soviet Union.

Although losses on the Chinese side were greater, Mao believed that China could afford those losses better than the United States. The Chinese troops were highly motivated, much more so than their American opponents, and Mao wanted to demonstrate that China could sustain the fight indefinitely if necessary. Despite China's economic and military weakness, the CCP had a few trump cards domestically, namely, control over the media and the lack of political opposition. In the United States, the government had to deal with media and political pressure to end an unpopular war, with growing casualties and no progress at the front.

There was a lot of confusion in Washington about the extent to which China was an instrument of the Soviet Union. Douglas MacArthur rightly believed that China was acting largely independently. His conclusion was therefore that the risk was very small that a limited attack on China, if necessary, would lead to a war between the United States and the Soviet Union. MacArthur thought the People's Republic of China was so vulnerable that targeted attacks on Chinese industry and infrastructure would likely spell the end of the CCP regime. But Truman and other military leaders were concerned that MacArthur would single-handedly start the third World War by attacking or overprovoking China. In April 1951, Truman dismissed him from all military positions. The president felt that MacArthur was not showing enough loyalty and had become an unreliable factor. It was not until 1953 that the warring parties agreed on a ceasefire, which is still in force today. The new border between North and South Korea was more or less the same as the old one before the war. A peace treaty never materialized.

China had failed to prevent entering into a military conflict with the United States. Until the beginning of October 1950, that had been the commitment of the CCP leadership. But the Chinese warnings to the United States had been ineffective because MacArthur and Truman had failed to take China's ability and willingness to fight seriously. It also didn't help that the warnings weren't immediately passed on to the United States due to the lack of a Chinese ambassador in Washington. China had also not succeeded in conquering South Korea, while some 200,000 Chinese soldiers were killed or missing (more than five times the number of United States dead and missing). Still, the war had provided some strategic advantages for Mao and the CCP. They had succeeded in seizing the initiative for geopolitical action in East Asia. Moreover, China now knew what it was like to wage war against the United States. Mao saw this as an important advantage: 'We have now been able to gain a lot of experience with the US forces. If you don't come into direct contact with them, you might be afraid of them. But we fought them for thirty-three months, and now we know them inside out. American imperialism isn't very scary, it just is what it is and that's all.'[7]

Particularly important to him was that China had acquired a more favourable position vis-à-vis the United States in the long run. The Americans now knew that a conflict with China would not bring them a quick victory. As powerful as the United States was, China was no longer the weak prey it had been during the Opium Wars. Meanwhile, the Chinese leadership had not failed to notice the usefulness of the UN Security Council to the Americans. The latter used the council as an instrument to support their strategic interests. Thanks to its influence in the Security Council, the US government was able to present itself as a defender of the international legal order and more easily obtain support from other countries in the fight against North Korea and China. It was important for the People's Republic of China to become a member of the UN and take over the seat of Taiwan and thus the veto right in the Security Council. It would then be less easy for the United States to claim to be morally and legally right in any subsequent conflict. For the time being, however, the United States used its power within the UN to block Chinese membership.

According to Shu Guang Zhang, an expert on Sino-American relations during the Cold War, it is striking how little the two countries understood each other. While the Chinese viewed the crisis in Korea from a regional perspective, the Americans placed developments in a global perspective. For the United States, the conflict in Korea was part of the geopolitical confrontation with the Soviet Union. They wanted to discourage communist governments anywhere from attacking American allies. They largely failed to notice that North Korea and China were largely independent actors, driven by local factors. But according to Zhang, the Chinese government also had limited insight into the motives of the opposing party. Mao and his colleagues mistakenly believed that the US military intervention in Korea was directed against China. In his work, Zhang points to a 'siege mentality' that has long existed in China and that he says was also very influential in the 1950s. The basis of this was the belief that China has always been, and still is, surrounded by barbarians who tried again and again to harm the country.[8] US actions unfavourable to China were quickly perceived as part of a targeted strategy to keep China down.

## Break with the Soviet Union

China had shown itself to be unafraid of even the greatest world power, drawing a new confidence from the Korean conflict. The CCP's willingness to engage in armed struggle was a signal not only to the United States, but also to the Chinese people themselves. The Party had shown that China, under its leadership, was able to keep foreign threats at bay. The Americans were confronted in Korea, not on Chinese soil. But while China had fought largely on its own initiative and on its own, the Soviet Union's role was essential. If there had been no risk for the United States of a conflict with the Soviet Union, and thus of a nuclear war, it might well have carried out bombings or blockades against China. The United States could perhaps even have used nuclear weapons against China.

Immediately after the end of the Korean War, the CCP turned its attention back to China's economic reconstruction. Soviet aid also played a major role in this. Due to the trade embargo that the United States had imposed on China, Sun Yat-sen's strategy of economic development through close cooperation with the West was not an option for the time being. Especially for modern technology, the Soviet Union was now the only remaining source. At the request of the Chinese government, Moscow signed several economic cooperation treaties and sent large numbers of technical experts to China. As for military aid during the Korean War, the Soviet Union made China pay the full price for it.

Despite this cooperation, the ideological ties and the joint geopolitical struggle against the United States, things soon went wrong between China and the Soviet Union. After Stalin's death in 1953, following a brief power struggle in the Kremlin, he was succeeded by Nikita Khrushchev. From the mid-1950s, disagreements arose between China and the Soviet Union on issues ranging from the assessment of Stalin's role to what was the right model of development for China. Increasingly, the question arose of who had the deciding vote when it came to ideological differences of opinion. Mao felt he was a greater authority than Khrushchev in that regard. By showing this, he challenged the Soviet Union's traditional role as the leader of global communism. The very fact that the two countries were so similar in ideology now became a source of mutual tension. There could be only one correct version of communism, and Beijing and Moscow could not agree which one it was.

By 1959, tensions were so high that the Soviet Union withdrew all of its technical experts from China. All cooperation programmes were abruptly stopped. The rift between the two communist powers was widening so fast that American intelligence agencies had a hard time understanding what was going on. They thought that the quarrel did not go very deep and would soon be made up again. But during the 1960s, China and the Soviet Union drifted further and further apart.

The Cold War in East Asia took on a very different character than in Europe, where there was mainly a dichotomy between the United States and the Soviet Union (and their respective allies). Attempts by French President Charles de Gaulle to make Western Europe strategically independent from the United States came to nothing. The other Western European countries accepted American leadership in exchange for economic cooperation and security guarantees against the Soviet Union. The era of Europe as an autonomous global geopolitical player was over. China moved in the opposite direction. With both the United States and the Soviet Union as enemies, China developed into the third major geopolitical actor in Asia. The most important milestone in that process was 1964, when China successfully tested an atomic bomb for the first time. The Chinese government had managed to build its own nuclear weapon.

China depended on no one for national security. But without economic cooperation with the United States, the Soviet Union, Japan or Europe, it became very difficult for the CCP to modernize the Chinese economy. Mao launched a national campaign to motivate and mobilize the Chinese people to significantly increase agricultural and industrial productivity in a short period of time. Foreign technology was not necessary in his view. Instead, the large size and enthusiasm of the population should bring about the desired results. Mao Zedong called his campaign the Great Leap Forward. Among other things, the peasant population was instructed to produce steel from self-built furnaces, to compensate for the lack of a modern steel industry. Private ownership of farmland was abolished. Land was now farmed collectively by peasants. Such actions made little economic sense and undermined the ability of the agricultural sector to produce enough food. Political pressure on local governments to report high production figures, regardless of reality, exacerbated the situation. Grain, which according to the misleading statistics was available in abundance, was exported while it was badly needed at home. This economic mismanagement led to large-scale famines. Tens of millions of people perished. Another consequence of the failure of the Great Leap Forward was that the long-standing disagreement in the party leadership about the right economic policy further intensified. Mao's position was weakened after this debacle.

## Mao's leap

In order not to get sidetracked politically, Mao Zedong turned to the people. In traditional political thinking in China, the greatest source of political power is the population. The government or the CCP cannot resist the people when they revolt en masse. In 1966, Mao Zedong unleashed a new mass movement, the Great Proletarian Cultural Revolution. His aim was not to replace the Party, but to strengthen his position as Party leader by eliminating his rivals within the CCP. He made sure that everyone but himself was at risk of being accused of being ideologically impure. According to the CCP, the foreign powers and everyone who had collaborated with them, the Kuomintang, the large landowners, wealthy entrepreneurs, conservative middle classes and subversive intellectuals, were all enemies of the country. But those groups had already largely been eliminated by now. Now, according to Mao, the most threatening enemies were those within the government and the Party who were not fully committed to the ideals of Chinese communism. Especially when such persons had authority, they were dangerous.

The tracing of ideological enemies within the Party was not a new phenomenon. There were ideological differences within the CCP from the very beginning. Ideological discipline was taken very seriously. Party officials were constantly at risk of being accused of deviating from the prevailing (i.e. the 'correct') party doctrine. Measures in such cases ranged from intensive interrogation and the writing of self-criticisms to imprisonment and even the death penalty. It was inevitable in this context that competition among Party leaders for more influence within the Party took the form of a struggle for ideological purity. Whoever had the most influence could determine what was ideologically correct. It was tempting to eliminate competitors within the organization by accusing them of not being fully committed to party doctrine. Even when the CCP fought against the Kuomintang and Japan, there were constant purges within the Party. But during the Cultural Revolution, its scale and intensity were unprecedented.

Apart from Mao himself, no one, inside or outside the Party, was safe. Encouraged by him, students went out to 'expose' party leaders, civil servants, teachers, parents and random other people as reactionary saboteurs of the revolution. Many victims of the Red Guards, the revolutionary youth, were killed, often by being driven to suicide. Many more were exiled to small rural villages to be re-educated through hard labour. It was not long before it was the turn of many of the Red Guards to be sent to the countryside themselves. In this way, Mao prevented them from becoming a permanent factor of power.

The Cultural Revolution weakened in intensity after a few years, but ultimately lasted ten years. Society became highly politicized and traumatized during this period. No one knew whom to trust. This situation hampered China's economic development. But Mao achieved his goal. He remained in power as China's supreme leader. Many party leaders lost their positions and sometimes their lives. Mao's main rival and intended successor as party leader, CCP Vice Chairman Liu Shaoqi, was deposed in 1966 and died in prison as a result of his mistreatment. His place as Mao's successor was taken by Lin Biao, who participated wholeheartedly in the Cultural Revolution. But in 1971, Lin himself was killed when the plane he was travelling in crashed in Mongolia. It is believed that he had become embroiled in a power struggle with Mao and that he had just fled the country when his plane crashed. The exact cause of this incident has never become clear.

Another whom Mao viewed as a threat was Peng Dehuai, once the successful commander of China's forces in Korea. Some years before, Peng had dared to criticize Mao's policies during the Great Leap Forward. During the Cultural Revolution he was publicly humiliated and tortured for years. In 1974 he died sick and exhausted in a prison. Deng Xiaoping, now a member of the CCP leadership and proponent of moderate economic policies (and therefore distrusted by Mao), was dismissed from all his positions. The Red Guards were unleashed on him and his family. As a result of abuse, one of Deng's sons was paralysed. In 1969, Deng Xiaoping was sent to the countryside and employed as a factory worker. Even the popular Zhou Enlai, Mao's right-hand man, was criticized by his political opponents. However, he kept Mao's support and was able to remain in office.

Among the countless other victims of the Cultural Revolution was a boy in Beijing named Xi Jinping. His father Xi Zhongxun had joined the CCP in the late 1920s, rising to head the Party's propaganda department. In 1959, he became one of China's deputy prime ministers under Zhou Enlai. However, the elder Xi subsequently fell victim to rivalries within the CCP and was imprisoned during the Cultural Revolution. Xi Jinping was fifteen years old at the time. He was sent to the countryside, where he lived in primitive conditions and had to do hard labour.

For some, the chaos of the Cultural Revolution actually offered opportunities to move up. This was particularly true for Mao Zedong's fourth wife. Although she had been the country's first lady since the founding of the People's Republic, she did not play a prominent role in Chinese politics for a long time. When she first met Mao, she was twenty-three or twenty-four years old and a well-known film actress. Her stage name was Lan Ping ('Blue Apple'). As an actress, she lived in Shanghai and had been briefly married to another actor, who was also a director. When the film industry in Shanghai came to a standstill as a result of the Japanese occupation, Lan Ping fled to the area held by the Chinese communists. She started working as a drama teacher at the art academy that the CCP had just established and changed her name to Jiang Qing ('Blue River'). Soon she got into a relationship with Mao, who at the time was married to another woman with whom he had five children. He ended that marriage, and in 1938, Mao Zedong and Jiang Qing got married.

After the Communist takeover in 1949, Jiang worked for the CCP's propaganda office and oversaw the film industry on behalf of the Ministry of Culture. With these functions, she largely remained in the background. Although she remained married to Mao, the two grew apart during this period and no longer lived together. When the Cultural Revolution started, Jiang made her move and showed herself to be a passionate politician. Given her extensive experience in propaganda matters and her position as Mao's wife, she was appointed deputy director of the Central Cultural Revolution Group, the steering body of the Cultural Revolution. With great enthusiasm she set to work to realize for China the goals of ideological purity and total loyalty to Mao. Jiang Qing soon became the central figure within the radical wing in the CCP. Mao considered her very useful and supported her, but made sure not to become completely dependent on Jiang. He tried to strike a balance between the radical and moderate leaders within the Party, playing the two groups off against each other. On the moderate side, Zhou Enlai was the most important figure. When Zhou's health deteriorated, Mao brought Deng Xiaoping, who was known for his strong organizational skills, back from exile and made him first vice-premier.

## A new world vision

In the century since the Opium Wars, China's administrative and intellectual elite had gradually come to see the country as part of a global community. China increasingly sought the restoration of its sovereignty and recognition as a full member of the international community. In 1943–5, with the ending of the unequal treaties, membership in the UN and victory over Japan, these goals were realized. From a victim of colonialism, China was suddenly a leader of the Allies and co-founder of the new world order. The country needed a new vision of the world and China's place in it in order to define future foreign policy goals. Chiang Kai-shek and his associates had no opportunity to develop such a vision. From 1945 they had their hands full fighting the CCP. Nevertheless, the Kuomintang left behind a few important building blocks, which were adopted by the People's Republic of China from 1949 as starting points for its foreign policy.

The first of these was membership in the UN, as a follow-up to China's League of Nations membership. With this, China endorsed the idea that there was a global community of states and that it was necessary for them to cooperate on a number of issues. The most important of these was international stability. That cooperation required the establishment of permanent international organizations, financed and administered by the governments of those states. Moreover, by joining both the UN and the UN Security Council, China supported the idea that the world consisted of two kinds of states: ordinary countries and great powers with special rights (i.e. the five permanent members of the Security Council). China was not only a founding member of the United Nations, but also of the World Bank, the International Monetary Fund (IMF) and the GATT (the predecessor of the WTO).

A second foreign policy building block was that modern China adopted the Qing dynasty's land borders in their most expansive form. The government took the position that peoples such as the Tibetans and Uyghurs and the regions they inhabited were part of a China in which Han Chinese formed by far the majority. The same applied to Macau, Hong Kong and Taiwan, three areas largely inhabited by Han Chinese that had long been administratively isolated from the rest of China. In Taiwan, there was still an autochthonous minority that was not Han Chinese and who already inhabited the island before the arrival of Dutch and Chinese settlers in the seventeenth century. In Macau and Hong Kong, Europeans and people of mixed European–Chinese descent formed a small minority. The Kuomintang felt that these areas should be returned to Chinese rule and thus should not remain colonized or become independent. In 1945, Japan handed over control of Taiwan to China. Macau and Hong Kong remained Portuguese and British, respectively.

Finally, Chiang Kai-shek's government considered the islands in the South China Sea to be part of China. This became a third building block for the later policies of the People's Republic. In particular, this applied to two groups of islands, the Paracel Islands in the north and the Spratly Islands in the south of the South China Sea. At the time of the Chinese Empire, the ownership of these islands and the surrounding sea was not a concern for the Chinese government. The tiny islands were uninhabited and had no valuable strategic or economic function. In addition, the Qing dynasty regarded the lands surrounding the South China Sea as vassal states. In that respect, it did not matter whether those countries made claims to the islands, because the ultimate control (from the point of view of the Chinese government) lay with China anyway. After the fall of the Qing dynasty, the new Chinese government announced that it considered the islands to be part of China.

In 1930, however, a dispute over the islands arose when France, as colonial ruler of what would later become Vietnam, claimed the Paracel and Spratly Islands. The French move was prompted by concerns about possible Japanese plans to establish military dominance in the South China Sea using Taiwan (then a Japanese colony) as a springboard.[9] The Chinese government responded by publishing a map in 1935 indicating that the islands belonged to China. After the Second World War, the Kuomintang regime resumed such efforts by sending warships to the largest Spratly Island and placing a stone with an inscription there to record the naval visit. Soon after, the government published another map. It stated that not only the disputed islands, but also most of the South China Sea's maritime area belonged to China.

All these things the CCP took over from the Kuomintang. They formed important starting points for China's foreign policy from 1949 onwards. This also illustrates the contours of China's vision of its own place in the modern world. The basic premise of that vision is that China is an independent state that rejects all forms of foreign interference. Modern China adopted the borders of the former Qing Empire, with the exceptions of (Outer) Mongolia and what had become the Russian Far East. Parts of Central Asia that had been conquered by the Qing dynasty were incorporated into the new China. Former neighbouring peoples such as the Tibetans and Mongols, who had been regarded by the Manchus as part of the Qing empire, again became subjects (mostly only on paper) of the Republic of China and then (also in practice) of the People's Republic. In this way, China retained the spacious, sparsely populated buffer zones between the main Han territories and its two large neighbours, the Soviet Union and India (which gained independence from Great Britain in 1947).

The South China Sea was also a potential buffer zone in the eyes of the Chinese government. The maritime interests of neighbouring countries such as Vietnam (once a part of China, later a vassal state and eventually a French colony) and the Philippines (for a long time a Western colony, independent from the United States since 1946) were seen as subordinate to China's own strategic interests. Moreover, China viewed itself as a country that, through the UN, deserved (but did not yet have) special rights on a global level. The People's Republic objected to Taiwan being a member of the UN Security Council. Not because there was anything wrong with the dichotomy between regular members and permanent Security Council members, but because China wanted to take Taiwan's place.

The CCP's foreign policy is rooted in that of the Kuomintang on these important points. There were also similarities between China's international position after the Second World War and the two major powers of the time, the United States and the Soviet Union. For example, all three countries rejected the overseas colonialism of Europeans and Japanese, but they did maintain broad (exclusive) spheres of influence outside their own borders. The United States viewed Central and South America, Western Europe and parts of East Asia and the Pacific as a zone where other great powers had no business. The Soviet Union had the same attitude towards large parts of Central and Eastern Europe. China also aspired to have its own sphere of influence, as reflected in its attitude towards the South China Sea.

From the ideological perspective of the People's Republic, the world consisted of countries that were already communist and countries that would become so. Through revolution, sooner or later all countries would adopt a communist system. The capitalist countries, led by the United States, tried to stop and reverse this process. The United States was therefore China's main enemy. The two great communist powers, the Soviet Union and China, together formed the core and natural leaders of an ever-expanding communist world. At least, the latter was what Mao wanted. In practice, China was the Soviet Union's junior partner.

In the 1960s, after the break with Moscow, China's world view had to be adjusted again. A simple dichotomy between communism and capitalism no longer sufficed. Mao then developed the concept of the three worlds. According to him, there was a First World consisting of the two superpowers, the United States and the Soviet Union. There was no major difference between these two countries. Although the Soviet Union pretended to be a communist country, it really wasn't. Both superpowers, according to Mao, were imperialistic. There was also a Second World, made up of the other industrialized countries in Europe and elsewhere. These were oppressed by the two superpowers, but at the same time they were the co-oppressors of the developing countries. The latter together formed the Third World. Mao now presented China as part of the Third World. As the only great power among the developing world countries, China was the natural leader of the Third World. As the representative of true communist ideology, China would lead the world revolution that would liberate the Third World from the first two, and the Second World from the First. The American and Russian people would, of course, eventually rise up and put an end to the imperialist behaviour of their own governments.

## Beginning of the relationship with Africa

A consequence of this vision of the world and China's place in it was that the country increasingly focused on developing countries. Not only in Asia, but also in Latin America, the Middle East and Africa. For the first time, China was seriously interested in countries that were neither a great power nor in its immediate vicinity. During the Ming dynasty, China had sent maritime expeditions to the Indian Ocean. These were led by the eunuch Zheng He. Zheng and his fleet visited the Middle East and East Africa, among other places. He probably aimed to explore the possibilities for China to gain more influence on the maritime trade routes between East Asia and the countries around the Indian Ocean. However, none of these expeditions had led to lasting diplomatic contacts between China and distant countries.

As early as 1955, when relations with the Soviet Union were still friendly, Mao had already laid the foundations for closer ties between China and developing countries in Asia and Africa. In that year, Indonesia organized a conference together with India and a number of other countries. The aim was to strengthen cooperation between African and Asian countries that were neutral in the Cold War. Moreover, these countries jointly wanted to put an end to Western colonialism. Although China clearly belonged to the communist camp, as the largest Asian country and declared opponent of colonialism it was nevertheless invited to the conference, which was held in the Indonesian city of Bandung. Mao saw an opportunity to give his country a role beyond the reach of the Soviet Union, which had not been invited. He sent Zhou Enlai to Bandung, who made a great impression with his charismatic appearance and constructive attitude towards the developing countries. So on this occasion, China presented itself not as a representative of the communist camp, but as a member of the community of developing countries.

Africa in particular had the attention of the Chinese leaders. When many African colonies became independent states from the late 1950s, China was ready to enter into diplomatic and economic cooperation with them. The Chinese government was eager to show that it was a useful partner to these countries. It sent doctors to support the development of medical care in Africa. It also helped in building infrastructure. In 1967, China signed an agreement with Tanzania and Zambia for the construction of a rail link between the two African countries. The latter had initially tried to get funding for the project from Western countries, but these were unsuccessful. Although China itself was largely economically isolated and cash-strapped, as well as embroiled in the Cultural Revolution, it lent some $400 million to Zambia and Tanzania without interest for the railway. It was built in the first half of the 1970s with Chinese expertise and Chinese materials. A large part of the many thousands of railway workers also came from China. Of these, sixty-four died in accidents during the work. Upon completion of the project, ownership and management of the railway line passed to the governments of Tanzania and Zambia. Mao had made a gesture to Africa. The medical and infrastructure aid served no direct commercial goals but were a long-term investment in building up China's image and diplomatic contacts in Africa. Later on, this approach would indeed pay off.

## China's isolation

While China strengthened ties with African countries, it became increasingly isolated in Asia. In 1962 China and India had fought a short war with each other over disputed border regions. Relations between the two countries had become strained when India granted asylum in 1959 to the Dalai

Lama, the Tibetan spiritual and political leader who had fled Tibet after a failed uprising by ethnic Tibetans against the Chinese government. The 1962 border war with India was won convincingly by China. Although it withdrew from all conquered territories after a few weeks, Sino-Indian relations remained tense. Meanwhile, the United States used the tensions in Tibet to put pressure on China. The Central Intelligence Agency (CIA) had already provided covert support to the Tibetan insurgents in 1959. In subsequent years, the CIA trained Tibetan fighters who occasionally carried out attacks in Tibet. This did not change much to weaken the power of the Chinese central government and the CCP in Tibet, but it made it more difficult for China and India to stabilize their relations.

In Indonesia, the army seized power in 1965, after which the PKI, the Indonesian Communist Party that Henk Sneevliet had helped to found, was banned. The PKI was the third largest communist party in the world after those of the Soviet Union and China. Many PKI members and sympathizers were killed in and after 1965 by the military and paramilitary organizations, allegedly in response to a failed coup attempt by the PKI. For the US government, which secretly encouraged the killings, this was a major victory.[10] Previously, due to the many ethnic Chinese in Indonesia and ties between the CCP and PKI, there were close relations between the two countries, but in 1967 Indonesia suspended its diplomatic ties with China. In the same year, Indonesia, together with other anti-communist countries in the region, founded a new organization, the Association of Southeast Asian Nations (ASEAN). The other members were Thailand, Malaysia, Singapore and the Philippines. ASEAN focused on economic cooperation, with the aim of increasing resilience against communist influence.

The United States had troops stationed in Japan, South Korea, Taiwan, Thailand and the Philippines. In addition, it sent more and more soldiers to South Vietnam. After France withdrew from Indochina in 1954, four new states had emerged there: North and South Vietnam, Laos and Cambodia. The two Vietnams subsequently came into conflict with each other. The communist north was supported by China and the Soviet Union, which competed for the role of North Vietnam's main partner. Meanwhile, South Vietnam received military aid from the United States and various US allies. Unlike in the Korean War, Mao did not send Chinese combat troops. China (like the Soviet Union) did supply arms and food. In addition, Beijing sent large numbers of Chinese soldiers who stayed behind the front to perform support services in North Vietnam. They focused on issues such as transport, infrastructure construction and defence against American air raids. The United States, which did send combat troops to Vietnam, was not mandated by the UN to participate in the war this time. The Soviet Union used its veto power in the Security Council and blocked such a mandate. By the late 1960s, the Vietnam War had grown into a large-scale conflict with no end in sight. In addition, the fighting spread to Laos and Cambodia.

China's geopolitical situation was not favourable and was set to get worse. Relations with the Soviet Union had deteriorated rapidly from the late 1950s. After the Korean War, Mao Zedong wanted China to have its own nuclear weapons to deter a possible American nuclear attack. The Soviet Union initially provided the necessary technological knowledge, but had stopped that aid in 1959. The Chinese government then continued its nuclear weapons programme independently, becoming a nuclear power five years later. In 1969, fighting broke out in several places on the Chinese border with the Soviet Union. Mao and several CCP military leaders were deeply concerned about a possible Soviet attack on China. Soviet forces had invaded Hungary in 1956 and Czechoslovakia in 1968, in order to bring these fellow socialist countries back under Soviet control. The Chinese leaders were very concerned that the Soviet Union, now led by Leonid Brezhnev, would sooner or later also intervene militarily in China. They were particularly concerned that the Russians would attempt to destroy China's modest arsenal of nuclear weapons in order to shift the balance of power back in favour of the Soviet Union.

Faced with two hostile world powers, China increasingly sought support from the world outside Asia. In order not to become more isolated, China built relationships with developing countries in Africa and elsewhere. The Chinese government sent (on a relatively limited scale) money and weapons to many countries. Sometimes the aim was to support the government, in other cases the aid went to groups that had rebelled against the government. Often China did not choose its partners based on ideology. Only at the beginning of the Cultural Revolution, in 1966 and 1967, did ideology briefly become a decisive factor in China's foreign policy. More important was whether foreign partnerships strengthened China's international influence over that of the United States and the Soviet Union.[11] Non-Communist political organizations and governments were therefore also eligible for Chinese support.

Looking for opportunities to weaken the Americans and Russians in their own spheres of influence, China also became interested in Europe. Mainly through propaganda, the Chinese government tried to undermine the ideological appeal of the United States and the Soviet Union in Western and Eastern Europe, respectively. A special relationship developed between China and Albania. The leader of that country was Enver Hoxha, who, like Mao, had once worked as a teacher and who had been a member of the resistance against Italy and Germany during the Second World War. After the war, Albania, as a socialist state, joined Stalin's anti-Western policies. However, Hoxha got into a row with the Yugoslav leader Tito (whose real name was Josip Broz) and with Stalin's successor Khrushchev. Isolated in Europe, Hoxha turned to China. Mao Zedong and Zhou Enlai were happy to provide economic support to tiny Albania. Conversely, Albania helped the Chinese cause in the UN by pointing out time and time again (but to no avail) that Taiwan was wrongly a member and that its seat should be given to the People's Republic of China.

Good relations with Albania and newly independent developing countries were very welcome, but did not remove the threat China was experiencing from the United States and the Soviet Union. Mao recognized that a drastic step was necessary. In his eyes, the Russians now posed a greater danger than the Americans. The latter had their hands full with the Vietnam War, which was unpopular in their own country, and with the global geopolitical competition with the Soviet Union. After almost twenty years of enmity between China and the United States, would it be possible to find a rapprochement? Mao was willing to try. Thanks to the Cultural Revolution, his rivals within the CCP had disappeared from the scene. If, after years of intensive anti-American propaganda, he suddenly started collaborating with the United States, it would be highly remarkable, but not impossible. No one in China dared to contradict Mao. The big question was whether the leader on the American side was interested in rapprochement, and if so, whether he could get everyone inside and outside the government on board.

## Unorthodox manoeuvres

Coincidentally, in 1969, when China was in a bad geopolitical position, the United States got a new president who took an unconventional view of China. The Republican Richard Nixon was a fierce anti-communist who had served as vice president under Dwight Eisenhower in the 1950s. In 1961, Nixon ran for president, but lost the election to John F. Kennedy by a narrow margin. Eight years later, the former lawyer and naval officer finally got what he wanted so badly. He was elected the thirty-seventh president of the United States. The greatest challenge he faced was to end the war against North Vietnam and against the communist insurgents in South Vietnam. The United States, despite all its military might, could not win that war. However, simply withdrawing was not an option, given the tens of thousands of American deaths that had already occurred and the belief that the credibility of the United States as a geopolitical leader was at stake.

Nixon was open to unorthodox strategic manoeuvres to solve the Vietnam problem and improve America's geopolitical position. A different China policy was one of the options as far as he was concerned. He had already written in 1967 in an article in *Foreign Affairs* magazine that China, provided it changed its foreign policy, should not remain isolated. The country was too big not to be part of the international community, Nixon argued. But this thought was not easy to put into practice. As president, he was confronted with the fact that there were no direct channels of communication between him and China's leaders, that many Americans saw China as the evil force behind the Vietnam War and that the Cultural Revolution made it even harder than usual to assess what was going on in China. The American and Chinese ambassadors in the Polish capital Warsaw held talks from time to time, so that the two countries still had some form of contact. Nothing came of these routine conversations, however. A breakthrough required direct contact at the highest level.

China's top diplomat, Zhou Enlai, sought an opening on Mao's behalf. In late 1970, Zhou sent a letter to Henry Kissinger, Nixon's National Security Adviser. Kissinger was Nixon's right-hand man for geopolitical matters, as Zhou was for Mao Zedong. He was born and raised in Bavaria, Germany, as Heinz Kissinger. Because he was Jewish, he had fled the country with his family during the Nazi era and ended up in New York at the age of fifteen. As a talented student, he was able to attend Harvard University, where he started working as a political scientist after graduating. When Richard Nixon became the Republican presidential nominee in 1968, Kissinger joined Nixon's team. After his election as president, Nixon appointed him National Security Adviser. Kissinger's main job was to help the president get the United States out of the Vietnam War quagmire in a politically acceptable way. Zhou's letter reached Kissinger through Pakistan and the Pakistani ambassador in Washington. The Chinese premier wrote that he invited a US special envoy to Beijing to discuss the withdrawal of US troops from Taiwan. A second letter from Zhou arrived soon after. This time the letter was not sent via Pakistan but via Romania. In his second letter, Zhou Enlai went one step further, inviting President Nixon to visit Beijing. Kissinger and Nixon noted with surprise that both letters were mild in tone and made no mention of the Vietnam War.[12] Apparently there was only one issue that really mattered to Chinese leaders, and that was Taiwan. Kissinger sent a letter back to Zhou on behalf of the president: Nixon declined the invitation, but he was willing to send someone else.

A few months later, China gave another signal. In the spring of 1971, the World Table Tennis Championships were held in Japan. One of the American players, Glenn Cowan, shared a shuttle bus with the Chinese men's team. During the short ride, Chinese star player Zhuang Zedong chatted with the American and presented him with a silk cloth with a traditional Chinese painting as a gift. A day later, Zhuang received a return gift from Cowan: a T-shirt with the peace symbol and Beatles lyrics on it ('Let it be'). Journalists present filmed and photographed the exchange. These friendly gestures attracted attention, as it was not common for sportspeople from the two countries to interact with each other. A journalist asked Cowan if he would like to visit China. 'Of course,' he responded. Subsequently, when Mao Zedong learned what had happened and saw the media attention, he ordered Zou Enlai to invite the US table tennis team. Shortly afterwards, the American table tennis players were warmly received in Beijing by the Chinese premier.

Nixon got the message: the CCP leadership was willing to seriously review its relationship with the United States. He informed the Chinese government that he would accept the invitation, and he sent Kissinger to Beijing to prepare the visit. But Nixon also wanted this to be done in the utmost secrecy. Making a rapprochement with China was extremely sensitive in the United States, especially as long as the Vietnam War was going on. Chinese military support to North Vietnam continued unabated. In July 1971, during a visit to Pakistan, Kissinger stated that he was ill and was taking a few days' rest. During that period, he flew to Beijing with three staff members and two security guards for a secret meeting with the Chinese leaders. In Washington, only Nixon and a close associate of Kissinger were aware of this mission.[13]

Kissinger spent 48 hours in Beijing. This gave him the opportunity to speak extensively with Zhou Enlai. It was the first time since the founding of the People's Republic in 1949 that China and the United States had direct contact at a high political level. Zhou wanted the United States to withdraw its troops from Taiwan. Kissinger, in turn, wanted China's cooperation in crafting an end to the Vietnam War that was acceptable for the United States. The two strategists concluded that there was sufficient room for cooperation. There was no concrete agreement, but it seemed feasible for both parties to give the other what they wanted. Satisfied, Kissinger flew back to Pakistan and from there to the United States. A few days later, as agreed by Zhou and Kissinger, China and the United States simultaneously announced that President Nixon would visit the People's Republic of China. The news came as a shock to the world. America's allies, including Chiang Kai-shek, who was still the leader of the Kuomintang and of the Taiwanese government, had not been aware that something like this was going to happen. The same was true of Enver Hoxha in Albania, who felt betrayed by Mao.

Richard Nixon's historic visit took place in February 1972. When he met Mao, the communist leader told him that abroad he favoured right-wing governments. He found them more reliable. That's why he was glad that the United States had a Republican president, not a Democratic one.[14] Moreover, he informed Nixon that the banners and posters calling for resistance to US imperialism, then pervasive in China, were meaningless. While the Chinese people were embroiled in a Cultural Revolution centred around ideological purity, Mao laughed at the thought of anyone taking the slogans on the banners seriously.[15] In other words, Mao made it clear that ideological contradictions were not an obstacle to cooperation with the United States as far as he was concerned. He also informed the US president that he did not intend to send Chinese combat troops to Vietnam. The two leaders agreed to issue a joint statement. It stated that neither would seek hegemony in East and Southeast Asia and that the United States would end its military presence in Taiwan in due course.

## Stabilizing China's domestic and foreign policy

The Cold War took a new turn as a result of this sudden rapprochement between China and the United States. As a direct consequence, in 1973 the United States felt confident enough to exit the Vietnam War. Now that the US government no longer had to fear that China was poised behind the scenes to establish its power in Vietnam and the rest of Southeast Asia (the long-feared domino effect), the war between North and South Vietnam became just a local conflict. South Vietnam was left to its own devices and was conquered by the communist north in 1975. In the longer term, the United States would recover from the Vietnam conflict and increase pressure on the Soviet Union. China and the United States became strategic partners and would coordinate their geopolitical activities vis-à-vis the Soviet Union in the 1980s.

China also benefitted from the rapprochement. That became visible in the months after Kissinger's first visit to China. In November 1971, despite being dissatisfied with China's new American policy, Albania once again proposed to the UN that the seat of Taiwan be given to China. The proposal received a lot of support, especially from developing countries in Africa and other parts of the world. The United States was now no longer holding back Chinese membership. It did try to keep Taiwan in the UN, so it would be a member along with China, but that failed, partly because Chiang Kai-shek thought just as much as Mao Zedong that there was only one China and that Taiwan was part of it (they differed only about which was the legitimate government of China). Thus, on 15 November 1971, the People's Republic of China became a member of the United Nations and of the UN Security Council. At the same time, Taiwan lost its membership in all UN bodies.

The United States ended its economic embargo against China, and the two countries began negotiations to establish diplomatic relations. Due to leadership changes on both sides, those negotiations dragged on for several years. Nixon was forced to resign as president in 1974 as a result of the Watergate scandal, when it was revealed that he had abused his presidential powers to spy on the Democratic party. In 1976, Zhou Enlai and Mao Zedong died shortly after each other. Both were weakened in the last years of their lives, Zhou due to cancer and Mao due to heart problems, among other things.

On 1 January 1979, China and the United States established diplomatic relations, now with President Jimmy Carter in the White House. The US military left Taiwan, and the United States no longer recognized the government on the island as the legitimate representative of China. The Cold War was not yet over, but for China, the geopolitical situation was now considerably less threatening. The United States was no longer a military threat, and the Soviet Union was now less dangerous because China was much stronger with the United States as its strategic partner.

With Mao's death, the Cultural Revolution ended. Shortly before his death, he had appointed the relatively unknown, loyal Hua Guofeng as his successor. Hua saw Jiang Qing as a threat, and shortly after Mao's death, he had her and her political allies (together known as the Gang of Four) arrested. She was unpopular and, without her husband's protection, she disappeared from the scene surprisingly quickly. Subsequently, however, Hua Guofeng himself was sidetracked by Deng Xiaoping. Deng was popular and had sufficient support within the Party and the military to gradually seize power. By 1978, Deng was the new supreme leader of China. He had big plans. Just as Mao and Zhou had radically changed China's geopolitical strategy in 1971, Deng would steer the country's economic course in a new direction. Now, after the Cultural Revolution and the rapprochement with the United States, China was finally able to develop economically on a large scale.

FIGURE 17 *Mao Zedong proclaiming the founding of the People's Republic of China, Beijing 1 October 1949 (photo by Bettmann/Getty Images).*

FIGURE 18 *Chiang Ching-Kuo (right) with Chiang Kai-Shek and Song Meiling, Taiwan* circa *1955 (photo by Hulton Archive/Getty Images).*

FIGURE 19 *Communist soldiers and captured American soldiers during the Korean War, Wonsan, North Korea 1951 (photo by Chinese government/ PhotoQuest via Getty Images).*

FIGURE 20 *The film star Lan Ping (right) with her mother,* circa 1936. *She would later marry Mao Zedong and become known as Jiang Qing (photo by Hulton Archive/Getty Images).*

**FIGURE 21** *US National Security Advisor Henry Kissinger (front right) and his entourage visiting the Summer Palace in Beijing, 1971 (photo by Bettmann Archive/ Getty Images).*

**FIGURE 22** *President Nixon meeting Chairman Mao, Beijing 21 February 1972 (photo by AFP via Getty Images).*

# 6

# Wait and observe (1979–2008)

At noon on 15 May 1989, a plane carrying Mikhail Gorbachev, the leader of the Soviet Union, and his wife Raisa landed at Beijing airport. For the first time in thirty years, a summit was to be held between the leaders of China and the Soviet Union.[1] Just as Nixon's visit in 1972 had led to the restoration of relations with the United States, the Chinese government now hoped to also normalize relations with the Soviet Union. A short welcome ceremony was held at the airport to reflect on this historic moment. Originally, a larger ceremony on Tiananmen Square was planned. However, a massive demonstration was going on there. Hundreds of thousands of students had been coming to the square every day for several weeks. They demonstrated for better governance, more freedom of expression and political reform. Some of them camped permanently on the square. Several thousand students had gone on hunger strike.

Tiananmen Square is of great symbolic significance to the Communist Party. Not only did Mao proclaim the People's Republic of China there in 1949, but it was also the square where students demonstrated against the Treaty of Versailles in 1919. That student protest strengthened political awareness among students and intellectuals, enabling the establishment of the CCP two years later. In the 1950s, Mao had the square enlarged considerably by the demolition of surrounding buildings. Beijing's central square has since been large enough to accommodate a million people. Facing the square are the entrance to the Forbidden City (on the north side), the National Museum (east side) and the Great Hall of the People (west side). The latter is where the most important political meetings and ceremonies take place. Mao's mausoleum is located in the southern part of the square.

The central object in the square is a gigantic granite column, the Monument to the People's Heroes. This is China's most prominent national monument, dating from the 1950s and designed by a son of the political thinker Liang Qichao. A text on that monument makes it clear to whom it is dedicated. Part of it reads: 'Immortal Glory to the People's Heroes who, since the 1840s, have given their lives in the many struggles to resist the enemy, domestic and foreign, to strive for the independence of the nation and the freedom of the people!' The text was devised by Mao and carved into Zhou Enlai's handwriting.[2]

After Zhou died in 1976, a large crowd spontaneously gathered around the monument to lay wreaths and remember the prime minister. The same thing happened in April 1989 following the death of Hu Yaobang. Hu had been Secretary General of the CCP since 1980, making him the intended successor to Deng Xiaoping. In 1987 he lost that position because he was seen by the other CCP leaders as too liberal and insufficiently able to protect party interests. Hu was very popular with students and liberal intellectuals. The memorial gathering at the Monument to the People's Heroes grew into the student demonstrations for political reform that were still going on when Gorbachev arrived in Beijing.

Until the last moment, the Chinese government had tried to persuade the students to leave the square. The CCP leadership did not want the Soviet leader's visit to be overshadowed by the protests. The state visit was a major milestone on China's long road to acceptance by the other great powers. In the late 1950s, the Communist Party of China had rebelled against its mentor, the Soviet Union, whose leader was now coming to Beijing to mend the relationship. Years of negotiations had preceded this moment. Deng Xiaoping had reason to be proud because the world could now see that his role of geopolitical strategist was on par with that of Mao Zedong.

Deng wanted to show Gorbachev (and the Chinese people) that China, having chosen its own path and abandoned the ideological leadership of the Soviet Union, was in excellent shape. A large crowd of dissatisfied students in the heart of Beijing did not fit that picture. For the students, Gorbachev's visit was an opportunity to get more attention for their cause. The Soviet leader had initiated a process of political reform at home that pushed back the previously dominant role of the Soviet Union's Communist Party. Some of the Chinese students regarded this as an example for China to follow. Moreover, a major inconvenience for the Chinese government was that hundreds of foreign journalists had come to the Chinese capital to report on Gorbachev's visit. The whole world could see on television that the CCP did not have its affairs in order.

The Chinese authorities did everything they could to keep Mikhail Gorbachev away from the demonstrators. Because they also lined the route from the airport to the city with signs and banners, the Soviet leader was taken to his residence via a shortcut. The next day, his long-awaited meeting with Deng was scheduled. It took place in the Great Hall of the People. Gorbachev was ushered into the grandiose building through a back door. The talks between the two leaders went as planned, and afterwards it was announced through a press conference that the two communist powers would gradually restore their relations.

This outcome was a geopolitical turning point that was to have major consequences. But the foreign reporters were paying much more attention to the students in the square than to the summit meeting behind closed doors. Everyone sensed that something was about to happen. The demonstrators were determined to continue their protest until the CCP allowed political changes. They received support from many ordinary citizens. Students from other parts of the country came to the capital or organized demonstrations in their own cities. The Party could only hold on to power by giving up part of it, it seemed. Could this be the beginning of the end for communist regimes around the world?

## Deng's long-term strategy

From the late 1970s, Deng Xiaoping was firmly established as the leader of the Party and thus of China. After more than half a century in the shadow of Zhou, Mao and other top figures within the CCP, it was now his turn to lead China's resurrection as a strong country. His former rival Jiang Qing and her radical supporters were charged and convicted of undermining the Party. During the trial, Jiang refused to admit she had done anything wrong. 'I was Chairman Mao's dog. I bit whoever he asked me to bite,' she said. She was sentenced to death, which was later commuted to life imprisonment. She would eventually commit suicide in 1991, by which time she was seriously ill.

From 1978, Deng Xiaoping mainly focused on two goals. First, rapid economic growth through domestic reforms and opening up to foreign trade and investment. And second, to maintain and strengthen the dominant position of the CCP. This was in line with Sun Yat-sen's blueprint. Deng passionately believed in the importance of both goals. One should not be at the expense of the other. The CCP had to provide prosperity to the people in order to remain in power. Ideology was not a priority for Deng: for him the CCP was first and foremost a political organization that represented the national interest as Sun had originally envisioned with the Kuomintang. The core function of the Party was to safeguard the unity of the Chinese nation. With a fifth of the world's population, China would be an enormous power in the world, as long as the people were united. Deng was also an advocate of strategic flexibility. China had to be prepared to take losses or sacrifice certain interests in the short term, as long as the larger strategic goals were achieved.[3]

Those strategic goals, in turn, were necessary to Deng's long-term pursuit: China's resurgence as a strong and prosperous country. His view on this was directly in line with that of Sun Yat-sen and Chiang Kai-shek. While Mao saw a major role for revolution and socialism, Deng, like the former Kuomintang leaders, was mainly concerned with a gradual evolution of China as a nation. China's revival, in Deng's view, would be realized when the country was economically prosperous and developed and secure from harmful actions from other great powers.[4] Deng's economic policies ultimately served a geopolitical purpose. He believed that countries that do not develop fall prey to countries that do. 'Those who are backward get beaten,' was Deng's sober assessment.[5] The time horizon of his vision was extensive. He expected China to be moderately prosperous only by the middle of the twenty-first century. How long it would take, according to Deng, before his country was fully prosperous and beyond the reach of malicious powers, is not known. In any case, the completion of China's process of revival was still a long way off.

But also the threat of war with other great powers was not acute for the time being. Under Mao, China had been preoccupied with survival. But Deng noted that the country had now entered calmer waters. That is why he thought it was not wise to enter into direct confrontations with major powers. While the Soviet Union and the United States were engaged in an expensive arms race, China was to waste as little energy as possible on geopolitical adventures. Deng strove for stable and good relations with the United States, the Soviet Union and other major countries such as Germany, France, Great Britain, Japan and India – not because he believed that good relations with these countries would last, since the world order was unstable and ever-changing, but to buy time for China to become stronger.

## The return of foreign investors

The most important innovation under Deng's leadership was the large-scale process of economic reform that he initiated. Farmers and companies were given more space to develop commercially, which gave a powerful boost to the economy. These domestic reforms were accompanied by a new 'open door' policy, announced in December 1978. Deng carried out what Sun Yat-sen had already proposed around 1920: to modernize the Chinese economy through intensive cooperation with the West. China would open up to foreign investment and establish close trade relations with foreign countries. Exports, especially of cheap consumer products such as clothing, toys and electronics, would become the growth engine of the Chinese economy. Since the 1960s, Japan, Taiwan, South Korea, Hong Kong and Singapore had shown how successful this strategy could be. China was poised to follow in their footsteps, but on a larger scale.

Deng now faced the same dilemma that Qing dynasty officials had already wrestled with. How could China modernize without giving up its own identity and independence? The role of foreign companies was particularly important here. They had the organizational skills, technology and access to markets and capital that China desperately needed. Deng Xiaoping was looking for a way to allow them into China without the Party and government losing control of the Chinese economy. China's past experience helped Deng and his allies find a solution to this dilemma.

Foreign companies had been very active in China before the Second World War, despite the political instability. But due to the Japanese occupation and the subsequent civil war, many foreign companies had disappeared from the country by 1949. Those that remained, mostly British companies that had been in China for a long time, now had to deal with a difficult communist government in combination with international sanctions against China. The Chinese government did not allow foreign workers to leave the country. That made it impossible for the companies to wind down their Chinese activities and withdraw from the country. The purpose of the CCP was to let foreign enterprises contribute to the economic reconstruction of the country. These were forced to transfer their technical knowledge and management experience to their Chinese employees. The companies incurred costs and even had to make additional investments in their Chinese subsidiaries without making a profit. With their expat workers in China being held hostage in this way for several years and having transferred relevant knowledge to local staff, foreign companies were eventually allowed to repatriate their employees if they relinquished their Chinese assets. They cut their losses and left.

Despite this background, foreign companies were eager to re-enter the Chinese market by the late 1970s. When Deng Xiaoping opened the door for Western companies, it was the Americans who were the first to use it. In December 1978, a few days after China announced that diplomatic relations with the US would soon be restored, it was announced that the Coca-Cola Company had been authorized by the Chinese government to sell a batch of 20,000 cases of Coke in three cities in China. Coca-Cola had established some bottling plants in China from the 1920s but had withdrawn from the country after 1949. For the first time since the Korean War, a United States product would be made available in the country again. And not just any product, but the ultimate symbol of the American consumer society. In addition, Boeing entered into an agreement with the Chinese government for the delivery of three 747 aircraft.[6]

Importing American products was a big step, but it didn't bring in capital or technology for China. The batch of cola delivered to China in 1978 had been produced in Hong Kong on behalf of Coca-Cola by Swire, one of the British companies with a long history in China. A Chinese state-owned company called COFCO, specializing in trading agricultural products, did the distribution in China. The next step for Deng was to get foreign companies to actually establish themselves in China in a way that worked for both the Chinese government and the investor. But what was the right way, and which company would make the first move?

The answer to that last question was the China Merchants Steam Navigation Company. Founded more than a century earlier by Li Hongzhang as China's first Western-style company, China Merchants now proved particularly well-suited for launching direct investment in China. In 1949, this shipping company was split into two parts, both of which were located outside the People's Republic. The main body of China Merchants had transferred to Taiwan with Chiang Kai-shek. The company's Hong Kong branch, China Merchants Hong Kong, had remained in the British colony. Its ownership had somehow been obtained by the communist government in Beijing. Thus a curious situation had emerged. China Merchants Hong Kong was based outside of Mainland China but owned by China's Ministry of Transportation while having no ties to its former parent company, which was now in Taiwan.

During the Cold War, China had left the Hong Kong company undisturbed. In 1978, the Ministry of Transport turned its attention to China Merchants Hong Kong and began exploring how the company could be used to modernize China. A ministry official, Yuan Geng, was appointed chairman of the board of China Merchants Hong Kong and tasked with making proposals on how to proceed. Yuan had joined the CCP in 1938, at the age of twenty-one and had fought against the Japanese army as a guerrilla fighter in southern China.[7] In that capacity, he had also collected military intelligence on Japan for the United States. He later worked as a Chinese intelligence officer in Vietnam and Indonesia. Born in a district in South China bordering Hong Kong, Yuan knew the British colony well. The office of the Chinese state news agency Xinhua ('New China') in Hong Kong was originally set up by him. That office served as China's informal embassy in Hong Kong during the Cold War. Now that he was CEO of China Merchants Hong Kong, he suggested that the company purchase a piece of land on the other side of the border, in the area where he came from. There the company was to establish an industrial zone where it could produce shipping-related equipment. In Hong Kong, land and personnel costs had risen rapidly, but in China those costs were very low. Leaders in Beijing approved the proposal, and China Merchants Hong Kong set up a subsidiary in the People's Republic to operate in the new industrial estate.

This first instance of foreign direct investment in China since the 1950s set an example for other Hong Kong companies looking for ways to lower their production costs. The local government of Guangdong province also went into action. China Merchants Hong Kong's new industrial park was located in that province, whose capital was Guangzhou. There resided the party secretary of Guangdong, the highest boss of the province. In 1979, this position was held by Xi Zhongxun, Xi Jinping's father. The elder Xi had made a new career after his imprisonment during the Cultural Revolution. He proposed setting up special zones in a few places along the coast where foreign companies would be allowed to invest. This would allow China to keep the influence of the companies manageable while still benefitting from their investments. Like Yuan's proposal earlier, Xi's plan was in line with what Deng and the other top leaders envisioned and was approved.

Four locations were designated where foreigners could invest. Three of them were in Guangdong and one in the other southern coastal province of Fujian. All four locations bordered on port cities where Europeans used to have (Shantou and Xiamen) or still had (Hong Kong and Macau) colonial influence. By far the most important of the four 'Special Economic Zones' was the one next to Hong Kong. The initial core of this area was the China Merchants Hong Kong Industrial Park, but its area was considerably larger and included the city of Shenzhen. As hoped, many companies from Hong Kong moved their production to the area around that city. Ethnic Chinese companies in Singapore and other countries in Southeast Asia also started investing in Shenzhen and the other three Special Economic Zones. In the early years of China's economic opening, overseas Chinese investors played a vital role. Western, Japanese and Taiwanese companies would follow later. The Chinese government responded by gradually opening such zones in more locations, including eastern and northern coastal cities such as Shanghai. The inflow of foreign investment allowed China to produce and export consumer products. The country proved to be very competitive on the global market, especially with clothing, toys and electronics, often initially made by local branches of foreign companies.

This successful approach was based partly on development models developed by other Asian countries but also on China's own historical experience. During the imperial era, China designated Macau and later Guangzhou as places where European traders were allowed to operate under controlled conditions. Later, several other coastal cities had developed into centres of foreign trade and investment. Hong Kong, Shanghai and other major cities were the gateways to the Chinese market for the outside world and China's gateway to the world market. Foreign trade had provided the Chinese government with an important source of income in the form of customs revenue. Investments had formed the basis for the emergence of China's first industrial enterprises. Foreign loans had enabled the construction of railway lines. Capital came not only from Western and Japanese investors, but also from ethnic Chinese who had built successful businesses abroad. Deng Xiaoping now continued the pre–Second World War pattern of China's integration into the world economy, with coastal cities, foreign multinationals and overseas Chinese as connecting factors. But he made sure that everything now happened on Chinese terms.

The main condition was that foreign companies would cooperate with Chinese partners through joint ventures. This created a new category of companies that were part foreign and part Chinese. The foreigners mainly contributed technology and advanced business skills. Their Chinese partners provided the local contacts necessary to obtain land, personnel and the necessary permits. The Chinese government also drew on the experience of the 1950s that foreign companies could be used to modernize Chinese enterprises. Companies with advanced skills and technologies from Asia, Europe and the United States thus played a major role in China's economic development.

Another important condition was that American and Western European companies should not in any way be a vehicle for political influence by their home governments. As early as the 1920s and 1930s, it had become clear that the interests of foreign companies did not always coincide with those of their own governments. Multinationals at that time cooperated with all political actors whose support they needed, including the Kuomintang and the Japanese military. Political power had proved decisive, not nationality. The rise of shareholder capitalism in the 1980s would further weaken the bond between Western companies and their home countries. Modern listed companies increasingly identified their interests with those of their shareholders, and increasing stock market value became their overriding objective. This trend made it easier for the Chinese government to do business with multinationals from the West. China mainly had long-term political interests, while the multinationals were strongly guided by their short-term commercial interests.

Due to the influx of foreign investment, China's coastal cities were able to develop very quickly. The ultimate symbol of the success of Deng Xiaoping's open-door policy was Shenzhen. In thirty years' time, from 1978, Shenzhen's economy grew by 1.2 million per cent.[8] The previously insignificant provincial city is now the country's third largest city by economic size, after Beijing and Shanghai.

## China in the world during the late Cold War

Deng Xiaoping paid much attention to improving relations with the outside world. Good foreign relations brought the stability, albeit temporary, necessary for China's economic development. In April 1974, during the Cultural Revolution, Deng had travelled to New York on Mao's instructions to address the United Nations General Assembly. It was the first time that a leader of the People's Republic of China addressed the UN. Referring to China's emergence as a new world power, Deng said the Chinese government had absolutely no intention of dominating other countries. He invited the rest of the world to act against Chinese dominance should the need ever arise: 'If one day China should change her colour and turn into a superpower, if she too should play the tyrant in the world, and everywhere subject others to her bullying, aggression and exploitation, the people of the world should identify her as social-imperialism, expose it, oppose it and work together with the Chinese people to overthrow it.'[9]

Deng Xiaoping's message was that no one should be afraid of China's rise. Allaying other countries' suspicions was a necessary step towards stabilizing China's foreign relations. Unlike the ideologically oriented Mao, Deng was very pragmatic. While in China the Cultural Revolution was aimed at destroying everything capitalist and Western, in New York in 1974 he bought toys for his grandchildren. And on his way back to China, when he spent a few days in Paris, he bought French cheeses and 200 croissants there.[10] Those were also gifts to take to China. They were intended for

Zhou Enlai and other CCP officials who, like himself, had lived in France in the 1920s.

A few years later, in 1978, Deng visited Japan. Sino-Japanese relations were now more friendly than ever. Deng made the relationship with Japan even better. He did not put much emphasis on what had happened during the Second World War and stated that the main current dispute between the two countries, namely, disagreement over several uninhabited islands in the East China Sea, was not an urgent issue. New infrastructure was built in China with Japanese financial support. During his visit, Deng took a ride in a shinkansen, a Japanese high-speed train, which he was very excited about. The shinkansen existed since 1964 and, together with the Tokyo Summer Olympics of the same year, was an important symbol of Japanese development and modernity. For China, high-speed trains and the organization of the Olympic Games were still a bridge too far for the time being. It did not go unnoticed by Chinese experts that the Japanese government was able to invest heavily in economic modernization because it had relatively little defence spending. The US guaranteed the security of Japan, which played only a limited geopolitical role.[11] This observation may have strengthened Deng's conviction that China should invest primarily in the economy, not in defence. Deng Xiaoping's foreign policy in the 1980s focused heavily on stabilizing relations with major powers, limiting the likelihood of a full-scale military conflict.

In January 1979, immediately after the People's Republic of China and the United States had established diplomatic relations, the then seventy-four-year-old Deng left for America. His wife Zhuo Lin travelled with him. It was the first time that a Chinese top leader paid a state visit to the United States. On 29 January 1979, a state banquet was held at the White House in honour of Deng and his wife. In addition to President Carter, former President Nixon was also present. This was against Carter's initial wish, but Deng had insisted he meet Nixon on his trip. This was a way for Deng to show that he recognized Nixon's role in restoring Sino-American relations. On the same night, Carter treated his Chinese guests to a show featuring numerous American performers, including a ballet troupe, the singer John Denver and the Harlem Globe Trotters. Deng also visited other locations in the United States. These included a Ford car factory (he had worked at a Renault factory himself in France when he was young) and NASA's Johnson Space Center in Houston (where Deng sat in a model of a lunar rover vehicle). In Houston he also attended a rodeo show. During that show, Deng Xiaoping was presented with a cowboy hat, which he accepted and without hesitation put on his head. The Chinese leader clearly enjoyed the performance of the rodeo riders, to the delight of the American public.[12]

During his visit, the Chinese leader urged the Americans not to relax their military pressure on the Soviet Union. China and the United States, he said, had a duty to work together for international stability.[13] The Chinese government was still very concerned about the threat from the Soviet Union.

In 1975, North Vietnam had conquered the southern part of the country. The now reunited Vietnam had greatly strengthened strategic ties with the Soviet Union and had become estranged from China. Something that worried Deng deeply was that the Vietnamese army had invaded Cambodia in late 1978. Cambodia, ruled by that country's Communist Party (the Khmer Rouge) and its leader Saloth Sar (better known as Pol Pot), was an ally of China. The Khmer Rouge exercised a reign of terror that killed an estimated 1.5 to 2 million people, or a quarter of the Cambodian population. China nevertheless continued to support Pol Pot's government for ideological and strategic reasons.[14] After the invasion, Vietnam occupied a large part of the country, and Pol Pot retreated to the jungle with his allies.

For Deng, it was unacceptable that Vietnam attacked pro-Chinese Cambodia with military support from the Soviet Union. The fact that the Vietnamese invasion ended the Khmer Rouge massacres was not a major factor for China. During the imperial era and again today, the Chinese government's position has been and is that it does not interfere in domestic affairs in neighbouring countries, but it does demand that they do not engage in activities that threaten China's security. The Cambodian genocide was not a reason for Chinese interference, but the Vietnamese alliance with the Soviet Union was.

Deng decided to attack Vietnam, which was to take place after his visit to the United States. He wanted to inform the Americans, as China's strategic partners, about this so that they would not be taken by surprise. However, he did not do so through President Carter but through a bank manager in Houston called George H. W. Bush. He was the former ambassador to the UN and director of the CIA, businessman, Republican and candidate for the US presidency. Deng knew him because Bush had worked in Beijing for over a year as the de facto US ambassador (this was before China and the United States had resumed formal diplomatic relations). The Chinese leader found Bush trustworthy because, he would later explain, he rarely said anything that was meaningless or that he did not mean.[15] Apparently he also saw George Bush as a promising contact in which he wanted to continue to invest.

Shortly after Deng returned from the United States, Chinese troops did indeed invade Vietnam. From a military point of view, the short Chinese war with Vietnam was not a success. Deng's plan was for the Chinese army to demonstrate its superiority in a brief campaign and then retreat, as it had done in the 1962 border war with India. Although the People's Liberation Army succeeded in capturing all five capitals of the northernmost Vietnamese provinces, this came at the cost of heavy losses on the Chinese side. After destroying much infrastructure in the occupied territory, the Chinese troops withdrew to their own country.

Deng had failed to force Vietnam to withdraw from Cambodia, but he had made a point nonetheless. The Chinese government had sent a clear signal to all countries around China what to expect if they sought strategic cooperation with the Soviet Union. Equally important, Deng had shown the United States that China was a serious strategic partner in the geopolitical battle with the Soviet Union. Pol Pot and the Khmer Rouge, though pushed on the defensive, continued to wage a guerrilla war against the Vietnamese with Chinese support. To keep up the pressure, the Chinese army continued smaller attacks along the Vietnamese border as long as there were still Vietnamese troops in Cambodia.

When the Soviet Union invaded and occupied Afghanistan, a neighbouring country of China, in late 1979, China responded by providing financial and military support to Afghan guerrilla fighters. The Chinese government was not alone in doing this, as the United States provided similar support.[16] Part of the Afghan fighters they armed, the mujahideen, would later form the Taliban. The war in Afghanistan cost the lives of about 15,000 Soviet soldiers, while China's growing strength forced the government in Moscow to remain on the alert for developments in Asia. As a result, the Soviet leaders had less attention and resources for the confrontation with the United States. Ronald Reagan, who became president of the United States in the early 1980s, further increased the pressure through the arms race, including by announcing in 1983 a missile defence programme, the Strategic Defense Initiative, popularly known as Star Wars. The aim was to develop new weapons that would be capable of intercepting Soviet nuclear missiles. With this, the United States, which had a financial and technological advantage, forced the Soviet Union to make costly investments to develop similar weapons. If the Soviets did not, they might end up in a situation where their own nuclear arsenal was no longer a guarantee against a US attack and the whole principle of mutual deterrence, upon which the arms race had been based for decades, would be of no value to them.

In 1982, Soviet leader Brezhnev gave a speech in Uzbekistan. Hidden among the usual negative remarks about China, his speech contained some tentative signals that he was interested in better relations with the People's Republic. When Deng learned of this, he immediately ordered the Chinese Ministry of Foreign Affairs to respond. That was not easy, because diplomatic contact with the Soviet Union had been broken for some time. Qian Qichen, one of the top officials at the ministry, was tasked with finding a solution for this. Qian came from a family of prominent officials and scholars. During the Second World War, when he was about fourteen and attending school in Shanghai, he secretly joined the CCP. Later he lived for a long time in the Soviet Union, where he first studied and later worked at the Chinese embassy. During the Cultural Revolution he, like so many others, got into trouble and was sentenced to years of forced labour. From 1974 he was allowed to resume his career and Qian rose within the Ministry of Foreign Affairs.

To let Brezhnev know that Deng had understood the message from Uzbekistan, Qian Qichen organized a press conference. That by itself was a challenge, because the ministry had never done that. As he later described in his memoirs, Qian had about seventy to eighty journalists come to the ministry.[17] In the entrance hall, surrounded by the journalists, Qian made a three-sentence statement criticizing the Soviet Union. After that the press conference was over. No questions were taken. Deng's message to Brezhnev was subtle: the tone and wording of Qian's three sentences were a little different than usual. In addition, the press conference itself was very unusual. The journalists understood that apparently China wanted to send a message to the Soviet Union and wrote about it in their newspapers. This was the beginning of renewed rapprochement between the Soviet Union and China. After some time, diplomatic negotiations began. China set three conditions for normalizing the relationship: the Soviet Union had to stop supporting the Vietnamese occupation of Cambodia and withdraw militarily from Afghanistan and Mongolia. Although nothing concrete came out of these negotiations for the time being, the fact that negotiations were taking place was in itself a big step.

Meanwhile, Sino-US relations continued to improve. The US government allowed arms sales to China and supported Deng's programme of economic reform. The only problem remained Taiwan. Although the United States had withdrawn its troops from Taiwan and had ended diplomatic relations with the government in Taipei, it continued to provide arms to Taiwan. The Kuomintang still ruled the island, and the United States was still influencing the military balance of power between China and Taiwan from a distance. Joint action against the Soviet Union, continued extensive US military presence in Asia and close cooperation with Taiwan were the three pillars of US China policy in the 1980s. The military presence could be seen, at least in part, as necessary to keep Russian influence out of the region. But the continued military support for Taiwan made it clear that the United States wanted to maintain leverage against China. After difficult negotiations, the US government promised in 1982 that arms deliveries would gradually be phased out but there was no time schedule specified. Deng decided to accept this situation for now.

# Hong Kong and Macau

Around the same time, the question arose of how to proceed with Hong Kong. In 1898, Britain had forced the Qing dynasty to make available land for the expansion of Hong Kong. This happened in the aftermath of the Chinese defeat against Japan. As a result of the Opium Wars, Hong Kong Island and the Kowloon Peninsula had been annexed and thus been fully separated from the Chinese state. But the additional territories (known as New Territories) that were added to the colony of Hong Kong in 1898 were only leased by Great Britain. While the British did not have to pay for the use of the New Territories, the lease term had a ninety-nine years limit. This meant that it would end in 1997. Foreign investors in Hong Kong wanted to know where they stood. Would the leased territories be returned to China, and if so, what would that mean for the rest of the colony?

To put an end to this uncertainty, the British government had no choice but to start negotiations with China. It fell to Prime Minister Margaret Thatcher to find a solution to this issue. She was known as the Iron Lady for her hardline attitude towards the Soviet Union. In 1982, under her leadership, the British won the Falklands War against Argentina. In doing so, they had shown their willingness and ability to protect their overseas possessions, in this case a few tiny islands in the South Atlantic. And Thatcher had shown that, in the tradition of Churchill, she had no intention of giving up Britain's status as a colonial power without a fight. However, it was clear that China held some important trump cards. The Japanese attack in 1941 had already shown that Hong Kong was indefensible against superior military forces. In addition, the city of millions depended on the People's Republic for its water supply. Thatcher had to go to Beijing to talk to Deng about the future of the colony. She arrived there in September 1982, determined not to give up Hong Kong.

The conversation between the two leaders lasted two and a half hours. Thatcher pointed out that in 1997 Britain only had to return the leased area. The harbour and most of the city itself were owned indefinitely by the British. According to Thatcher, British rule was also a precondition for attracting foreign investment. Without the continued presence of investors, Hong Kong would be of little value to China. Her proposal was therefore that the lease be extended, while Hong Kong might be decolonized in the future. The British Prime Minister expected that with these arguments she could persuade the Chinese to cooperate.

But Deng Xiaoping made it clear to Thatcher that there was nothing to negotiate regarding the ownership of Hong Kong. The situation was the reverse of that in 1840, when Palmerston would not negotiate with China, but simply demanded that the country give up an island. In 1997, China would take over the administration of Hong Kong, one way or another, Deng now told Thatcher. And to be clear, China would not just take over the leased part but the entire colony. Deng's plan was for Hong Kong to gain autonomous status from 1997, with its own political system and legislation. That would reassure investors and provide sufficient foundations for Hong Kong's economic future. He was willing to coordinate with the British on the way in which the transfer was to take place, but there was nothing else to talk about. Possibly to reinforce his argument, Deng, who was dressed in a Mao suit, during the meeting frequently spat into a spittoon next to his chair.[18] The Iron Lady returned to London empty-handed.

Thatcher and her government continued to struggle for two years after her visit to Beijing, but eventually gave in. In September 1984, China and Britain signed an agreement on the future of Hong Kong. On 1 July 1997, the city was to be incorporated into the People's Republic, while retaining a high degree of autonomy as Deng had indicated. The opinion of the more than 5 million inhabitants of Hong Kong was not asked and there was no question of the territory becoming an independent state. In view of the forthcoming negotiations with China, the British government had already established in 1981 that Hong Kong residents were not entitled to a British passport. The emergency exit for many Hongkongers who did not want to come under Chinese rule was nailed shut: they were not welcome in Britain. Chris Patten, Hong Kong's last colonial governor, acknowledged in retrospect that the British decision was 'hardly edifying'.[19] But it was a harbinger of future relations between China and Europe. The British had once set out to dominate the world, but now they took a defensive stance. Immigrants from Hong Kong were not wanted.

In 1987, China also signed an agreement on Macau, which had been under Portuguese colonial rule for some 430 years. Like Hong Kong, Macau was dependent on the People's Republic for its water supply and was militarily indefensible against a Chinese attack. The Portuguese government had no problem ceding Macau but hoped to do so sometime in the twenty-first century. However, that did not fit into the time frame that Deng had in mind. The transfer was to take place in the twentieth century. Thus, the two countries agreed that Portugal would hand over the city to China on 20 December 1999, eleven days before the end of the century. Like Hong Kong, Macau would be granted autonomous status within the People's Republic.

The handover treaties of Hong Kong and Macau were great successes for Deng. Hong Kong was especially important. As an economy, that city was much larger than Macau. In addition, as a British colony, Hong Kong was a prominent symbol of the First Opium War. Just as the Daoguang Emperor had been responsible for the loss of Hong Kong, Deng would go down in history as the man who returned the territory to China. What China got back was much more than a piece of land. While Hong Kong was barely inhabited at the time of the British occupation in January 1841, in 1997 it was a prosperous, stable and highly internationalized economy, one-fifth the size of China's economy. Macau's return in 1999 was a nice bonus. That city was smaller, less international and less modern, but it did have a sizeable gambling industry that brought in a lot of money for the city. With the transfer of Macau to China, the phase of European colonial presence in East Asia would be definitively closed.

## Tiananmen

The period from 1982 to 1989 was a favourable time for China from a geopolitical point of view. China's economic isolation had been lifted and the country was now developing very rapidly economically. There was also cautious rapprochement with the Soviet Union. Moreover, Soviet troops left Afghanistan and Mongolia, and Vietnam withdrew from Cambodia. Gorbachev personally came to Beijing as a sign that relations with China were now stable again. That was the May 1989 visit, a moment of triumph for Deng. But unfortunately for him, the student protest on Tiananmen Square spoilt the situation. Although the talks with Gorbachev went well, and it was decided that the two countries would fully restore their diplomatic relations, China suddenly found itself in the middle of an acute political crisis. After the Soviet leader returned to his home country, the students continued their protest.[20]

On 3 June, when the square had been occupied by students for weeks, tensions in Beijing peaked. The government had previously made an attempt to send soldiers into the city to clear the square. In response, many citizens of the capital had taken to the streets in support of the students. They set up barricades and stopped the columns of military vehicles by their massive presence. That night, the military was ordered by the political leadership to advance and clear the square regardless of any opposition. The population was warned to stay indoors, but many did not comply.

Fierce fighting broke out on the access roads to the centre of the city. Armed soldiers, trucks, tanks and armoured vehicles moved towards Tiananmen Square from all directions. The soldiers used tear gas and sticks to disperse people, but also fired AK-47 assault rifles into the crowd and drove their vehicles over barricades and over people. Civilians fought back by throwing firebombs and stones. Many military vehicles were set on fire, but that did not stop the advance. After the army seized the access roads with brute force and threatened to do the same with Tiananmen Square, the demonstrating students decided to give up the occupation and leave the square. In the chaotic night of 3 to 4 June, an unknown number of civilians and students lost their lives. Estimates of the number of fatalities vary, from a few hundred to a few thousand. It was the most violent moment in the city's history since the Boxer crisis and the sack of Beijing by foreign troops in 1900. In the days and weeks that followed, peace returned there and in the rest of the country. Student leaders and intellectuals were arrested and given prison terms. Thousands of others involved in the protests were also imprisoned, some of them sentenced to death.

Deng Xiaoping has never shown any sign of regret or doubt about his decision to deploy the army against the protest. He strongly believed in the need for the CCP to remain in power and thought that giving in to the students' demands would be the beginning of the end of that power. The armed intervention secured the position of the Party in the short term, but it was uncertain whether the population would turn away from the Party in the longer term. When Commander Everson opened fire on demonstrating students in Shanghai in 1925, it marked the beginning of the end of British influence in China. And now it was not foreigners, but it was the CCP itself that had fired on students (thereby causing many more victims than the Shanghai police had in 1925).

## Turning point

The spring of 1989 was a turning point for China's geopolitical position. From now on, relations with Russia would keep improving, especially after the Soviet Union broke up in December 1991. But relations with the US deteriorated. Public opinion in the United States, like in other Western countries, had reacted with shock at the violent crackdown on the student protest. The US government imposed diplomatic and economic sanctions against China. High-level contacts, arms transfers and loans through the World Bank (in which the United States had much influence) were cut off. Relations were not to be restored unless the Chinese government took steps towards political reform. America's allies, Japan and the Western European countries, pursued similar policies in coordination with the United States.

George Bush had been sworn in as the forty-first president of the United States a few months earlier, after eight years as vice president under Ronald Reagan. He was looking for a new balance in the relationship with China. On the one hand, there were the sanctions and the associated demand that China take steps in the field of democratization and human rights. On the other hand, China was still a valuable strategic partner against the Soviet Union. Bush also believed in the importance of good relations with China. He therefore sent a personal letter, and shortly afterwards his National Security Adviser Brent Scowcroft, to Deng. Scowcroft's journey, like Kissinger's in 1971, had to be done in the greatest secrecy. After all, all high-level diplomatic contacts had been suspended. On 2 July 1989, Scowcroft met with Deng Xiaoping. As Thatcher had experienced earlier, Deng was a tough negotiator. The Chinese leader informed his American guest that he was not impressed by the sanctions. 'The sanctions don't affect us,' he said. 'We're not afraid of them.'[21]

Bush's explanation, conveyed by Scowcroft, that Americans, based on their own values, could not stand by passively when human rights were violated as grossly as during the Tiananmen crisis, was waved off by Deng. The Chinese leader was not interested in the fact that, according to Scowcroft, the American government had to take the views of the American people and of Congress into account. The Chinese leader held the American government responsible for its China policy regardless of what Congress and the media did in the United States. The bottom line, according to Deng, was that China could only be safe under the leadership of the CCP and that the United States had tried to undermine the Party's position during a moment of crisis. He said he was convinced that the US government had supported the demonstrating students, but he did not specify how it had done so. In any case, as he saw it the United States added fuel to the fire by imposing sanctions and setting conditions for their ending. Deng said that he still considered Bush a friend, but that he would not give in to American pressure. He said the relationship between the two countries could only be restored if the United States lifted its sanctions.[22]

Deng Xiaoping and China's other communist leaders were disturbed by what they had seen. At a time of great crisis, the Americans and their allies seemed to be actively trying to undermine the CCP's rule. This happened in a context where China and the US cooperated on security policy and economic matters, China posed no military threat to the United States and the US president was someone Deng got on well with. If the United States could not be trusted even under such favourable circumstances, then for the CCP it was clear that it should always remain on its guard.

Some other developments contributed to the feeling that also other Western countries were out to weaken China when the country was vulnerable. A few months after the Tiananmen Crisis, the Norwegian Nobel Prize Committee announced that the 1989 Nobel Peace Prize was awarded to the Dalai Lama. The latter was still in exile in India. One of the motives of the Nobel Prize committee for this choice seemed the desire to encourage the pro-democratic forces in China. At least that's how the Chinese government saw it. And after June 1989, the negotiations between China and Great Britain on the handover of Hong Kong suddenly became much more difficult than before. According to China, the British were making demands that they had not previously had, aimed at introducing more democracy in Hong Kong. It seemed as if the West was trying to put pressure on all of China's sensitive issues to force the country into political reform.

After some time, relations between China and the West improved somewhat. In the summer of 1990, the Iraqi army invaded Kuwait. The United States then needed China's support to obtain a mandate through the UN Security Council to liberate Kuwait by military means. China provided that support, after which diplomatic and economic relations with the West recovered. While the ban on arms transfers from the United States and the European Community remained in force, the effect of the Tiananmen crisis on Sino-Western relations seemed limited. Beneath the surface, however, China's mistrust of the United States would continue to grow.

A series of incidents contributed to this. In the fall of 1992, Bush authorized the sale of 150 F-16 fighter jets to Taiwan. Bush did this partly because he was accused by his opponent Bill Clinton during the presidential election of being too friendly with China. But the president probably also wanted to increase pressure on China. At that time it was already clear that the Cold War was over and that the United States was the great victor. The Soviet Union disbanded in December 1991. Its main heir was Russia, which took over the Soviet Union's permanent seat on the UN Security Council and its nuclear arsenal. In the face of a now relatively weak Russia, China and the United States no longer needed each other's support. Thus, the foundation for the strategic cooperation that the two countries had had with each other since 1972 disappeared. Instead came great uncertainty.

The United States, which now was the undisputed global leader, had some frustrations with China. The most important was the US trade deficit. China, as Deng Xiaoping had hoped, was fast becoming the world's main industrial hub. Many articles for Western and Japanese consumers were no longer made in the United States, Europe, Japan or in low-wage countries elsewhere, but in China. Large international companies moved their factories to China and were now part of the Chinese export sector. The result for the United States and many other Western countries was the loss of jobs at home and a negative trade balance with China. Another frustration was that China was supplying countries like North Korea with technology that could be used for nuclear weapons. There was a risk that such countries might one day use those weapons against the United States.

Bush lost the presidential election and in January 1993 Bill Clinton took up residence in the White House. Clinton was Democrat, lawyer, young and the former governor of the state of Arkansas. He wanted to give human rights a major role in his foreign policy towards China. The new US Secretary of State, Warren Christopher, declared on taking office that he intended through peaceful evolution to ensure that China would become more democratic. The United States would not intervene harshly in China, but would use its considerable economic and cultural influence to gradually steer the country towards a different political-economic system. In American eyes this was a logical and necessary step towards a world based on liberal values and led by the United States.

It was now clearer than ever to the Chinese government that the United States would not rest until the CCP was overthrown. Democratization in China automatically meant an end to the CCP's autocratic rule. Moreover, peaceful evolution was a term the United States had used in the 1950s to describe its strategy against the Soviet Union. The core of that approach was that the United States tried to bring down the Soviet Union by non-military means. Simply ensuring that information about the prosperity and freedoms of Western society could reach the people of the Soviet Union, for example through radio broadcasts, would undermine support for the Communist Party. To both China and the United States, the student protest of 1989 seemed evidence that the Chinese people were susceptible to political ideas from abroad. And the fall of the Soviet Union seemed to prove the effectiveness of this strategy.

But US foreign policy in the Clinton era was not just about influencing public opinion in China. From 1993 onwards, the United States tried to put pressure on the Chinese government by threatening higher import tariffs on Chinese exports. In doing so, the Clinton administration not only wanted to reduce the trade deficit with China but also to force the Chinese government to improve the human rights situation in China. After a few years, the US abandoned these attempts because they had insufficient effect on the behaviour of the Chinese government. But China had learnt yet another lesson: the US viewed China's economic dependence on access to the huge US market as a tool to influence its domestic politics. The suppression of all forms of opposition in China was seen by the United States as a violation of basic human rights, but the Communist Party saw this as a necessity to avoid chaos and to remain in power. What was a matter of adhering to universal principles to Washington was an act of aggression to Beijing. Chinese leaders were probably aware that the First Opium War was justified by Palmerston on the basis of a principle that the then world power regarded as universal, namely, the right to free trade. Whereas Britain had used brute force in 1840 and 1857, the United States now used more subtle tools to force China to conform: the power of ideas and economic pressure.

## Deng's legacy

With the Cold War over, many Americans and Europeans thought that democracy and the free market had finally become the norm for the entire world. Francis Fukuyama coined the term often used in those days: end of history. Sooner or later, but probably sooner, all countries would adopt the Western political-economic model. Liberalism would dominate. As China had more contact with the outside world, and as a result became more prosperous, more and more Chinese would demand good governance and personal freedoms. At least, that was the prevailing expectation in the West. Indeed, China's foreign trade increased, more foreign companies invested in China and more Chinese students studied at foreign universities. A new middle class emerged in the big cities. The 1990s also brought the Internet to China, and with it a new channel through which information about the world came to Chinese citizens.

Deng Xiaoping saw the American attempts to change China as a great danger. Henry Kissinger writes in his book *On China* that in the final stages of his role as China's supreme leader, Deng circulated a short text to top officials that read: 'Enemy troops are outside the walls. They are stronger than we. We should be mainly on the defensive.'[23] The main foreign policy guideline that Deng passed on to his successors was derived from this and can be summarized as: wait and observe.[24] China should not take initiatives that unnecessarily attracted the attention of stronger countries.

The belief that the United States was trying to undermine the CCP regime through increasingly intensive contacts was no reason for Deng to isolate China. On the contrary, within the Party, he continued to press for an acceleration of economic integration between China and the rest of the world, even in the early 1990s, when he had already formally retired. After the deep political crisis in the spring of 1989, conservative party officials had slowed the pace of China's economic reforms. Although Deng was still a very powerful man even after his official retirement, his prestige within the CCP had been damaged by Tiananmen. In 1992, when Deng was eighty-seven, he resorted to an unexpected approach to get economic reform back on track: he left Beijing politics and went on vacation.

Travelling by private train, he visited cities such as Shanghai, Guangzhou and Shenzhen. Everywhere he went, he visited local administrators. In

Shenzhen he was guided through the city to get an idea of the local economy. Media from the region and especially from Hong Kong started to pay more and more attention to Deng's holiday trip. He did not give official press conferences, because he was no longer in office and only on vacation, but where possible he addressed citizens and journalists. He kept repeating the same message: continue with economic reforms and focus on rapid economic growth. His solo action had the desired result: with the support of local officials and companies in the southern provinces, the Chinese economy was further modernized. The government loosened the reins in the economic field and there was increasing room for market forces. Exports and foreign investment played a central role in the now very-fast-growing Chinese economy.

Deng Xiaoping died on 19 February 1997. He did not witness the transfer of Hong Kong from Great Britain to China, which occurred a few months after his death, but his legacy was huge. The long-term effects of his view on China's resurgence were similar, in key respects, to those of Sun Yat-sen. Deng took the threat from the outside world, especially the United States, very seriously, but he did not believe that either isolation or confrontation was the solution. Instead, he wanted China to integrate into the international system. Deng did not believe that China was destined to adopt the liberal values of the West. He focused on making the potentially harmful side effects of foreign economic activities in China manageable through special zones, joint ventures, censorship of foreign media and maintaining a major role for the Chinese government. In addition, Deng focused on gradually expanding China's influence in international organizations in order to temper any undesirable influences on China from there. China had already joined the United Nations, the World Bank and the IMF in the 1970s. Under Deng, negotiations were initiated that would culminate in China's membership of the World Trade Organization (WTO) in 2001, the last major international organization of which the People's Republic was not yet a member.

As Deng lived a secluded life in his last years, China continued to follow his strategic course. His successor as the top leader in the Communist Party was Jiang Zemin, a former mayor and party chairman of Shanghai. He was an at times flamboyant figure, who was known to spontaneously burst into song on some occasions. Jiang supported Deng's two main goals: strengthening the position of the CCP and modernizing the economy. As general secretary of the Party, commander-in-chief and president of China, he was Deng's undisputed successor as leader of China. The prime minister of China in the 1990s was Zhu Rongji, also a former mayor of Shanghai and an even more enthusiastic proponent of economic reform than Jiang. Zhu worked on the economic reform policy with great dedication.

In 2002, when Jiang and Zhu's terms expired, they were succeeded by Hu Jintao (as party leader, commander-in-chief and president) and Wen Jiabao (as prime minister). Hu and Wen, in office from 2002 until 2012, had already been chosen during Deng's lifetime as the future successors to

Jiang and Zhu. Hu Jintao and Wen Jiabao would also implement Deng's strategy and focus on economic modernization and maintaining the CCP's dominance. They, too, would avoid unnecessary confrontations with the United States or other countries. Deng had ensured a stable succession not only for himself, but also for the leaders who came after him (who, however, would fail to achieve his high degree of authority). The Deng era lasted until 2012, when he himself had been dead for fifteen years.

## Taiwan

In the 1990s, the Sino-American geopolitical relationship slipped further. The biggest problem was Taiwan. In 1978, when Deng Xiaoping became the top leader of China, his former fellow student from Moscow, Chiang Ching-kuo, became president of Taiwan. Like his father Chiang Kai-shek, who had died a few years earlier, he had no intention of allowing Taiwan to become part of the People's Republic. Chiang Kai-shek's widow, Song Meiling, had a difficult relationship with her stepson Chiang Ching-kuo. After her husband's death, Song moved to the United States, where she died in 2003 at the age of 105. The new first lady of Taiwan was Faina Vachrava, who had adopted the Chinese name Chiang Fang-liang. Meanwhile, the Kuomintang still ruled Taiwan. As in China, political opposition was not allowed in Taiwan. From the 1960s, the island's economy had developed very quickly, increasing the level of prosperity. For a while, therefore, the blueprint that Sun Yat-sen had devised for China also seemed to apply to Taiwan. At the end of his life, however, Chiang Ching-kuo took the first steps towards democratization. When an opposition party, the Democratic Progressive Party (DPP), was created, Chiang decided to turn a blind eye rather than suppress it.

He appointed Lee Teng-hui as his successor. That was a striking choice, because Lee was born in Taiwan. Most members of Taiwan's political elite came from mainland China. They had fled the CCP in 1949 with Chiang Kai-shek. In the years before, they had fought against Japan. Lee Teng-hui grew up when Taiwan was a Japanese colony. Like many other Taiwanese, he generally had positive memories of the Japanese era. He had studied in Japan and had volunteered in the Japanese army in 1944. In the 1970s, Lee became mayor of Taipei and then vice president under Chiang Ching-kuo. After the latter's death in 1988, Lee became president.

When Taiwanese students took to the streets en masse in 1990 to demand democracy, Lee reacted very differently than Deng had done in China a year earlier. Lee gave the students what they asked for and promised that a general election would be held several years later. With his pro-Japanese background and promise of democratization, Lee was not exactly a leader with whom the CCP felt comfortable. Chiang Kai-shek may have been the arch-enemy of the Chinese communists, but he was also a familiar and predictable person who had also fought for China's revival. Chiang Kai-shek and his son had always rejected the idea that Taiwan could be an independent country. Their position was clear: Taiwan was an inseparable part of China. The only point of contention with the Beijing government was whether the Kuomintang or the CCP was the rightful ruler of China.

Lee, however, seemed to be heading in a different direction. He felt that Taiwan had its own identity, which was different from China's. Lee was a Taiwanese, not a Chinese, nationalist, deviating from Sun Yat-sen's tradition. In China, Jiang Zemin was concerned that Lee would use the upcoming election to turn Taiwan into an independent country. After all, there was a chance that a majority of voters would be in favour of this when presented with the choice. The Chinese army was not powerful enough to conquer Taiwan. The Kuomintang had modern American weapons, and in addition, the United States was likely to intervene if the mainland would attempt to attack or impose a blockade on the island.

Chinese leaders had long made it clear how important Taiwan was to them. The reunification of the island with mainland China into a single state was one of the main goals of the CCP. In 1949 the Party had succeeded in bringing almost all of China under centralized control, as it had been during the Qing dynasty (Tibet was occupied by CCP troops in 1950 and annexed to the People's Republic). Reuniting China and reducing the influence of the great powers were the most basic goals of Chinese nationalism. Both the Kuomintang and the Communist Party grew out of that nationalism. For many Chinese, the fact that Taiwan had remained beyond the reach of the People's Republic meant that the 'century of humiliation', as the period from 1840–1949 was increasingly referred to, was not quite over. China had ceded Taiwan to Japan in 1895. The island thus had become a symbol of China's defeat against Japan. Hong Kong and Macau were to be reunited with China in the late 1990s, but Taiwan's future was uncertain. It was impossible for the CCP to accept that Taiwan would formally declare itself independent, because then the chances of the island joining the mainland would be greatly diminished. The CCP would have failed as a champion of Chinese nationalism. And that would seriously undermine the Party's legitimacy as China's indefinite ruler.

## The Cornell crisis

In 1995 Lee received an invitation from Cornell University in the United States to give a lecture. He had obtained his doctorate there in 1968 with a dissertation on agricultural economics. The US government had not issued visas to senior Taiwanese officials since the late 1970s, in the interest of good relations with China. Qian Qichen, the official who had organized the press conference with the subtle message for Brezhnev in 1982, had now risen to become foreign minister and deputy prime minister. As China's top diplomat, Qian was personally informed by Warren Christopher that the United States would not allow Lee Teng-hui to come to Cornell. A month later, however, the US government reversed this decision. Bill Clinton gave permission for Lee to visit the country in a personal capacity. Subsequently, Lee gave a lecture at Cornell in which he emphasized that Taiwan was a democracy and had its own identity.

Christopher informed Qian that Clinton had no choice: the US Congress had demanded that Lee, representing democratic Taiwan, give his lecture. Clinton risked reputational damage if he had not issued a visa, because American public opinion would see him as soft on China. Qian, however, felt that the US government was not a reliable partner because in the end it was not Congress but the government that made the visa decision.[25] What mattered most to China was that the stable period in relations with America had now apparently come to an end.

In the summer of 1995, after Lee's trip, the Chinese navy conducted exercises near Taiwan. As part of the exercises, the Chinese ships fired missiles. They caused no damage, but the action made it clear that China was also prepared to fire missiles at Taiwanese targets if necessary. The Chinese state media reported extensively on the exercises, which were an unsubtle message to Taiwan (independence is unacceptable) and the United States (don't use Taiwan as a weapon against China). Qian Qichen spoke to Henry Kissinger, when he visited Beijing at this time, about the crisis. Long retired, Kissinger's prestige and top-level contacts in both China and the United States served as a communication channel between the two countries. Qian indicated to Kissinger that the Chinese government had no room for manoeuvre when it came to Taiwan. Good relations with the US were very important, but Taiwan was even more important.[26] In another conversation, Jiang Zemin told Kissinger that China was in no hurry: Taiwan eventually had to be reunited with China, but it didn't necessarily have to happen in the short term.[27] This meant that China did not intend to force the situation and accepted the status quo as long as Taiwan did not attempt to declare formal independence from China.

At the end of 1995, tensions rose further. The Taiwanese people went to the polls for the first time to elect a parliament. The Chinese government wanted to send another clear signal to voters in Taiwan that a pro-independence policy would lead to war. Again, Chinese troops held exercises clearly aimed at simulating a possible attack on Taiwan. The US government responded by sending an aircraft carrier plus other warships to pass through the Taiwan Strait. The crisis reached a climax a few months later when another election was held in Taiwan, this time for the presidency. When China again conducted military exercises near Taiwan, President Clinton decided to escalate the US response. The United States this time sent two aircraft carriers plus two destroyers, a frigate, a cruiser and several smaller warships to the Taiwan area. It was the largest display of US military might in Asia since the Vietnam War. With this, the United States made it clear that if it wanted to, it could protect Taiwan against a Chinese invasion. More importantly, the US showed its unwillingness to relinquish its place as the main military power in Asia to China. No one doubted that an armed confrontation at sea or in the air would be won by the United States.

After the elections and after all those involved had made their point, calm returned to the Taiwan Strait. Lee Teng-hui won the presidency and continued his policy of democratizing Taiwan and strengthening its identity. However, he did not strive for formal independence. The US government, having demonstrated its military might, refused to guarantee Taiwan's security under any circumstances, because then Taiwan would have free rein to declare independence. The United States did not want to be played off against China by Taiwan. Jiang Zemin and the CCP had learned that military power was still decisive in determining the regional order. This meant that the most important lesson of the Opium War still applied. China therefore started to invest more vigorously than before in its navy and air force, both of which were still very underdeveloped. However, building them up would take many years.

Nobody wanted a war. Also, now prosperous Taiwan had a lot to lose. China stuck to Deng's strategy: to stay focused on economic growth and avoid confrontations as much as possible. Meanwhile the United States, in Kissinger's view, lacked goals that were both achievable and worthy of war.[28] China was too big for any other power to change, and Taiwan's independence was not a priority for the Americans.

## More incidents

While the US and China would, at least for now, not come as close to an armed conflict as in 1995–6, there were still some dramatic incidents in the following years. In 1999, during the Kosovo war, NATO aircraft bombed the Serbian capital Belgrade. In one such raid, an American B-2 bomber dropped bombs on the Chinese embassy. The building was destroyed, while three Chinese journalists were killed and twenty-seven other Chinese were injured. Public opinion in China reacted with shock and fury. Despite an apology from President Clinton, who assured that it was a mistake, the prevailing opinion in China was that the attack was deliberate. The Chinese government gave diplomatic support to Serbia, not NATO, during the Kosovo war. It was possible that the Chinese embassy also passed on military intelligence to Serbia. The view that prevailed inside China but which has remained controversial in the West was that the US deliberately bombed the embassy to put an end to this.

Two years later, on 1 April 2001, a United States and a Chinese military aircraft collided over the South China Sea. The American navy plane, an EP-3E Aries II, which flew at a distance of some 70 miles off the coast of the Chinese island of Hainan, had twenty-four crew members on board. It was capable of gathering communications intelligence and electronic signals. There are several bases of the Chinese military on Hainan. As Chinese fighter jets approached the US spy plane they probably wanted to scare or drive it away, but one of them came too close and collided with the American plane. The Chinese jet crashed into the sea, the pilot was never found. The American plane managed to make an emergency landing in Hainan despite significant damage. The crew was arrested, to be released only after ten days. The damaged surveillance plane was also eventually returned to the United States after Chinese experts removed all electronic equipment on board. The US government declined to apologize in the case but said it was sorry a Chinese pilot had been killed and a US military plane had entered Chinese airspace without permission. Once again, tempers in China's public opinion became very heated. The events in Belgrade and in the South China Sea showed how little trust there was between China and the United States. In both cases, the perception on the Chinese side was that American military superiority allowed the US to harm China's security interests and prestige with impunity.

## Quiet before the storm

This series of incidents between China and the United States came to an end for the time being. On 11 September 2001, major terrorist attacks took place in the United States, in the aftermath of which the US invaded first Afghanistan and then Iraq. In the following years, American attention was strongly focused on the fight against terrorism and on geopolitical developments in the Middle East. The period from 1989 to 2001 had shown that the rise of China did not lead to direct confrontations with other powers, but that deep tensions between the United States and China were building beneath the surface.

But for now, there was geopolitical calm in East Asia, and Chinese leaders had the chance to focus on their country's further economic growth. George W. Bush served as president of the United States from 2001 until 2008. Unlike in the case of his father and Deng Xiaoping, Bush had no personal relationship with China's leader. Hu Jintao was an unobtrusive personality, who dutifully carried out Deng's directives. The younger Bush had no great interest in East Asia. But while there was no special bond between the two leaders, they did not get in each other's way either.

In 2008, China reached a landmark on its lengthy path to national revival. In that year, the Olympic Games were held in China for the first time. That was a moment for the CCP and the Chinese people to reflect on how far the country had come. The once massive poverty in the country had been significantly reduced, and growing numbers of Chinese were prosperous residents of modern megacities. The country was now the world's third-largest economy after the United States and Japan and was on the verge of surpassing Japan in that regard.

There were no more military tensions with Russia. All border disputes with that neighbouring country had now been resolved. The United States was still preoccupied with the wars in Afghanistan and Iraq and needed China's help in stopping North Korea's nuclear weapons programme. The US remained the biggest foreign threat in the eyes of the CCP, led by Hu Jintao during these years of geopolitical calm, but for now tensions with the United States had largely faded into the background. On Friday, 8 August 2008, at 8 pm (the number eight being seen as a sign of prosperity in China), the opening ceremony of the Olympic Games in Beijing started. Only later would it become clear that this day marked the end of the geopolitical lull that had begun in 1990. A new period of tensions between the world powers began, and this time China would take centre stage.

FIGURE 23 *Soviet leader Mikhail Gorbachev and his wife Raisa Gorbacheva meeting Deng Xiaoping, Great Hall of the People, Beijing 16 May 1989 (photo by Peter Turnley/Corbis/VCG via Getty Images).*

FIGURE 24 *The Chinese military deploying tanks against protesters, Beijing, the night of 3 to 4 June 1989 (photo by Jacques Langevin/Getty Images).*

FIGURE 25 *Flag lowering ceremony during the handover of Hong Kong by the United Kingdom to the People's Republic of China, 30 June 1997 (photo by Bill Rowntree/Mirrorpix/Getty Images).*

# 7

# Confrontation (2008–24)

On 25 September 2012, the Chinese Navy held a ceremony at Dalian Port to celebrate commissioning its first aircraft carrier. President Hu Jintao was there, as was Premier Wen Jiabao and the commander of the Navy. The 300-meter-long aircraft carrier was named *Liaoning*, after the name of the province in which Dalian is located. That is the strategically important port city from which the Japanese army launched the invasion of Manchuria in 1931. The name of the aircraft carrier seems to suggest that if it is up to the Chinese navy, no country will ever launch a full-scale attack on China again.

Since the Second World War, aircraft carriers have been the ultimate symbol of the United States as a world power. The US Navy was able to act in all parts of the world thanks to its aircraft carriers. These can not only be used against targets at sea, but are also very useful for attacking targets on land. This makes them an instrument that can be used against other great powers as well as against weaker countries, even in remote parts of the world. The carriers are the modern equivalent of the frigates and gunboats Britain used to impose its will on China in the nineteenth century. But now China was to going have that instrument at its disposal, although it would take several more years before the *Liaoning*, and its fighter planes, would be operationally deployable. And for now, China's only aircraft carrier would remain in close proximity to its homeland. Still, the commissioning of the *Liaoning* was a signal that China was in the long run on its way to becoming a world military power similar to the United States, and Britain before that.

The *Liaoning* was not originally intended for the Chinese navy at all. The keel was laid in 1985 at a shipyard in Mikolaiv, a city in Ukraine. The ship would be called *Riga* and was meant to be part of the Soviet fleet. The hull was launched in 1988. But when the Soviet Union collapsed in 1991, construction of the ship, by now renamed *Varyag*, was halted. The newly independent state of Ukraine now owned an aircraft carrier about two-thirds complete and had no intention of finishing the ship. It was put up for sale, but no one was interested. That included the Chinese government, which did not want to jeopardize relations with the United States by buying an aircraft carrier. China might potentially be able to complete construction of the ship, but the US government would likely see that as threatening. In line with Deng Xiaoping's guideline, China focused on economic growth and avoided unnecessary tensions with the United States.

For years the unfinished and rusting *Varyag* remained moored, until a Chinese businessman came forward in 1997. Xu Zengping had started his career in the 1970s as a basketball player in the service of the Chinese army. He later set up his own business and moved to Hong Kong. Xu told the Ukrainian authorities that he planned to take the *Varyag* to Macau to turn it into a floating casino. In exchange for $18 million he bought the ship, and for an extra $2 million he acquired the original construction plans as well.

In reality, Xu had no intention of converting the ship into a casino at all. He had been approached in April 1996 by the deputy commander of the Chinese Navy, He Pengfei, and the chief of China's military intelligence service, Ji Shengde, with a request to purchase the *Varyag* and bring it to China. They appealed to his patriotism, but also informed him that the transaction should not be done openly. Officially, the Chinese government was to have nothing to do with it. The United States had recently sent aircraft carriers to China in response to the Lee Teng-hui crisis and the Taiwanese elections. This probably reinforced the belief within the Chinese navy that having its own aircraft carriers was desirable in the long term. It is possible that Ji Shengde and He Pengfei, anticipating a possible later decision to add an aircraft carrier to the fleet, wanted to ensure that the *Varyag* would be available. There was always the option to turn it into a casino if such a decision did not come. It seems unlikely that the involvement of Xu Zengping and the attempt to buy the *Varyag* was not known to the CCP leadership, and that He and Ji acted entirely on their own initiative. On the other hand, then-President Jiang Zemin and Premier Zhu Rongji are known to have been at least hesitant about the Chinese navy's possible purchase of an aircraft carrier. They did not want to damage relations with the United States.

After extensive negotiations in Ukraine, Xu became the owner of an unfinished Cold War aircraft carrier. Now he had to get the ship, which did not have its own propulsion, to China. He hired a tugboat from a Dutch company to tow the *Varyag* from the Black Sea to China. Shortly after the start of the journey in June 2000, Turkey proved unwilling to allow the ship to pass through the Bosphorus. The official reason was that the floating colossus could ram the bridges over the strait. It is possible that behind the scenes the United States, which probably understood Xu's true plans, was pressuring its NATO ally Turkey not to allow the passage. The tugboat had no choice but to sail circles on the Black Sea with the aircraft carrier, waiting for permission to continue.

After the American bombing of the Chinese embassy in Belgrade in 1999, the Chinese government became more interested in obtaining its own aircraft carrier. Although Chinese diplomats firmly denied that the *Varyag* would be used for military purposes, China entered into negotiations with Turkey. Meanwhile, the ship was attracting the attention of the media in various countries. While some journalists questioned whether it would really be used as a casino, many experts maintained that the idea that this rusting hull could ever be made into a functional warship was far-fetched. Perhaps the Chinese navy wanted to study it in order to one day build an aircraft carrier of its own?

Only after difficult negotiations did the Turkish government change its position. China had promised to ensure that Chinese tourists would come to Turkey in greater numbers from now on. It is also possible that the fact that US-Chinese relations were somewhat improving helped. After the terrorist attacks of 11 September 2001, the United States was planning to invade Afghanistan. The Chinese government did nothing to hinder these plans, even though it had vigorously opposed the Soviet invasion of Afghanistan in 1979. After almost a year and a half of sailing in circles, the *Varyag*, which by now was known as the ghost ship of the Black Sea, was finally allowed to pass through the Bosphorus on 1 November 2001. After a long journey around the Cape of Good Hope (Egypt did not allow passage through the Suez Canal) and a severe storm in which the ship drifted and a crew member of the tug lost his life, it finally reached China. Not Macau, but Dalian turned out to be its destination. The journey had taken 627 days. And that was just the beginning. Removing the rust and completing the aircraft carrier would take another ten years.

Xu Zengping came to be seen in China as a hero because he helped the country acquire its first aircraft carrier. However, he never received official recognition for his role from the Chinese government. He didn't even get his money back. According to Xu, buying the *Varyag* and transporting it to China cost him a total of about $120 million. His two contacts in the army could not help him. He Pengfei, the deputy commander of the Chinese navy, died of a heart attack in 2001. Ji Shengde, the head of military intelligence, was sentenced to death around the same time for large-scale corruption. That sentence was later commuted to twenty years in prison.[1]

In the end, what counts for China is not the length of the process to get the *Varyag*, but the final result. Sea trials were made in 2011, and from the end of 2012, fighter aircraft practiced landing on the ship, now called *Liaoning*. Although the ship has been fully operational since 2016, it is mainly used for training purposes. Training pilots to take off from and land on an aircraft carrier takes a lot of time. Making the *Liaoning* into China's first aircraft carrier was mainly a learning process for China, which is now able to build new carriers independently. In 2015, the keel was laid at the Dalian shipyard for a ship that closely resembles the *Liaoning*. The yard only needed three years to build this second aircraft carrier. The first sea trials were made in 2018, and the navy commissioned its second aircraft carrier at the end of 2019. This ship, the *Shandong*, was named after the province where the naval port of Qingdao is located. The ship's name also refers to the period around the First World War, when China was too weak to prevent part of Shandong, including the port of Qingdao, from falling into Japanese hands. Construction of a third aircraft carrier, this one larger than the other two and based on a new design rather than a copy of an old Soviet ship, started in 2017. That became the *Fujian* (the name of the province opposite to Taiwan), whose first sea trials were made in May 2024. By that time, a fourth carrier was on the way.

The once wide gap between the United States and China in terms of naval vessels is narrowing. The same goes for fighter jets. Since 2017, the Chinese Air Force has J-20 fighters, a combat aircraft with stealth technology, similar to the F-22 and F-35 of the US Air Force. China has also been developing a second stealth fighter, the J-35. Cyber weapons and missiles also play a major role in the Chinese armed forces. These are relatively cheap weapons that China can deploy from its own soil to counter the threat posed by American ships and airfields in Asia. The Chinese military has ballistic missiles (that fly in a high arc towards their target), specially designed to hit aircraft carriers and other surface ships. China also has missiles with which it can strike targets on land (such as the US military bases in Japan, South Korea and Guam) and satellites (essential for military communications and observation). The Chinese arms industry is not only catching up with existing weapons. There is also a strong focus on building a head start in the weapons of the future. China spends more money developing hypersonic missiles than the United States or Russia.[2] Such missiles fly over great distances at least at five times the speed of sound. The short response time makes it extremely difficult for the opponent to respond to an attack in time.

## New tensions between the great powers

During the opening ceremony of the 2008 Olympic Games, George W. Bush and Vladimir Putin sat with Hu Jintao in Beijing's National Stadium, also known as the Bird's Nest. Like many television viewers around the world, they saw a spectacular show put together under the supervision of Chinese film director Zhang Yimou. After that, the athletes entered the stadium, each team with their national flag with the host country China last. During the festive ceremony, however, it became increasingly clear that a crisis was escalating in the Caucasus. Fighting had broken out in the region of South Ossetia, an enclave in Georgia that borders Russia. Ossetians fought against Georgian government troops, after which Russia intervened on the side of the Ossetians. Some TV viewers in Western countries saw coverage of the Olympic ceremony interspersed with live footage of Russian tanks crossing the border into Georgia.

At the stadium in Beijing, Putin and Bush spoke briefly about the crisis in Georgia. The United States was alarmed by the Russian intervention in pro-Western Georgia but stayed out of the conflict. It is unknown whether the Russian government aimed for the South Ossetian crisis to coincide with the opening ceremony in Beijing. In any case, the extra attention the conflict received was good for Russia (and bad for the Chinese government). Because even though the Russo-Georgian War lasted only five days and the international media soon turned back to the Olympics, Putin had used a small-scale local conflict to maximum effect. The Russian intervention was aimed at blocking Georgia's accession to NATO. That country was no longer an attractive asset to the Western alliance now that South Ossetia remained a source of instability and military tension with Russia.

With the war in Georgia, geopolitical rivalry between Russia and the United States returned to an active phase after an eighteen-year pause. In 2014, the Russian government did in Ukraine what it had done in Georgia in 2008, but on a larger scale. Russia then gave military support to separatists in eastern Ukraine. Moreover, the Russian government went one major step further by occupying Crimea and then annexing it. Russia now also started to take a more active stance outside its immediate neighbourhood. In 2015, Russia sent troops to Syria to assist President Anwar al-Assad in his fight against various rebel groups, some of which were supported by the United States. In the following year, Russia interfered in the US presidential election, partly by influencing online media. US-Russian relations have deteriorated sharply since 2014. But that was only part of the story, as the centre of gravity of global geopolitical tensions had by that time shifted to the relationship between the United States and China.

In the fall of 2008, Barack Obama had been elected the new president of the United States. Obama wanted to reduce the US military role in the Middle East and focus more on Asia. He believed that Asia would be the economic centre of the world in the twenty-first century. The United States therefore had to ensure that it would continue to play a leading role in that region. The big problem was the rise of China, which became increasingly stronger economically, and therefore also militarily. China's role as the 'factory of the world' had resulted in high economic growth and large currency reserves through massive exports of consumer products. Chinese exporting companies received support from the Chinese government in various ways to strengthen their competitive position in the global market. As a result, they grew larger and more profitable in relation to many foreign competitors. The export success gave the Chinese government ample resources to invest in military modernization. Moreover, China's rapid economic growth has made it an important export destination for many other countries, which have become more dependent on that country. Concerns grew in the United States about the possibility that China would sooner or later reduce US geopolitical influence in Asia.

Obama and his team of Asia advisers therefore decided that addressing China's rise would be a central element in US foreign policy.[3] Instead of fighting China or giving it free rein, they focused on a combination of the two approaches. On the one hand, the US started to pay greater attention to China's Asian neighbours. They had seen that as China grew stronger, neighbouring countries had a greater need for American support. Those countries did not want to be at the mercy of an all-powerful China. So the emergence of China naturally created a need for a continued geopolitical role for the United States in the region. From then on, the US government gave clear signals to Japan, South Korea and the countries in Southeast Asia that they could continue to count on US support. In a sense, America's Taiwan policy was now extended to the rest of the region. The United States had the ability to intervene in relations between China and other Asian countries, for example by providing them with weapons and other forms of protection, thereby increasing pressure on the Chinese government if necessary.

On the other hand, the Obama administration made it clear to Chinese leaders that they had nothing to fear and that there was plenty of room for cooperation. The United States needed China as a partner on all kinds of international issues. These ranged from putting pressure on Iran and North Korea to end their nuclear programmes, to combating climate change and stabilizing the global economy. The latter was an urgent goal of the Obama administration. A few weeks after the end of the Beijing Olympics, the bankruptcy of the American bank Lehman Brothers had accelerated a global financial crisis. The world economy was hit hard. China also ran into problems but recovered quickly and was able to resume the pace of rapid growth. In 2010 it overtook Japan as the second largest economy in the world. In doing so, China replaced Japan as a crucial partner in managing the international economic order. China was allowed to continue to grow as a great power as far as the United States was concerned, as long as it was done in a way that suited US strategic interests.

President Obama's strategy, which came to be known as the Pivot (or Rebalance) to Asia, was avidly put into practice by his secretary of state Hillary Clinton. The former first lady had competed with Obama for the Democratic nomination for president in 2008. After Obama's victory, she was invited by her former rival to join his administration. In early 2009, shortly after being sworn in, Clinton made her first foreign trip as secretary of state. To show the world which region the US wanted to focus on from now on, she flew not to Europe (as US secretaries of state almost always did on their first foreign trip) but to Asia. She visited China, but also Japan and South Korea (the main US military allies in the region) and Indonesia (the largest country in Southeast Asia).

In the months and years that followed, both Obama and Clinton would reiterate in public speeches that the United States was open to cooperation with China, but also that there was no question of the United States ever withdrawing as a leading geopolitical player in the region. To show that it was serious about the latter, the US government took various measures. It became an active member of regional organizations. The administration also announced that it would station 60 per cent of overseas US naval and air force units in Asia. There were new arms sales to Taiwan. And the United States began talks with countries in the region (but not China) to create a giant free trade zone, the Trans-Pacific Partnership (TPP).

Perhaps what alarmed China most was a statement made by Hillary Clinton in the summer of 2010. On 23 July, she was in the Vietnamese capital of Hanoi, where she participated in the meeting of the ASEAN Regional Forum, an international conference on regional security. China and most of China's neighbouring countries were also represented at the conference with their foreign ministers. Beforehand, US officials had encouraged neighbouring countries to speak out strongly about their views on the situation in the South China Sea. That maritime region had been the scene of a series of disputes between China, Taiwan, Vietnam, Malaysia, the Philippines and Brunei for decades. The quarrels concerned the ownership of the Paracel and Spratly Islands and the demarcation of the economic zones of the countries bordering the South China Sea. These disputes were partly caused by the fact that after the end of the Second World War, the US deliberately left the issue of ownership of the islands in the South China Sea unresolved. China's growing power made other countries fear that sooner or later they would be forced to give up their maritime interests in the South China Sea. This seemed an ideal situation for the United States to position itself strongly as the custodian of the balance of power between China and the other Asian countries.

As the Americans had hoped, many of the Asian foreign ministers spoke out against China's claim to the South China Sea at the Hanoi conference. Vietnam in particular took a strong stand. Clinton used the opportunity to make it clear that the United States would henceforth become actively involved in this matter. The US government would not allow obstruction of free passage in the South China Sea and demanded that maritime disputes be resolved in accordance with international law. Clinton did not mention China, but everyone in the room understood what she meant.[4] If China were to engage in activities to seize control of the South China Sea by force, the US reserved the right to intervene. That could also include military action, because Clinton had made it clear that obstructing the presence of US warships or fighter jets in or over the South China Sea was not acceptable.

China's foreign minister, Yang Jiechi, was also at the conference and listened to the speeches by Clinton and the other ministers present. He saw how the mood turned against China under American encouragement. After everyone else had spoken, Yang delivered his response, a 25-minute thunderous sermon. He warned the other Asian countries not to get involved with the United States over the South China Sea. 'China is a big country. Bigger than any other country here,' Yang said.[5] The tone for regional geopolitical relations had been set. The American strategy was partially successful. It played on growing unease in Asia about China's rise. The Chinese government's foreign policy failed to allay that unease. On the contrary, China's international actions, in Hanoi but also at other times, fuelled that unease. The country was on a course for quite some time from which it could no longer easily deviate.

## China's new nationalism

The Tiananmen crisis of 1989 had revealed that the CCP's power base, beneath the surface, was far from solid. The Party had therefore started to focus on strengthening feelings of patriotism among the population in order to solidify the acceptance of the CCP's leadership. Central to this approach was mobilizing the historical awareness of Chinese citizens. They had to become convinced that the country, led by the CCP, had a long-term mission. They were reminded that China had been hit hard in the past by the imperialism of Britain, Japan and the other great powers. The Chinese people must not forget the terrible consequences of foreign imperialism, so that they would never again be its victim. As long as its former status as a great power was not restored and China remained vulnerable, the CCP had a task to fulfil and the people had to unite behind the Party.

The political scientist William A. Callahan has described how the Chinese government has taken multiple initiatives for this purpose since the 1990s. For example, several annual days of commemoration were established to reflect on the foreign aggression against China. State television began broadcasting historical drama series much more extensively than before, centring on Japanese aggression during the Second World War. School materials devoted increasing attention to the crimes committed by the great powers in China since the Opium Wars. A new generation grew up being told over and over that China was a country with a great past, but that the great powers had tried again and again since 1840 to destroy Chinese civilization.

Nationalism, which had also been an important political force in China under Mao, was now emerging from the shadow of communism. Chinese nationalism, and the drive to keep alive the memory of foreign aggression, is not a product of the CCP. The first call for a national day of remembrance on foreign aggression against China dates back to 1915, six years before the founding of the Communist Party. Moreover, the call did not come from the government, but from the National Teachers Union.[6] As in the case of anti-foreign consumer boycotts, which had begun a decade earlier, this expression of nationalist activism originated with civil society groups. The CCP, like the Kuomintang before it, took advantage of nationalist sentiments that were already there by amplifying them and redirecting them in a way that suited its political agenda. After the Tiananmen crisis, the political energies of students and other citizens who had demanded administrative reform, insofar as they had not turned away from politics, were thus channelled in towards increased nationalism.

That energy found a new outlet. In China, as elsewhere, the Internet emerged in the 1990s. Although the Chinese government exercises strict censorship to prevent the Internet from being used by political dissidents or foreign governments to weaken the CCP's legitimacy, it allows public expressions of patriotism. Especially since 1999, when the Chinese embassy in Belgrade was bombed, Chinese internet users have become very active on discussion platforms regarding the historic 'national humiliation' and the (as they see it) still current foreign aggression against China.[7] On these platforms they give their views on the behaviour of the United States, Japan and other countries, but also on the reaction of the Chinese government. As nationalistic feelings among the Chinese people have grown stronger, it has become more difficult for the government to contain them completely.[8] Cyber-nationalism has taken on a life of its own to some extent, which is not entirely without risks for the CCP. Criticism of foreign countries can easily turn into criticism of one's own government, if people feel that it reacts too weakly to (alleged) humiliations such as a bombing of a Chinese embassy or inciting neighbouring countries against China. With the increasing use of social media after the turn of the century, more and more Chinese people were able to get involved in these discussions, even if only a small minority did so in practice. The way in which memories of the past play a role in current public opinion in China is to an important extent, yet certainly not entirely, the result of government policy.[9]

In the decades since the Tiananmen crisis, China's leaders had created a context in which they had limited room for manoeuvre to respond to the new US strategy. The price the CCP paid for blocking political reform at home was the loss of strategic flexibility abroad.[10] The room that Deng had in the 1980s to stabilize relations with Japan, the United States and the Soviet Union was now shrinking. Obama's Pivot to Asia strategy increased pressure on China through closer US cooperation with its neighbours, thus pushing the Chinese government towards a tougher stance on regional disputes over the demarcation of maritime areas. In both the East China Sea (with Japan) and the South China Sea (with Vietnam, the Philippines and other countries), China has been embroiled in such disputes for decades.

Strong international action by the Chinese government led to stronger resistance to China's growing influence in the region. This in turn increased neighbouring countries' need for cooperation with and protection from the United States. Obama's strategy was a success in that it increased the pressure on China. However, the other part of Obama's strategy didn't work so well. He and his foreign policy team had reckoned that increased pressure would move China's leaders to act economically and strategically more in line with US interests. The expectation in Washington was that China would realize that it had no choice but to accept the outstretched hand and that it would, as Germany and Japan had previously done, focus on economic growth under US geopolitical leadership and in a manner that was not detrimental to the US economy. Instead, China's opposition to the US grew stronger. The Obama strategy only seemed to confirm to CCP leaders what they had always believed, at least since 1989: namely, that the US posed an existential threat, waiting for an opportunity to bring down the Communist Party and weaken China. After all, the ultimate consequence of the US strategy, if successful, would be that the Chinese government would no longer have room for manoeuvre vis-à-vis neighbouring countries. These would turn away from China, under the protection of the United States. Under such circumstances, China's ability to bring Taiwan under its rule also diminished. Given the now strong nationalism in China and the history of great power interventions in Asia, the CCP's legitimacy would be dealt such a severe blow that the Party might not survive.

To deal with this threat the Chinese government therefore focused its efforts on two areas. First, China's military modernization continued. The country was not yet ready for an armed conflict with the United States, but since the 1990s, and now more openly, it was preparing for a potential escalation of military tensions. The construction of aircraft carriers and modernization of other military equipment arose from this objective. Second, China sought to strengthen economic ties with other countries in the region. The country was now the second largest economy in the world and has been in good shape since the global financial crisis. China's Asian neighbours would be less likely to side with the United States if they were economically dependent on China. Indeed, China had quickly become the most important trading partner of many countries in the region.

Just as the United States had been able to exploit China's weakness (namely, neighbouring countries' fears of Chinese dominance), the Chinese government was able to capitalize on the biggest weakness of the United States in the region. This weakness stems from the fact that the United States is an external power. China's neighbours have no assurance that the United States will always be there for them. The signal that the Chinese government therefore sent to the other countries in East and South-East Asia was that the only certainty for the future was that China would be a great military and economic power. China would not allow itself to be pressured by the United States and would not accept that countries in the region let the United States to use them as a tool against China. The withdrawal of US troops from South Vietnam in 1973 and from Taiwan in 1979 supported China's message. As much as Obama insisted time and again that the United States would never leave Asia and abandon its regional allies, there was no guarantee that the Americans would or could continue to protect the balance of military power in Asia well into the distant future. China's neighbours therefore adopted a cautious attitude. They welcomed a continued major American role in the region, while at the same time trying to maintain good relations with China.

# Xi Jinping

The most influential political event in China since 1989 took place in October 2007 in Beijing. Then the Communist Party held its five-yearly national congress. It was the seventeenth time the Party had held such a congress since its founding meeting in 1921. At each edition, the leadership for the next five years is announced. The big question in 2007 was not who the leaders would be in the period 2007–12. That would be Party Secretary and President Hu Jintao and Premier Wen Jiabao, because they had only completed one five-year term and therefore had a second to go. The big thing was the announcement of their successors in 2012. Hu's favourite to succeed him as supreme leader was Li Keqiang. With his protégé Li as CCP chief for the period 2012–22, the continuation of Deng Xiaoping's strategic line would be secured for another ten years. But Hu Jintao was seen as a relatively weak leader, who had little grip on the policy areas of the other party leaders or on the large state-owned companies that played a central role in the Chinese economy.

Before the party congress, extensive negotiations took place between the most influential persons in the top of the CCP about Hu's succession. The outcome of those negotiations was that not the intended crown prince Li Keqiang, but a relative outsider was appointed as successor to Hu.[11] That outsider was Xi Jinping, the son of former CCP top official Xi Zhongxun. After being exiled to the countryside during the Cultural Revolution, young Xi had returned to Beijing where he studied engineering chemistry at Tsinghua University. That was the university founded in 1908 on the initiative of the United States with part of the reparations after the Boxer crisis and which is now one of China's top universities (Xi's daughter and only child later went to study in the United States at Harvard University). Xi Jinping had joined the Communist Party with some difficulty (he was rejected the first nine times he applied) and subsequently made a career as a Party official and administrator in various parts of China. At the time of his election as Hu Jintao's successor, he was party secretary of Shanghai. Xi was now on track to become China's new supreme leader from 2012. Li Keqiang would get the less prominent post of prime minister.

The CCP needed a strong leader who could keep Deng's policy going but who could also adjust the country's strategic direction when necessary. Conditions had changed quite a bit since the early 1990s. China was now in a much better economic position, but it was not clear how further economic reform could be carried out without the CCP losing its grip on the process. With the rapid economic growth, corruption, which greatly eroded citizens' confidence in the government, had become a major problem. In addition, China had become significantly more dependent on foreign raw materials, markets and technology, making it more vulnerable to international instability or foreign sanctions.

Xi seemed like the right man for the job. As a regional top official he had already shown that he dared to take risks and was able to get things done. He was the son of a former leader in the CCP but not a direct threat to the current party leadership. His father Xi Zhongxun had played a role in starting Deng's economic reform process in the late 1970s. However, Xi senior was forced to retire by Deng in 1987 because he remained loyal to Hu Yaobang when the latter was under pressure to resign as party leader.[12]

With the appointment of Xi in 2007, the Party had shown that strong leadership and a partial reassessment of strategy were desirable. Indeed, from 2012, when he actually succeeded Hu as party leader, Xi would not disappoint on these points. To strengthen his position as leader, Xi launched a large-scale anti-corruption campaign. This had the dual effect of somewhat restoring popular confidence in the government, while giving Xi a tool to get rid of his political opponents and rivals. In China, government and business are so intertwined, and personal contacts are so central to most professions, that corruption is very widespread. Since the government, judiciary and media are at the service of the CCP, there is no independent mechanism to track down and convict corrupt officials. The leaders of the Party ultimately determine, based on their views and interests, who should be punished, especially in the case of senior officials. Several prominent politicians and senior military personnel were sentenced to long prison terms. Their places were taken by individuals loyal to Xi.

In 2018, he further cemented his position by ensuring that the limit on his tenure as president was abolished. Previously, a person could be president of China for up to ten years. The other top positions, that of party leader and military commander in chief, had no time limit. The 2018 adjustment has made it easier for Xi to maintain his overall leadership position indefinitely. The ascent of Xi Jinping from outsider to the political leadership in Beijing, to achieving tenure for life in little over a decade was astonishing, and shows his success at outmanoeuvring his rivals and previously powerful political factions. A consequence of the high degree of concentration of power in the person of Xi Jinping is that all important strategic decisions are made by himself. This gives him flexibility, but also increases the risk of administrative failure or wrong political decisions because no one dares to contradict him or even report on matters that are displeasing to him.

The fact that Xi has become China's unrivalled top leader does not mean that he develops the country's strategy all by himself. Among his advisers, one in particular stands out. Wang Huning, a former political science professor who had grown up and worked in Shanghai. In 1988, he stayed in the United States for half a year as a visiting scholar. Upon his return he published a book about his observations of America's strengths and weaknesses. Later he moved to Beijing where he became a political theorist working for the Communist Party. From the late 1990s, Wang has been closely involved in formulating China's key strategic and ideological concepts. Jiang Zemin was the first top leader to work with Wang as one of his main advisors. Both Hu Jintao and Xi Jinping did the same after coming to power.

In Wang Huning's view, it is essential for China to have a strongly centralized system of government in order modernize and prevent internal chaos. He is also thought to believe that Western cultural influence poses a significant threat to the Communist Party's ability to maintain centralized political control. Wang is more than just an influential theorist and advisor. As one of the top ranking members of the Party, he is one of China's leading politicians. He is also involved in Chinese foreign policy and in charge of political relations with Taiwan.

# China in the world according to Xi's dream

As Xi's 2012 museum speech – referred to in the introduction to this book – showed, he presented the idea of national revival (or 'rejuvenation', the term used by the Chinese government in English-language publications) as the common long-term goal of the Chinese people. This was in line with previous generations of CCP leaders. At the same time, no political leader in China since Sun Yat-sen and Chiang Kai-shek had so openly and emphatically made the notion of revival central to his policies. This term would become strongly associated with Xi Jinping's reign. High-speed trains in China, for example, were called 'revival' (*fuxing*). The older high-speed trains of Hu Jintao's time were all called 'harmony' (*hexie*), the Confucian term by which Hu identified his reign.

The time was right for a self-confident and forceful leadership style, and the strongly nationalistic concept of national revival was a good fit. Xi's Chinese dream was that the increasingly prosperous country would take its rightful geopolitical place and thereby offset past humiliations. Since 1989, emphasizing that past, known in China as the 'century of humiliation', has been part of the core of the CCP's strategy to minimize the distance between the Party and the population (and the risk of a popular uprising). Xi's political strategy was consistent with the direction the Party had taken more than two decades earlier. At the same time, he emerged as China's most nationalistic leader since the founding of the People's Republic in 1949. The increasing emphasis on nationalism as a binding force within China had major consequences for the country's foreign relations. It contributed to the escalatory course of events in which the foreign policies of the United States and China were increasingly caught up. US geopolitical pressure on China, in response to that country's growing power, strengthened nationalist sentiment among the population and thus the position of Xi and the CCP. This gave Xi a stronger incentive to act decisively abroad, especially when it came to territorial disputes and issues that China believed to be internal affairs. This in turn exacerbated concerns in the United States's and China's neighbouring countries.

Xi Jinping has expressed his views on China's place in the world on several occasions. According to him, China will contribute to global economic development and a stable international order, never threaten or dominate other countries and will ensure that each country is free to choose its own development model (and thus its political-economic system). What Xi expects from the world is international stability and that no one tries to undermine China's interests.¹³ He refers to the international dimension of the Chinese dream as 'building a community with a shared future for mankind.' This term and the idea behind it are reminiscent of the Great Harmony, Sun Yat-sen's utopian vision of the future, and of the traditional concept of *tianxia*, a world in which the Chinese emperor was the ultimate custodian of order. One question that China's growing international power raises is where to draw the line between a defensive China that safeguards its core interests with restraint and an offensive China that intervenes anywhere in the world to protect its broader interests.¹⁴ Xi's view does not clarify whether or how the Chinese government defines that border.

What is clear to see is that the Chinese government and Chinese businesses have become increasingly active outside their own region. China established its first embassy in another country as early as 1876, later co-founding the League of Nations and the United Nations. The Chinese government began to engage with countries in Asia, Africa and Latin America from the 1950s. It sent troops on a UN peacekeeping mission for the first time in the 1990s. At first such missions comprised only medical, engineering and logistics units, but from 2012 China also sent infantry to Africa as UN peacekeepers. Since 2009, the Chinese navy has been patrolling the Gulf of Aden permanently to deter Somali pirates. Chinese multinationals have been on the rise for several decades. In 2004, IBM announced that it was selling its PC division to Lenovo. Volvo has been owned by Geely since 2010. The process of China's expanding role in the world is not new. But soon after Xi took office as leader, a new phase in China's presence and visibility in the world began.

## Globalization with China at the helm

On 7 September 2013, Xi Jinping visited Nazarbayev University in the Kazakh capital Astana. At 11:30 that morning, Xi walked into the university's auditorium with his host, President Nursultan Nazarbayev. On the occasion of the honorary doctorate that Xi received that day from Nazarbayev University, he treated the students present to a speech on relations between China and Central Asia. In it he proposed creating a modern version of the ancient Silk Road. What he envisioned was a 'belt' of economic cooperation, supported by improved transport links, from China to Eastern Europe. In the distant past, Central Asia had been the connecting link for the caravan trade between China and the Middle East and Europe. Now Xi proposed restoring the region's central role in trade flows between China and Europe.

It soon became apparent that Xi Jinping had something even bigger in mind than just better transport links between China and Europe via Central Asia. The following month he was visiting Indonesia. In Jakarta he gave a speech to the Indonesian parliament. There he recalled that Southeast Asia had been an important link in the maritime dimension of the Silk Road. In addition to the ancient trade caravans that passed through Central Asia, there was indeed a network of sea routes that connected China to the Middle East via Southeast Asia and the Indian Ocean. Xi proposed making a modern version of the maritime side of the Silk Road as well. At first glance, this proposal seemed strange, because the vast majority of modern trade flows between China and Europe already went by sea, via the Indian Ocean and the Suez Canal. What Xi apparently meant is that he wanted to help Indonesia and other countries around the Indian Ocean benefit more from that trade route. Many container ships sailing between China and Europe call at the port of Singapore, but other Asian ports along the route receive much less traffic. Xi's proposal was in line with Indonesia's own plans and those of other Southeast Asian countries, which aimed to improve transport infrastructure within the region.

In the next few years, Xi's initiative for a modern Silk Road became increasingly grandiose. Plans for a new east–west trade corridor through Central Asia, and for new connections between China and the countries of Southeast Asia and the Indian Ocean, were merged. In addition to improving transport infrastructure (railways, roads, ports), China would also help modernize energy and telecom infrastructure and help industrialize and modernize cities. The geographic scope of the initiative was expanded to include the Middle East, Europe, Africa, Europe, Latin America and the Caribbean. Better connections between China and other parts of the world were also to be created through aviation, space travel and new shipping routes via the Arctic. Moreover, China would improve its foreign connections through new international organizations, cultural and educational institutions, and cooperation in healthcare.

Xi referenced the ancient Silk Road in his speeches to suggest that his initiative is about reviving ancient trade networks centred on China. After all, the name Silk Road implies that the export of Chinese silk was the basis of those ancient trade networks. The connotation of a past in which the West was not yet dominant and European explorers such as Marco Polo were impressed by the richness and sophistication of Asian civilizations also made the term attractive. But despite this China-centric connotation, the term did not come from China. The German geographer Ferdinand von Richthofen introduced the name *Seidenstraße* in an 1877 book, in which he wrote about the trade contacts between the Han dynasty and the Roman Empire. The term coined by Von Richthofen, who, incidentally, was a strong supporter of Germany acquiring colonial possessions in China, caught on and has remained popular.[15]

The term New Silk Road was also not invented in China. It was introduced by Hillary Clinton in July 2011 when she gave a speech in Chennai, India. As US Secretary of State, she proposed improving connections between Afghanistan and neighbouring countries through new infrastructure. Clinton's idea received little support from President Obama, and not much came of it. But the idea of a New Silk Road offered interesting prospects and was reflected in Xi Jinping's ambitious plan. From 2013, this became its (informal) designation in many countries. The official name used by the Chinese government is *yidai yilu* (literally 'One Belt, One Road', referring to the land and sea dimension of the modern Silk Road, respectively) in Chinese and 'Belt and Road Initative' (BRI) in English.

BRI is much more than an attempt to revive old trade routes. Above all, it is China's very ambitious plan to put the world economy on a more stable footing by integrating developing countries more into it in a way that is economically and geopolitically beneficial to China. In the years before 2013, the country was already the main driver of global economic growth, but now it sought a more guiding role in the globalization process. The Communist Party, because of its great influence over both government and business, is able to use the Chinese economy to some extent for strategic objectives at the international level.

The principle of *guandu shangban* (commercial management under government supervision) that Li Hongzhang had once applied to new business ventures in the nineteenth century had grown under the Kuomintang and the CCP to become the basis for the relationship between the government and especially the larger companies. Banks in China are owned by the state, as are the largest construction companies, oil companies and makers of transportation equipment such as ships and railway equipment. The chief executives of the largest state-owned companies are appointed by the government on the instruction of the CCP. But also Chinese multinationals that are privately owned cannot escape a certain degree of political control. If they contribute to politically desirable goals, such as the New Silk Road, they can count on financial and other support from the government. That everyone in society should participate in strengthening the country is a norm originally set by Sun Yat-sen. The position of power of the CCP is such that it can make life very difficult for companies and entrepreneurs who deviate from that norm. Incidentally, foreign companies with subsidiaries or major interests in China are also expected not to undertake or support activities that are harmful to China or the CCP.

The Chinese government mobilized China's considerable financial reserves and Chinese business potential for the Belt and Road Initiative. Developing countries could borrow large amounts of money for the construction of new transport infrastructure and for energy projects such as coal-fired power stations and dams. Typical for developing countries is that they have a major shortage of infrastructure, which greatly hinders attracting foreign investors, the development of their own companies and the export of local products. The demand for infrastructure financing is many times greater than what is available from international development banks and Western countries. In many dozens of countries around the world, transport or energy projects have been started with Chinese funding. Partly as a result of this, China's international loans exceeded those by the World Bank or the IMF. Some 150 countries have borrowed from China in the past 20 years, some of which now owe China more than 20 per cent of their gross national product.[16]

China's infrastructure construction loan agreements generally state that the majority of construction activities will be carried out by Chinese companies. These companies, already large because of their huge home market, were able to benefit greatly from the BRI and grow into the largest in the world.

Large-scale financing and construction of infrastructure in developing countries is certainly not without risks for China. The reason many countries cannot get funding from Western banks is that there are many uncertainties surrounding major construction projects, particularly as to whether borrowing countries will be able to service their debts. Chinese companies and the Chinese government also run the risk of reputational damage through the involvement of large-scale corruption, because the interests of local communities are not respected, damage is done to the environment or unforeseen local problems prevent projects from being carried out properly. All these problems have indeed occurred frequently in practice. Finally, the Chinese government has faced criticism that local suppliers and labour are insufficiently benefitting from major construction projects. It has also been accused of building ports in developing countries for the hidden purpose of being used as Chinese naval bases in the future and of intending to use infrastructure loans to exert political influence on the recipient countries. How successful projects are and how they are assessed by local governments and communities varies from case to case. The implementation of the New Silk Road has led to numerous complications in China's relations with many developing countries, but that hasn't stopped Xi Jinping from pushing ahead with the plan.

Modern China shows two faces to the world. On the one hand, the country is a great power, with a gigantic economy, nuclear weapons and a permanent seat on the UN Security Council. On the other hand, it also has characteristics of a developing country, with a level of prosperity for the majority of its citizens that is still far below that of Western or other East Asian countries. The Chinese government is using this ambiguous nature of China's identity to present itself as a champion of the developing world. Ever since the 1950s, the Chinese government has propagated the idea that each country should be free to choose its own political economic model. According to this idea, major powers or international organizations should not interfere, even if that choice means that a country is not democratic or leads to serious human rights violations. With this attitude, the People's Republic has been trying to protect itself against Western influence for decades. At the same time, this is an instrument to increase China's own influence in developing countries at the expense of the West.[17] Foreign interference is sensitive in any country, but this is especially the case when it comes from former colonial powers. Therefore, the ideas that the Chinese government propagates are often well received by non-Western governments. China does not object to countries having a democratic system or adhering to high human rights standards in their domestic affairs but to governments and organizations that try to export these values to other countries. The international space for norms based on liberalism, with a limited societal and economic role of governments, is shrinking as China's global influence grows. This increases the ideological distance between Western and many non-Western countries. The BRI also contributes to a reorientation of developing countries away from the West and towards China.

There are consultative groups within the United Nations that aim to arrive at joint positions because individual countries, apart from the permanent members of the Security Council, have little influence. By far the largest consultative group is called 'G77 and China', with 134 of the 193 UN member states as members. The group, which consists of developing countries, once started with 77 members, but has since grown almost twice as large. If the G77 form a bloc, they automatically have the majority of the votes in the UN General Assembly. China has no formal power over the G77, but it does have significant influence within the group. Thanks in part to China's support in the General Assembly, it has become possible for the Chinese government to play an influential role in various UN organizations. One of the most important for China is the UN Human Rights Council. It has a major influence on the setting of international standards in the field of human rights. Especially since 1989, the Chinese government has been harshly criticized by human rights groups and Western governments. Because China has gained more control over the norms that define what exactly human rights violations are, the Chinese government is less vulnerable to international criticism and sanctions. What it is betting on is support for the idea that human rights are not absolute ('universal') rights but depend on the level of development of countries. According to this idea, governments of countries that are still poorly developed economically should have the scope to determine for themselves how they deal with human rights.

China's influence in the UN is not only growing through economic cooperation and coordination with developing countries. The country is the second largest funder of the UN after the United States and is the largest supplier of troops to UN peacekeeping operations among the permanent members of the Security Council. The top positions of some UN bodies are held by Chinese. The BRI is an important part of China's approach to global governance, as its government tries to derive moral authority from the initiative as it acts as a spokesperson for much of the world in the UN and other international organizations. China primarily uses economic resources to build the BRI and supports it with diplomacy. However, there is also a military dimension. In 2016, China signed an agreement with Djibouti to build its own naval base in the East African country. The base was commissioned by the Chinese Navy in 2017 and is the first (and so far only) Chinese military base outside the territory that the Chinese government considers part of China. (By comparison, the United States has about 750 military bases abroad.)

# Investing in Europe's shipping and rail connections

Another consequence of the Belt and Road Initiative has been that Chinese companies started making direct investments in transport and energy infrastructure abroad. They knew that the Chinese government considered it highly desirable that they did so and made financial support available for this. State-owned companies, in particular, but also large private companies, responded to the call to contribute to the BRI. Unlike loans and construction activities, direct investment involves operational control over companies in foreign countries. Another difference is that Chinese companies direct their direct investments to Western economies more so than to developing countries.

Europe in particular became a destination of direct investment related to the BRI. The most visible of these are the stakes Chinese companies have taken in container terminals in European ports. Partly driven by the BRI, two Chinese state-owned companies have become active in European ports in recent years. One is China Merchants (now known without the 'Hong Kong' suffix as in 1995 the Taiwanese branch of the company became part of the Yang Ming Marine Transport Corporation), the company once created by Li Hongzhang to reduce the European presence in Chinese waters. Through a joint venture with the French shipping company CMA-CGM called Terminal Link, in which China Merchants holds 49 per cent of the shares, the Chinese company is involved in eight European container terminals. The other state-owned company with investments in European ports is China COSCO Shipping, founded by the Chinese government during the Cold War and now one of the largest shipping companies in the world. In addition to a number of minority interests, COSCO has majority interests in container terminals in Valencia, Bilbao and Zeebrugge. Moreover, the Hong Kong–based private enterprise CK Hutchison is also a major investor in European container terminals. Its Rotterdam subsidiary ECT is the largest terminal operator in Europe's busiest seaport.

But the most important BRI project in Europe concerns the role of COSCO in the port of Piraeus, Greece. The company had already signed an agreement with the Greek government in 2008 to take over the operational management of part of the container terminal in Piraeus for a period of thirty-five years. With an investment in 2016, COSCO not only acquired the entire container terminal, but also the rest of the port. The ferry port, from which tourists depart for the Greek islands, and the cruise terminal are also covered by the agreement.

The container terminal is located on the Salamis Strait, where Greek city-states in 480 BCE defeated a Persian invasion fleet. In 2016, however, the Greeks had little choice when it came to Chinese influence in the port. As a result of the global financial crisis, the country was deeply indebted after

2008 and was forced by the European Union and the IMF to privatize state-owned companies such as the Piraeus Port Authority in order to service its debts. COSCO was ultimately the only bidder for the 51 per cent interest in the port company that was up for sale. Due to the involvement of the Chinese company, the port was able to develop very quickly. Piraeus grew from a medium-sized port in 2008 to the busiest container port in the Mediterranean in 2020. COSCO achieved this by investing in the container terminal, but above all by ensuring that many ships call at the port. The company is the largest player in a Sino-French-Taiwanese alliance of shipping companies that currently holds the largest market share in container shipping between Asia and Europe. The company directed its own ships to Piraeus, creating more activity at the port and thereby making it more appealing to other shipping companies.[18]

Because of COSCO, Piraeus has become an important hub for the trans-shipment of containers to and from smaller ports in the Eastern Mediterranean. What the Chinese company also aspired to is for Piraeus to become a primary gateway for China's trade with Central Europe and Germany. However, this proved more difficult to achieve, because the distances are great and the port's hinterland connections are not very good.

In addition to international loans and direct investments, Chinese domestic government subsidies also played a major role in the development of BRI. Starting around 2013, Chinese regional governments began making substantial subsidies available for rail freight transport between China and Europe. HP, the American technology company, and other multinationals then started using trains to transport part of their products from factories in China to consumers in Europe. The necessary rail connections already existed for a long time, but now freight trains were running between China and Europe on a regular basis for the first time. Dozens of Chinese and European cities are now connected by fixed train services.

The number of containers transported has increased very quickly. The most used route passes through Kazakhstan, Russia and Belarus. A total (both ways) of 26,000 40-foot (or 52,000 TEU) containers were transported on this route in May 2020. That is about twice the number of containers that the very largest container ships can transport in one go. But although the trains carry only a fraction of the total trade between China and Europe, they are still interesting for certain products such as electronics, cars, wine and highly fashion-sensitive clothing. The trains are faster than ships, and cheaper than air transport. In order to achieve a sufficiently large scale, the local governments of the Chinese cities and provinces that have train services with Europe have initially provided massive financial support. After the start of the Russian-Ukrainian War in 2022, the number of trains between China and the EU declined. The number of China–Russia trains, meanwhile, has continued to increase.

## Obstacles to China's economic expansion

In addition to investments in Europe that are part of the BRI project, from 2013 the volume of other direct investments from China also grew very rapidly. Chinese companies took over numerous European companies, from French Club Med to Swiss Syngenta and Italian Pirelli. The same happened in the United States. In the European Union and the United States, the value of Chinese direct investment reached a peak of US$46 and US$41 billion in 2016, respectively.[19] Many of these investments went to Western companies that had high-quality technological knowledge.

This was in line with the economic strategy developed by the Chinese government after the financial crisis of 2008. Due to the economic problems in Europe and the United States, China's most important export markets partially disappeared. The government's short-term response to that crisis included accelerating the construction of infrastructure in China, such as roads, airports, subways and railways. In just a few years, the country built a nation-wide network of high-speed trains. Large-scale investments by the government brought back economic growth. But it was also clear that this could not be maintained for long and that Deng Xiaoping's old export-oriented model was becoming less relevant. Production costs in China had become increasingly high and there were now many other countries where things like clothing and shoes could be made at a lower cost. The government therefore focused on developing China's domestic spending as a future growth engine. The country already had a sizeable middle class, but a large share of the profits from sales of consumer products went to foreign manufacturers of luxury products and advanced goods such as iPhones. To capture the most profitable segment of the market (and become more influential in global supply chains), Chinese companies had to become competitive, especially in technology. The Chinese government set up support programmes to help Chinese companies achieve that goal.

This disrupted the economic equilibrium that had existed between China and the advanced economies since the 1980s. Companies in Japan, the United States and Europe had benefitted from China's rapid growth by selling large volumes of products there. The best example was Germany, which exports cars and precision machinery to China. In 2016, China became Germany's largest trading partner. The rapid increase in Chinese investment in Germany now gave rise to fears that the German companies that were the source of the export success would end up in Chinese hands. Alarm bells went off on a national level when, in 2016, a Chinese air conditioner manufacturer, Midea, bought a German maker of robots, Kuka. As the maker of the robots used by German industry to assemble cars, Kuka was seen as a strategically important company. After the Kuka takeover, the German government took action to make such takeovers more difficult. Together with France and Italy, Germany also initiated a process in 2017 to get the other EU member states to move in the same direction. Partly against the background of the BRI investments in Piraeus and elsewhere, the European Commission has been taking steps to push national governments to increase their supervision of Chinese takeovers of European companies. In the meantime, changes were taking place in the United States, as a result of which the scope for Chinese direct investment was considerably more drastically curtailed there.

## Trump

On 6 and 7 April 2017, Xi Jinping was in Florida where he spent the night at Mar-a-Lago, Donald Trump's estate in Palm Beach. The former real estate mogul and host of a reality show on TV had been president of the United States since early 2017. Trump felt that previous presidents had been too soft on China. During the election campaign he had announced that as president he would end China's trade surplus in relations with the United States. Immediately after the election, when Trump had defeated his Democratic opponent Hillary Clinton against all odds, Trump previewed his upcoming China policy.

When Taiwanese President Tsai Ing-wen called him to congratulate him on his victory, Trump took the phone call. This was contrary to the policy followed by successive US administrations for decades. There have been no diplomatic relations between Taiwan and the United States since 1979 and no contacts at a high political level. The Chinese government has since tried to manoeuvre Taiwan into international isolation, expecting the US government to adhere to the agreed principle of not recognizing Taiwan as a state. Only a handful of countries maintained diplomatic relations with Taiwan, but Taiwanese leaders continued to try to break through their isolation. Tsai's attempt to call Trump was an example. Usually the US side would politely decline a request for a phone conversation with the president. But Trump did have a chat with the president of Taiwan, thus showing his willingness, if needed, to fundamentally overhaul the US-China relationship to get his way. He was unconventional and unafraid to offend the Chinese government.

For his first meeting with Xi, president Trump invited the Chinese leader to Mar-a-Lago. The estate's massive main building was commissioned nearly a century before by an extremely wealthy businesswoman, Marjorie Merriweather Post. Trump had bought it in 1985, after driving the price down by announcing that he would build an ugly condo between the mansion and the beach (the condo was never built).[20] At Mar-a-Lago Xi and his wife, Peng Liyuan, met with Trump and his family. Arabella (5) and Joseph (3) Kushner, the children of Trump's daughter Ivanka, sang a song in Chinese for the guests on that occasion. Not just any song, but a traditional Chinese song that Peng Liyuan had often performed. Xi's wife has been a popular singer in China since long before the Chinese people even knew who Xi Jinping was. The two Kushner children also proved to be able to recite a Confucian text from memory. To top it off, Arabella also recited two classic poems from the Tang dynasty in Chinese.

In addition to singing and poetry, Trump had another surprise for Xi. During dinner, just after dessert had been served, the US president informed the Chinese leader that he had launched an attack on Syria. Indeed, two American warships fired a total of 59 cruise missiles at a Syrian air base around the same time. Trump said this was in retaliation for an attack by the Syrian army with poison gas on territory held by Syrian rebels three days earlier. Trump may have wanted to carry out the attack anyway, but he probably knew very well that Xi would take the coincidence with his visit as a signal. Trump wanted China to put pressure on North Korea over its nuclear weapons programme. The attack on Syria therefore seemed to be a reminder to China that the United States might also deploy military assets against North Korea.[21] Trump was trying to establish a friendly relationship with Xi, but at the same time, as with the call from Taiwan, he showed that he was not afraid to resort to drastic measures if necessary. On Twitter, Donald Trump spoke very positively about his relationship with China's Supreme Leader, but also pointed to what he regarded as the biggest problem in Sino-US relations: 'President Xi and I will always be friends, no matter what happens to our trade dispute.'

Trump's approach seemed promising at first. He seemed to have found a way to put pressure on the Chinese government without being too direct about it. In doing so, he left open the possibility that the Chinese government would make trade concessions to the United States without giving the Chinese people the impression that the CCP was showing weakness towards a foreign power. As a presidential candidate, he had been more popular in China than Hillary Clinton, and he now continued to emphasize that he got on well with Xi. However, as it turned out, Trump did not get what he wanted. Instead, the relationship between the United States and China was about to enter a phase of rapid deterioration.

## Escalation

During Obama's eight years in office, relations with China had worsened as the United States increased pressure but failed to change China's behaviour. On the contrary, under Xi, the Chinese government became more authoritarian at home and more expansionist abroad. The Chinese government was now becoming so powerful that it provoked a strong response from the United States, but at the same time it was not strong enough to convince the United States that there was no point stopping China's rise. Despite Trump's new approach, the same thing happened under his leadership as under Obama: China stayed on track and grew more powerful, but relations with the United States became even more disrupted. By the end of Trump's presidency, those relations were worse than they had been since Nixon's 1972 visit to China.

Although the Taiwan issue remained a problem after 1972, and new points of friction had emerged since 1989, there has always been a willingness on both sides to prevent mutual distrust from getting the better of them. Especially in the economic field, the two countries were closely integrated. This changed in 2018 when Donald Trump launched a trade war with China. He had believed for decades that the United States should raise import tariffs to reduce the trade deficit and prevent industrial production from being moved abroad. Because US companies had started to produce en masse in China, it had become more difficult for the United States to maintain its technological lead.

Negotiations with China did not yield the result Trump desired, and in 2018 he took action. On several occasions from July to September of that year, the US government increased import taxes on a wide variety of Chinese products. The trade in these products represented about half the value of China's annual exports to the United States. In response, the Chinese government imposed higher import tariffs on US products. However, the value of affected Chinese exports was considerably higher because the US imported more from China than vice versa.

Trade was not the only area in which the US government took action against China. The Chinese high-tech sector in particular became the target of new measures. The opportunities for Chinese companies to access high-quality technology partly or wholly developed in the United States were limited. American technology companies were no longer allowed to sell chips to Huawei, maker of mobile phones and telecom equipment and one of China's most successful private multinationals. Later, steps were also taken to force non-US companies that use American technology to stop supplying chips to Huawei. Also, in the fall of 2018, Meng Wanzhou, the chief financial officer and daughter of the founder of Huawei, was arrested in Canada while transferring from a flight from Hong Kong to a connecting flight to Mexico. The arrest was made at the request of the US government.[22] The Chinese company was also locked out of the US market for 5G telecom networks, and the US government started to put pressure on other countries to keep Huawei out of their 5G networks there as well. The attack on Huawei is a signal that the US government intends to win the competition with China in the high-tech field by extreme means if necessary. The American concerns are partly related specifically to Huawei (many Western governments regard the company as a potential tool for Chinese espionage activities), but also mainly to the fear that the United States and third countries will become dependent on Chinese companies and technology in the future. It also became more difficult for some other Chinese ICT companies to purchase foreign products incorporating American technology.

Gradually, President Trump discovered that despite the trade war and measures to curb technology transfers, China showed no intention of complying with his wishes. However, he also found that his China policy was growing in popularity, with his Republican base as well as Democratic Party supporters (with whom he was otherwise extremely unpopular). Continuing to increase pressure on China was therefore an attractive political strategy. If he won the trade dispute and forced China to take a technological step back, he could claim to have averted the Chinese threat. That would not only be an economic, but also a geopolitical victory, because Chinese international power was largely based on economic factors. According to former national security adviser John Bolton, Trump had asked Xi in 2019, when both were attending an international conference in Japan, to help him win re-election as US president in 2020 by importing large quantities of agricultural products from the United States.[23] That would make Trump popular in the states where those products came from. If the trade war dragged on and he took firm action against China, that would also boost his popularity.

Xi Jinping was in an awkward position. The most favourable approach for China was to buy time and avoid direct confrontation so that domestic consumption and technology could develop further and China's dependence on the United States would decrease. In the longer term, the rest of the world would become more dependent on the Chinese market and on Chinese technology, and China would also become increasingly powerful militarily. But the US increasingly steered towards an economic showdown. The US government wanted more access to the Chinese market and to slow down Chinese economic expansion in the rest of the world. In the military field, Trump continued his predecessor's policy: the United States used its military power in Asia to influence the balance of power between China and its neighbours. Under Trump's leadership, the United States had now seized the initiative.

The trade war and the measures taken against Huawei were so drastic that Trump's continued positive attitude about his relationship with Xi made little difference. For China it was clear to see what was happening. Also for the Chinese public it was not hard to see a parallel with British actions against China in the nineteenth century aimed at forcing open its market. Partially giving in to the United States to hold back escalation and buy time was possible, but giving up the role of geopolitical challenger was a tough choice. This would mean that the Chinese government would accept that the US remain the stronger party militarily and technologically and that Taiwan and the South China Sea would never be brought under China's control. That could undermine the domestic legitimacy of the CCP and Xi Jinping, given his stated aim of continuing the rise of China. For the Party, there also was the danger that the United States would use its position of power to further weaken China and at some point intervene to end the CCP's rule. For Xi and his colleagues at the top of the Communist Party, a more appealing course of action was to use the problems with the United States as proof that China continues to be threatened from abroad and that only the CCP can save the country. At the same time, Xi continued to be careful that the escalation did not get out of hand. China responded with countermeasures but left the initiative with the US government.

After intensive discussions, the two governments agreed in early 2020 that Chinese companies would purchase significantly more American products from now on and that the Chinese market would be made more accessible. This agreement only dealt with the trade dispute, not with the issue of technology transfers and was a shaky basis for a ceasefire. The relationship had now come under such strain that it didn't take much for it to deteriorate further. Just then, the coronavirus (COVID-19) pandemic broke out, with China as its source and with disastrous consequences for the US economy and public health in the run-up to the presidential election. The process of deteriorating the Sino-American relationship gained further momentum. China was the first to be hit hard by the coronavirus, which then spread to the rest of the world. Despite the trade agreement, China did not buy significantly more US products, and the tariffs remained in place.

Throughout 2020, the US government, under pressure from major social unrest caused in part by the COVID-19 crisis, took new measures against China. It responded to steps by the Chinese government to increase its authority in Hong Kong through a new security law by imposing sanctions on senior officials and financial institutions involved in the implementation of that law. Trump also revoked the special trade status of Hong Kong, which was increasingly brought under the control of the central government in Beijing. Another measure taken by the US government was the closing of the Chinese consulate general in Houston, the city where Deng Xiaoping had celebrated the new good relations with the United States in 1979 by attending a rodeo show. (China promptly responded by ordering the US consulate general in Chengdu to close as well.) The US government claimed the Houston consulate was being used for espionage activities. The existence of those activities was very likely, but the closure seemed primarily a symbolic act, aimed at showing that the US-China relationship was at a turning point.

A speech by US Secretary of State Mike Pompeo around the same time also pointed in that direction. On 23 July 2020, he stated that the confrontation between the United States and China was in fact a battle between freedom and tyranny.[24] The enemy of freedom everywhere in the world, Pompeo said, was the Chinese Communist Party. He called for an international alliance of democratic states and the Chinese people to change the behaviour of the CCP. The Secretary of State gave his speech at the Richard Nixon Library in California and made it clear that he believed that US-China policy since 1971, when Kissinger had travelled to China, was a failure. The implication seemed to be that as far as the US government was concerned, anything was now possible, including a return to a break in bilateral relations such as existed during the 1950s and 1960s.

## Russia's invasion of Ukraine

In the evening of Friday 4 February 2022, Vladimir Putin was back in the Bird's Nest Stadium to attend the opening ceremony for another Beijing Olympics. This time Beijing was hosting the Winter Games, thereby becoming the first city to have hosted both the Summer and the Winter Olympics. But on this occasion the US president was not attending. Under Joe Biden, who had succeeded Trump as president in January 2021, the United States had announced a diplomatic boycott of the Beijing 2022 Winter Olympics. The reason for the boycott was that, according to the White House, the Chinese government was responsible for 'genocide and crimes against humanity in Xinjiang and other human rights abuses'.[25] Leaders from most other Western countries also stayed away from the Olympic Games. Some of them declared that it was the COVID-19 pandemic that was still ongoing that kept them home. Unlike in 2008, there were very few foreign spectators at the games. Because of the pandemic, tickets were available only to people residing in China.

For Xi Jinping, the absence of Western leaders and foreign visitors was a setback. In 2008 he had been in charge of the preparations for the Games, but at that time, Hu Jintao was China's president and therefore the official face of the host country. The Beijing 2022 Winter Olympics should have been Xi's moment to shine. And potentially even worse than COVID-19 and the diplomatic boycott was the possibility that the games would once again be overshadowed by a Russian invasion in a neighbouring country.

Since the autumn of 2021, Russia had steadily built up large troop concentrations near the Ukraine border. On 3 February 2022, a day before the start of the Olympics, senior officials of the Biden administration briefed US lawmakers in Washington DC on the possibility of a Russian attack on Ukraine.[26] According to their presentation, which was based on US intelligence assessments, the Russian military had already gathered seventy per cent of the forces needed for a full-scale invasion. However, the US government was not sure whether Putin had made a final decision to go ahead with an invasion.

In Beijing, in the afternoon of the following day, Xi Jinping had a meeting with Putin. A small number of top officials from either side also attended the closed-door meeting. This was the first time since the start of the COVID-19 pandemic that Xi met face to face with a foreign leader. It was also one of the first times since then for Putin to travel abroad. Their meeting took place at a location known as the Diaoyutai State Guesthouse, a former imperial garden with multiple lakes and buildings. These include the villa where Kissinger stayed during his secret visit in 1971 and another one in which Nixon stayed when he visited China in 1972. The villa where Britain negotiated with China over the return of Hong Kong in 1985 was also part of the complex. The building in which Xi and Putin were now having their meeting had once been used by China to host the Six-Party Talks, a series of talks between North Korea, the United States and several other countries, including Russia, in order to discuss North Korea's plans to develop its nuclear capabilities. China hosted these meetings from 2003 until 2007, after which the negotiations broke down and North Korea accelerated its nuclear weapons programme.

Sitting across from each other at tables in a formal conference setting, Putin and Xi used the occasion to discuss relations between their countries. Both of them referred to the importance of coordinating with each other on international affairs.[27] After the meeting they had dinner together, during which they discussed in some detail 'major hotspot issues of mutual interest'. When the dinner was over, their two countries released a joint statement. Later the same evening Xi and Putin watched the opening ceremony of the Winter Games. No Russian tanks crossed the Ukraine border on that day. But on 24 February, just four days after the end of the Olympics (and eight days before the start of the Beijing 2022 Winter Paralympic Games), they did.

It is not known whether at their meeting in Beijing, Putin informed Xi about his plans regarding Ukraine. It is also unclear whether, if he did, he told his Chinese counterpart that he was going to launch a full-scale invasion aimed at capturing the Ukrainian capital Kyiv and possibly the entire country, rather than just the eastern regions where Russia had been fighting a proxy war since 2014. But given that international media had been reporting about a massive Russian troop build-up, and after the precedent of 2008 when Russia invaded Georgia during the opening ceremony of the Beijing Olympics, it seems very likely that the possibility of a Russian military action against Ukraine came up during the conversation.

## War in Europe and the Middle East

The joint statement that was released after their meeting was long and detailed and must therefore have been prepared in advance of 4 February. In the statement, Russia and China declared their relationship to be 'superior to political and military alliances of the Cold War era'.[28] In other words, China was now formally stating that it was closer to Russia than it had been to the United States during the later part of the Cold War. The statement also seemed to suggest that cooperation between the two countries might go beyond the one they had during the 1950s, when one (in that case the Soviet Union) provided the other (China) with technical assistance and weapons. The core element in this Sino–Russian expression of friendship with 'no limits' was their opposition to Western interventions in countries' internal affairs, the expansion of NATO and other US-led alliances into regions close to China and Russia, and the deployment of US missiles in Asia and Europe. Whereas Russia confirmed its stance that it regards Taiwan as 'an inalienable part of China', the Chinese government expressed support for Russia's desire for 'long-term legally binding security guarantees in Europe'.

Whatever Xi knew with regard to Putin's invasion plans, the joint statement reflected China's preoccupation with the United States as a threat, and its leaders' conviction that, in order to counter that threat, there was no alternative to aligning strategically with Russia. When Putin made his move against Ukraine, that alignment proved to have major consequences for China's geopolitical position.

Most importantly, China once more lost the initiative in great power politics. In 2018 the United States had put China on the defensive when it started a trade war and a process of partial containment in the technological domain. And now Russia, through a highly destructive and aggressive act against a neighbouring country, had re-established itself as a major player in great power politics. It was demonstrating that it was subordinate to no one and capable of influencing the relations between other leading powers. By attacking Ukraine, Putin was contributing to the already widening rift between China on the one hand and the United States and the EU on the other. The Western countries responded to the Russian attack by imposing wide-ranging sanctions against Russia. China, which had already been Russia's largest trade partner before the war, instead deepened its economic relations with Russia. As a result, China was now being seen by Western governments as undermining their sanctions. China–EU relations in particular became strained as European companies divested from Russia and European leaders referred to Russia as an existential threat.

The further Sino-US tensions increased, the more China has become dependent on Russia as a strategic partner, but also on the European Union as an economic partner. As a market and source of technology for China, the EU has remained a significant alternative to the United States. But because of the war in Ukraine, the Chinese government has come under growing pressure to prioritize either its relations with Russia or those with the EU. In an attempt to maintain good relations with both actors, China's support for Russia has primarily been economic rather than military. But at the same time, the Chinese government has clearly favoured Russia as its main partner, which unlike the EU is an autonomous geopolitical actor. As a consequence of the war, Europe has become more dependent on American military support, and thus, its ability to act independently has declined.

For the Chinese government, the war in Ukraine has greatly complicated its relations with Europe and Russia. While European leaders have made demands that China cannot meet without harming its partnership with Russia, the latter's behaviour has proven to be volatile and beyond China's control. At the same time, the war has also improved China's position in some respects. Many Chinese companies have been able to expand their presence in Russia after their western competitors withdrew. But perhaps more significantly, the United States has committed large quantities of weapons and strategic attention to the defence of Ukraine, which otherwise could have been available to support US interests in East Asia.

By late 2023, concentrating on East Asia had become even more difficult for the United States. Ever since the presidency of Barack Obama, the US government had tried to reduce its security involvement in the Middle East. Under presidents Trump and Biden, the United States withdrew militarily from Afghanistan. Although this had the unintended consequence of the Afghan government collapsing in August 2021, when the Taliban regained control of the country, it did indeed allow the US to turn its attention away from Afghanistan. But the large-scale attack on Israel by Hamas on 7 October 2023, the subsequent Israeli invasions of Gaza and South Lebanon, and escalating tensions between Israel and Iran kept US foreign policy very much engaged with the Middle East.

## China after COVID-19

Different from when Trump started his trade war in 2018, the Chinese government has done little to retaliate against the American efforts to block Chinese access to advanced technology. China itself has become a leading producer of technology. It is also by far the most important producer of many so-called rare earths, the minerals on which the semiconductor industry depends. But instead of retaliating against the United States and its allies, the Chinese government has focused on stimulating domestic capacities in semiconductors, quantum computing and AI. In spite of large-scale efforts, especially with regard to the making of the most advanced types of semiconductors, China is far from achieving self-sufficiency.

By the mid-2020s, China's economy was in worse shape than it had been during the financial crisis in 2009. Economic growth had been slowing, and local governments were burdened by large debts. During the COVID-19 pandemic, local governments exhausted their financial reserves as they paid for large-scale testing and control measures to keep the coronavirus from spreading. Xi Jinping's policy of concentrating political control in the Communist Party strongly favoured state-owned companies and undermined the dynamism of the private sector. The geopolitically motivated actions of the US government restricted China's access to foreign capital and advanced technologies, which further hurt mainly the private sector in China. Large property developers had trouble paying off their debts, and many building projects were stopped even if home buyers had already paid for them. Youth unemployment was high, and most crucially, consumers and businesses had become pessimistic about the economy and sharply reduced their spending. China's population had grown accustomed to a process of ever-increasing welfare, and now it had to adjust to the apparent end of that phase.

Despite the weaker economic situation, technological developments in China continued to advance at a fast rate. By the early 2020s, Chinese companies had become highly competitive internationally in sectors such as e-commerce and video sharing platforms, IoT (internet of things) applications, and solar and wind energy generation. The Chinese electric car industry in particular went through a highly rapid growth phase. In the last quarter of 2023, the Chinese manufacturer of electric cars BYD for the first time sold more vehicles worldwide than its American competitor Tesla. The rising competitiveness of Chinese companies in strategically important industries such as sustainable energy and cars led to further strains in Sino–Western relations. Governments in the United States and Europe often regarded Chinese competitiveness a result of state aid and worried about potential security risks involved in China-related products capable of collecting user data, such as the video sharing app TikTok and electric vehicles.

# Biden

When Joe Biden became president, America's strategy on China did not change substantially. His administration adopted three key components of Trump's approach to China: high duties on Chinese imports into the United States, restrictions on American technology exports to China and building international coalitions to counter China's influence. Regarding import duties, the Biden administration maintained the existing tariffs, thereby prolonging the trade war with China. In the area of building of coalitions, the United States under Trump had helped set up the Quadrilateral Security Dialogue, also known as the Quad, with Japan, Australia and India. The Biden administration went a step further when, in 2021, it established a security pact with Australia and the United Kingdom called AUKUS.

While the Quad is primarily a diplomatic platform and a series of leadership summits, AUKUS involves substantial commitments from and long-term implications for the participating countries. At the core of AUKUS is an arrangement according to which the United States and the UK will provide the Australian navy with the technology to build nuclear-powered submarines. Such vessels are able to operate under water longer at a higher speed and therefore at greater distances than conventional submarines. This would allow Australia to deploy its submarines close to China and potentially contribute to US efforts to deter China from attacking Taiwan. The programme involves not just the building of new submarines, a complex and long process, but also a high degree of technological dependence from Australia on the United States and the UK. Moreover, both the Trump and Biden administrations have promoted a greater orientation from NATO on China as a potential adversary.

But it was in the technological domain that the United States under Biden has been particularly active. The American government expanded and deepened measures introduced by the Trump administration that were aimed at limiting Chinese access to certain advanced technologies. It did this by limiting commercial and scientific transfers of semiconductors (also referred to as microchips), quantum computing and artificial intelligence (AI) technologies to China. The United States also took steps to end investments by American pension funds and other financial institutions in Chinese companies active in developing such technologies.

US strategy since Trump has been aimed at exploiting China's dependence on certain advanced technologies to slow down its military modernization. Artificial intelligence is now widely seen as a decisive element of military power. By limiting Chinese access to the most advanced AI algorithms and chips, the United States has been trying to maintain its own military superiority. It is difficult to separate this strategy directed at slowing down China's military development from efforts to do the same to its economic growth. Technologies such as semiconductors and AI are also crucial to China's efforts to make its economy competitive at the level where the United States is operating. Whereas China has become the world's manufacturing centre, economic activities that generate the greatest financial value are still primarily located in the United States. It seems likely that the US government is limiting China's access to technology in order to protect not only its military lead but also its main competitive advantages in the economic domain.

Semiconductor companies in Japan, Taiwan, South Korea and Europe have been under growing pressure from the United States to limit sales of their most advanced products to Chinese customers. The US government wants to make sure that China does not circumvent American restrictions by getting similar technologies from other countries. One example is ASML, a Netherlands-based company that builds the lithography systems that companies such as Samsung, Intel and TSMC need to manufacture microchips. ASML is also one of Europe's largest companies and a leading player in the global semiconductor industry. In 2019, pressured by the US government, the Dutch authorities withheld a permit for the export to China of ASML's newest equipment. In subsequent years, the US succeeded in also limiting sales to China of some of ASML's lithography systems that until then were not under restrictions. US authorities did so in part by inducing the Dutch government to introduce its own restrictions, and in part by using ASML's linkages to American technology to directly force the company to scale back its sales to China. America's China strategy was thus increasingly affecting not just companies in China and the United States itself, but also some in third countries.

In November 2023, Xi Jinping and Joe Biden met at the Filoli estate not far from San Francisco. It was only the second time for the two leaders to meet after Biden became president nearly three years earlier. Xi's meeting with Biden took place on the sidelines of the Asia-Pacific Economic Cooperation (APEC) forum. The estate's country house was more than a century old, and in the 1980s it had been used as a film location for the television series

*Dynasty*. By the time Biden and Xi were meeting there, China-US relations had become so tense that both sides deemed it desirable to make an effort to somewhat stabilize the relationship.

A symbol of the level that public anxiety about China had reached in the United States was the 'spy balloon' incident. On 1 February 2023, media in the United States reported that a high-altitude balloon was sighted drifting 18 kilometres above Montana, in the northwest of the United States, and heading southeast. The Chinese government subsequently made an announcement saying that it was a meteorological balloon which was launched from China and was blown far off its intended course. In the following days, American public opinion extensively debated how much of a threat the balloon posed to national security and what the government should do in response. Eventually, once the balloon had reached the Atlantic Ocean where falling debris would not cause damage, it was shot down by an American F22 fighter plane. The balloon appears to have been intended by the Chinese government to collect information from a flight path over the Pacific Ocean, perhaps aimed at covering US military bases on Guam or Hawaii, but probably not the continental United States. Due to the uproar about the balloon, US Secretary of State Antony Blinken decided to cancel a long-anticipated trip to China at the last moment. He had intended to re-establish high-level communication between the two countries after a more serious incident that had taken place a half year before.

## Taiwan again

In July 2022, Western media reported that Nancy Pelosi, the speaker of the US House of Representatives, was planning to visit Taiwan. Pelosi was one of the Democratic Party's most influential politicians, and as the presiding officer of the House of Representatives, she was second in line after vice president Kamala Harris to take over Biden's presidential responsibilities should something happen to him. The last time such a high-ranking US official had visited Taiwan had been in 1997.

Nancy Pelosi had a history of strongly criticising China. In 1991, when she was in Beijing as part of a Congressional delegation, she left the official programme to visit Tiananmen Square. There, in front of news cameras, she and two colleagues held up a banner and laid flowers to commemorate the victims of the violent crackdown two years before. Before she went to Taiwan, president Biden had tried to dissuade Pelosi from making the visit, and no formal announcement was made to confirm that she would actually go. But on 2 August 2022, after visits to Singapore and the Malaysian capital Kuala Lumpur, Nancy Pelosi travelled to Taipei. In order to avoid flying over the contested South China Sea, the US military transport plane that carried Pelosi made a detour by flying to the east of the Philippines. By the time the plane landed in Taipei, hundreds of thousands of people were tracking her flight trajectory online to see if she was really going to Taiwan and if there was no attempt by the Chinese air force to keep her from doing so. Two US aircraft carriers and military aircraft from Kadena Airbase on Okinawa were on standby in the waters and airspace near Taiwan just in case there was a sudden move from the Chinese military against Pelosi's plane.[29]

Nancy Pelosi stayed less than twenty-four hours in Taiwan, where she met with its president Tsai Ing-wen. Shortly after she left Taiwan to continue her Asian tour by going to South Korea, the Chinese military started several days of large-scale military exercises at sea and in the air in multiple locations around Taiwan. The deployment of large numbers of military vessels and aircraft underlined the resolve and ability of the Chinese government to attack Taiwan if needed. Unnoticed by most international media, but surely not by the Chinese military, was that the two US aircraft carriers were still in the vicinity of Taiwan during the military exercises. These ended without further incidents. But it was clear that the Taiwan Strait once again proved to be the dangerous place it had previously been in the mid-1990s and the 1950s.

After the meeting between Biden and Xi at the Filoli estate in California, Sino-US relations somewhat stabilized. Apparently both leaders wanted to prevent a further escalation of tensions in early 2024, when the Taiwanese population would choose a new president. The most likely winner of the election was Lai Ching-te, Taiwan's vice president. Lai was seen by the Chinese government as even worse than Tsai Ing-wen, the incumbent president of Taiwan. Like her, Lai was from the Democratic Progressive Party (DPP) which China views as pro-independence. But as a politician, Lai seemed to be somewhat more independence-leaning than Tsai. If China would respond with more large-scale military exercises after a victory by Lai Ching-te, President Biden would be under pressure from his political opponents to react in order to protect Taiwan, which could trigger further actions from China. Biden, who wanted to secure his re-election as US president in November 2024, probably preferred to avoid such a scenario.

Lai Ching-te was indeed elected as Taiwan's next president, although his party lost the majority in parliament. China did not initiate any special military activities. It seemed that, at least temporarily and under specific circumstances, the United States and China were still capable of controlling their relationship. Some months later when Lai Ching-te, during his presidential inauguration, made statements that seemed to signal his intention to take a more confrontational position towards China on Taiwan's autonomous status, the Chinese military did respond with drills around the island. The same occurred after a speech by president Lai at the occasion of Taiwan's national day in October 2024. On both occasions the Chinese military response was more limited in scope and duration than after the Pelosi visit in 2022. They also did not have a major impact on China's relations with the United States.

Despite Biden's success at preventing China-related tensions from derailing his attempt to win a second presidential term, by election day he was no longer running for president. He had dropped out of the race, pressured to do so by leading Democratic politicians after his disastrous performance during a presidential debate. On 5 November 2024, his successor as presidential candidate, Vice President Kamala Harris, was beaten by her Republican opponent. It was Donald Trump's turn once more to be Xi Jinping's counterpart in managing the world's most important geopolitical relationship.

FIGURE 26 *Prime Minister Vladimir Putin speaking with President George W. Bush before the start of the Opening Ceremony for the 2008 Beijing Summer Olympics at the National Stadium, Beijing 8 August 2008 (photo by Alexander Hassenstein/Bongarts/Getty Images).*

FIGURE 27 *Vice President Xi Jinping meeting US Secretary of State Hillary Clinton, US Treasury Secretary Timothy Geithner and other delegates, Diaoyutai State Guesthouse, Beijing 3 May 2012 (photo by Jason Lee/Pool/Getty Images).*

FIGURE 28 *President Donald Trump and his wife Melania Trump with President Xi Jinping and his wife Peng Liyuan, Mar-a-Lago, Palm Beach, Florida, 6 April 2017 (official White House photo by D. Myles Cullen).*

FIGURE 29 *Aircraft carrier* Liaoning *sailing into Hong Kong harbour, 7 July 2017 (photo by Justin Chin/Bloomberg via Getty Images).*

FIGURE 30 *President Vladimir Putin meeting with President Xi Jinping at the Diaoyutai State Guesthouse, Beijing 4 February 2022 (photo by Alexei Druzhinin/Sputnik/AFP via Getty Images).*

FIGURE 31 *Speaker of the US House of Representatives Nancy Pelosi (left) and Taiwan's President Tsai Ing-wen at the president's office, Taipei, 3 August 2022 (photo by Chien Chih-Hung/Office of The President via Getty Images).*

# Epilogue

There is no evidence that Napoleon Bonaparte ever actually uttered the words often attributed to him that China is a sleeping giant better left alone. But he did have an opinion about China's place in the world. We know that thanks to his doctor's diary. On 26 March 1817, less than two years after Napoleon's final defeat at Waterloo, he met with Barry O'Meara, an Irish physician assigned to him by the British authorities. The ex-emperor of France was exiled to Saint Helena, a remote (2,000 km from the African coast) and sparsely populated island, where he was under British supervision. One of his few interlocutors there was O'Meara, whom he saw daily. On this day the conversation was about China.

The reason was the upcoming visit to Saint Helena of the British diplomat William Amherst, who was on his way from China to Great Britain. Amherst had been sent to the Qing Empire to negotiate better access to the Chinese market for British products. But because he refused to perform the *kowtow*, the ritual of deep bows, for the Chinese emperor, negotiations had come to nothing. Napoleon knew of the failure of the Amherst mission and criticized the British government for sending an envoy who would not perform a *kowtow*. After all, that made the mission a pointless action in advance and actually caused more tension in British–Chinese relations.[1]

O'Meara then announced what was probably also the view of the British government: China had better adapt to the manners of the British because they were a world power. Britain would get what it wanted, one way or another, because it could send warships and thereby establish an economic blockade. But Napoleon did not agree at all. A military action against China would really be an unwise move, he thought. According to Napoleon, the British government would do better to create a trade monopoly by going to war with China's other trading partners, such as the US, rather than with China itself.[2] Certainly, the British navy would surely be able to deal a serious blow to the Qing dynasty. However, Napoleon pointed out what would happen next. The immense China would not accept that it was weaker than Britain and would gradually build its own power. Sooner or later China would beat the British. By attacking China, Britain would show the Chinese how potentially powerful their country really is. As Napoleon put it: *You would teach them their own strength*.[3]

What was special about Napoleon's vision was that he had an eye for the long-term dynamics in the geopolitical relationship between Great Britain and China. In the short term, the British could impose their will on China, but ultimately this experience would make China stronger. The central idea of this book is related to this: the emergence of China as a major global power today is the continuation of a process that began in the nineteenth and twentieth centuries with attempts to reduce the influence over China of other great powers.

In the Chinese government's representation of the country's history, it was the Communist Party under Mao Zedong that resurrected China as a great power after 1949. Although the Party and its leaders have played an important role, the emergence of China as a great power is the result of the actions of many people, also from outside the CCP and also before 1949. At the same time, the world's major powers – in particular Britain, France, Russia, Germany, Japan and the United States – have created and continue to be a significant part of the context in which that process has been taking place. As such they have contributed to the shaping of China's geopolitical role and are still doing so. Of particular long-lasting significance was their interaction with China before and during the time the country was unable to participate in great power politics, that is, from the middle of the nineteenth to the early twentieth century. This does not mean that the great power identity of today's China is the inevitable outcome of its experience as a target of Western, Russian and Japanese imperialism. For instance, many factors contributed to the fall of the Kuomintang government in the late 1940s, and China's communist leaders could at various points have made different choices about foreign policy and the role of nationalism and historical memory therein. Nonetheless, understanding the current relationship between China and the West requires knowledge of the historical role of the major powers throughout the process of China's resurrection as a leading actor in international affairs.

## China's role as great power

O'Meara's diary was published in 1822, a year after Napoleon's death, but it is unlikely that it had any influence on British policy towards China. In 1840 the British government did what Napoleon thought so unwise, namely to launch a military attack on China in order to force better access to the Chinese market. And what Napoleon had expected did indeed happen, albeit on a much longer term than he probably envisioned. The two opium wars marked the beginning of China's geopolitical transformation. The country has evolved from a regional power unable to defend itself against

Britain in 1840, to an emerging global power regarded as the greatest rival by America today.

The intention to end China's weakness in the face of modern great powers gradually became a driving force in China's foreign policy after 1870. Top official Li Hongzhang laid the foundation for this in the last three decades of the nineteenth century. Around 1920, Sun Yat-sen enshrined the same objective in his long-term plans for China's revival. The most powerful leaders since the country's political reunification from 1928 – Chiang Kai-shek, Mao Zedong, Deng Xiaoping and Xi Jinping – have maintained the central role of this objective.

What is striking is the long period that China needed and still needs to develop as a world power. As early as 1943, China joined the Big Four, the powers that institutionally shaped the world order that has existed since the Second World War, with the United Nations at its core. But even today, China lacks the resources to play a decisive military role outside its own region. China's influence in the world stems primarily from its economic power. China's return to the position of the world's largest economy (which it had two centuries ago) is still underway (and remains uncertain). The country only overtook Japan as the world's second largest economy in 2010. The large size of the Chinese market was a crucial factor in the British decision to attack China in 1840 and is now the main factor in making China a world power. The importance of access to the Chinese market makes China an essential economic partner for many countries. Other sources of Chinese power – military, financial, technological – are developing rapidly, but so far they have only been complementing the central role of the Chinese market.

The way the Chinese government exercises power internationally is largely the same as how other countries, especially large countries, do it. But the Chinese approach also includes methods that are different from those of longer-established major powers like the EU, the United Kingdom, Japan and the United States, as they stem at least in part from China's experience as a target of imperialism. Examples are the obstacles to foreign presence in the Chinese market by means that are not visible or predictable to the outside world, the use of consumer boycotts as a means of pressure against foreign governments or companies, the co-opting of large foreign companies to conform to China's political interests, the financing of infrastructure abroad as a means of strengthening diplomatic and economic ties and, above all, the strategic symbiosis between government and large Chinese companies that Li Hongzhang had started in the 1870s.

It is also remarkable that there is such a high degree of continuity in China's geopolitical objective. China has not been subjected to imperialist interference since the mid-1940s, when the unequal treaties were abolished and Japan lost the Second World War. And China's status as a regional great power was restored by 1953, when it had become clear that the United States was incapable of driving the Chinese army out of North Korea. Despite all these geopolitical changes, the determination of China's political leaders to make the country stronger internationally has remained.

China's revival as a regional power transitioned into China's emergence as a leading global actor. The long-term consequence of the series of military defeats against the great powers, from the First Opium War through the Boxer crisis of 1900, was a deeply rooted national sense of political fragility. That feeling was reinforced by the colonial-style Western presence until the Second World War, the Japanese invasion and occupation of 1931–45, and the conflicts with the two superpowers of the Cold War. The power differential between China and the great powers in the nineteenth and early twentieth centuries, and the way in which the powers abused it, contributed to a far-reaching and long-lasting destabilization of the country and ultimately of the entire region. Although China was never completely passive or defenceless even in times of great weakness, the Chinese people have suffered greatly from the economic, political and administrative consequences of this destabilization. This, together with the efforts of China's present rulers to promote the notion that the roughly one hundred years before they seized power in 1949 was an era of national humiliation, explains the persistence of Chinese mistrust and uncertainty about great powers. What first the Kuomintang and then the Communist Party offered to the Chinese people is primarily the promise of internal order through geopolitical security, or protection against great powers.

As far as the balance of power with other major powers is concerned, China has not yet returned to the level it was before the First Opium War. Then, the Qing Empire was the undisputed leader in the East Asian regional order. Today, however, the United States is a major factor in the relationship between China and its neighbours, including Taiwan. The United States has played the role of external balancer in Asia since the end of the Second World War, maintaining it during the 1980s when it strategically worked closely with China against the Soviet Union and also after the end of the Cold War. From 2010 onwards, in response to China's rapidly growing influence in Asia, the United States started using its regional role more actively to counterbalance Chinese power. One notable development at the time was that the US government started to become more involved in territorial disputes in the South China Sea. Greater American activism in Asia encouraged China's leaders to focus on building closer economic ties with countries in other parts of the world. Thereby the Chinese government increased its ability to influence relations between the United States and other countries worldwide, as a counterweight to US pressure in Asia. The Belt and Road Initiative and the strong increase in Chinese foreign direct investment in Europe from 2013 are important parts of this endeavour. For the United States, China's ability to win over many developing countries in international organizations and the seeming resignation of European countries to the shifting global balance of power were the undesirable outcomes of the Chinese strategy. In addition, China and Russia, since 2014 and even more so since 2022, have strengthened their strategic coordination and cooperation. With all this, the Chinese government had been undermining the US global leadership role.

The accelerated expansion of Chinese influence on a global level after 2010 had important consequences. First, the United States saw China's more active stance outside East Asia as a threat to its position as a leading world power. This partly explains the shift in US foreign policy around 2018, when actively countering Chinese international influence became a top priority. Second, the geographical centre of gravity of the confrontation between China and other powers is changing. As it shifted from the Chinese interior to the East Asian region after 1949, more recently it has been expanding from that region to the world as a whole. During the Cold War, Taiwan, Korea, Vietnam and Indonesia, among others, were the scene of geopolitical rivalry between China and the United States. Although East Asia remains the region that is central to US-China rivalry, countries and regions around the world have increasingly become involved.

As a modern great power, China is not simply a reincarnation of the empire that regarded itself as the centre of the world and other states as peripheral vassals. A consequence of the trajectory that China has followed since the Opium Wars is precisely its leaders' recognition that there are other 'centres', namely other great powers. China has also long accepted the principle that states are formally equals in international relations and that international organizations play a central role in managing them. On the other hand, the Chinese government likes to present the country as an ancient civilization and a source of great wisdom, including on international political issues. In addition, Xi Jinping's mission for China to help 'build a community with a shared future for humanity' seems to echo the ancient imperial role of guardian of the universal order. However, the image of China as a great civilization has only very limited relevance for the rest of the world. And the idea that China as an emerging global power has a mission for the rest of humanity is not unique to that country. Far more significant is that China is one of the five permanent members of the UN Security Council. As a fundamental characteristic of the existing international order, these countries have powers that the vast majority of states do not have. Although the main architect of this feature was the United States under president Roosevelt, for China it suits remarkably well with its imperial past and its present aims and interests.

# Geopolitical rivalry between China and the United States

At present, in the sphere of international relations, intense geopolitical rivalry with the United States is the main outcome of the long trajectory of China's rise as a great power. However, this is not the only consequence at the international level, nor is it likely to be the final stage of that process. For China, the United States today is the latest in a succession of individual, and groupings of, great powers that have exerted significant influence on China itself and on China's international position since 1840. As China interacted with the major powers, it gradually became a more active and influential participant in the global order. That China is now one of the leading actors in that order and that most of the world's countries regard it as a significant counterpart are also major results of China's rise.

In whatever way the China-US relationship may develop, that development takes place in a broader geopolitical context. Longer-existing geographic centres of economic and political power – Europe, Russia, North America, East Asia – are gradually being joined by new ones. Southeast Asia and India are the most prominent of these. India, in particular, is on its way to join the United States, China and Russia as one of the most influential independent actors in geopolitical affairs. Other non-Western countries with large populations may follow. Meanwhile, the European Union, Japan, the United Kingdom and South Korea remain geopolitically relevant as economically and technologically influential actors and close partners of the United States. How China is positioned in relation to all of these actors has fundamental implications for the long-term evolution of the global order. Still, for now the main geopolitical issue that involves China is the question of how it will manage its relationship with the United States, and vice versa.

The geopolitical positioning of China and the United States towards one another today is very different from the 1950s and 1960s, when their mutual relationship was at its lowest point. Unlike then, the two powers maintain diplomatic and economic relations, and they do not engage in armed conflict with each other as they did in Korea (directly) and Vietnam (indirectly). The present phase of deterioration in their relationship started in 2009, with the pace of deterioration accelerating from 2018. As a result, economic relations have been scaled back, while military tensions have been rising, most visibly in the South China Sea and in relation to Taiwan.

A further deterioration in the relationship between the two powers could lead to a complete break in economic relations, and possibly an armed conflict. But so far the confrontation has primarily been focused on the technological domain. Both countries have been trying to decrease their dependence on the other and strengthening their international influence by expanding their own technological strengths. In addition, the United States in particular has tried to maintain its lead in areas such as semiconductors and artificial intelligence by cutting off China's access to critical technologies in these fields. This technological dimension of their power struggle has major implications for the economic, military and diplomatic positions of not just China and the United States, but also of other countries in East Asia and West Europe.

While US-China rivalry has been intensifying, the underlying economic process that has triggered the United States to focus much of its strategic attention on China has become less prominent. The Chinese economy is still growing faster than that of the United States, but over the past decade, the difference has become much smaller. In 2023, the GDP growth rate in China was 5.2 per cent, while in the United States it was 2.9 per cent. Should China's economic growth rate continue to decline and come close to that of the United States, then it may take several decades for China to become the world's largest economy. Or it may never happen. China's economy has been its main source of international influence and the basis for its military and technological advancement. The prospects for the United States to maintain its leadership position in global affairs have thus been improving, while the urgency to respond to China's emergence as a great power has been diminishing. Great power competition between the United States and China is not likely to disappear anytime soon, but the prospect for it to enter a more stable and less directly confrontational phase seems to be growing.

Some of the features of China's rise discussed in this book are relevant in this regard. The high degree of consistency in the country's long-standing aim to become geopolitically autonomous means that, regardless of its leadership, China is likely to retain that aim. This means that the country highly values maintaining its current position among the world's leading countries and that it is likely to further increase its international influence whenever possible. At the same time, after a slow start, China has learned to be pragmatic and adaptive to its international environment. An implication of this would be that the Chinese government is not unchangeably committed to any particular construct or ideology of global order. Whether or not a system brings international stability and allows China to protect its main interests is probably of far greater importance to its leaders than the system's ideological and other features. A China that seeks geopolitical autonomy but that is also able to adapt to its international environment is not necessarily incompatible with the current global order.

A step that would put US-China relations on a firmer footing is an agreement between the two countries on each other's position in the global order and especially in the regional balance of power in East Asia. Henry Kissinger called for such an arrangement more than a decade ago in his book *On China*. Perhaps back then the time was not ripe as China's economy was growing at a high rate and was expected by many to overtake the US economy within ten to twenty years. But today, with China not growing so fast anymore and the United States seeing the limits to its ability to manage regional geopolitical orders, a deal by which the two great powers agree to accept and preserve the existing balance of power between them would be far more feasible. Trying to achieve the alternative would be costly and unrealistic. Just like China is not in a position to take over America's global leadership role or remove US strategic influence from East Asia, the United States cannot expect to achieve regional hegemony in East Asia by subduing China.

# NOTES

## Introduction

1 Xi Jinping, *The Governance of China I* (Beijing: Foreign Languages Press, 2014), 301.
2 English translation as published by the Chinese government. Xi Jinping, *Governance*, 37–8. Original text in Chinese: 自1840年以来，我们是持续奋斗，在中国大地上展现出了中华民族伟大复兴的光明前景。我们大家都能感到，我们现在比历史的任何时期都更加接近中华民族伟大复兴这个目标，我们现在比历史上任何时期都有信心、都有能力实现这个目标。回首过去，我们全党同志都要牢记：落后就会挨打，发展才能自强。… 我们展望未来，全党的同志也必须牢记，把蓝图变成现实，我们还将走很长的路，我们必须为之付出长期、艰苦的努力。… 我们为实现中华民族伟大复 兴去奋斗的历史任务光荣而艰巨，是需要我们一代又一代中国人不懈地为之共同 努力。… 我 坚信，中华人民共和国成立100周年时，把我国建设成富强、民主、文明、和谐的 社会主义现代化国家的目标一定能实现；我更坚信， 中华民族伟大复兴的梦想 一定会实现！
3 In a recent publication, Friso Stevens argues that China is currently in the final phase of the process of national revival, and what the implications are: Friso MS Stevens, 'China's long march to national rejuvenation: Toward a Neo-Imperial order in East Asia?', *Asian Security*, 2020.

## 1

1 Mao Haijian, *The Qing Empire and the Opium War: The Collapse of the Heavenly Dynasty* (Cambridge: Cambridge University Press, 2018), 133–4. Most of the information about the First Opium War in this chapter comes from Mao Haijian's book.
2 Paul Arthur Van Dyke, *The Canton Trade: Life and Enterprise on the China Coast, 1700–1845* (Hongkong: Hong Kong University Press, 2005).
3 Stephen Platt, *Imperial Twilight: The Opium War and the End of China's Last Golden Age* (London: Atlantic Books, 2018), 213.
4 Hosea Bailou Morse, 'Lord Palmerston to the Minister of the Emperor of China', International Relations of the Chinese Empire I (London: Longmans, Green, and Co., 1910), appendix A, 621–6.
5 Barend J. ter Haar, *Het Hemels Mandaat: de Geschiedenis van het Chinese Keizerrijk* (Amsterdam: Amsterdam University Press, 2009).
6 Haijian, *Opium War*, 147.
7 Jürgen Osterhammel, *China und die Weltgesellschaft: Vom 18. Jahrhundert bis in unsere Zeit* (Munich: CH Beck, 1989), 147.
8 Haijian, *Opium War*, 141.

# 2

1. Marie-Claire Bergere, *Sun Yat-sen* (Stanford: Stanford University Press, 1998).
2. Gordon Daniels, *Sir Harry Parkes: British Representative in Japan, 1865–1883* (Richmond, Surrey: Routledge, 1996, 4).
3. The name Elgin is best known today for the 'Elgin Marbles', the marble depictions of the Parthenon and other ancient Greek works of art owned by the British Museum. The Elgin who had these works of art shipped from Greece to London in the early nineteenth century was the father of the Elgin who had the Summer Palace destroyed in 1860.
4. Matthew Craven, 'What Happened to Unequal Treaties? The Continuities of Informal Empire', *Nordic Journal of International Law* 74, 2005, 335–82.
5. Haijian, *Opium War*, 502–3.
6. Osterhammel, *China und die Weltgesellschaft*, 155.
7. Hailian Chen, *Zinc for Coin and Brass: Bureaucrats, Merchants, Artisans, and Mining Laborers in Qing China, ca. 1680s–1830s* (Leiden: Brill, 2019), 147–9.
8. Manfred Görtemaker, *Deutschland im 19. Jahrhundert: Entwicklungslinien* (Leske +: Budrich, 1983), 300.

# 3

1. Gu Weijun became internationally known as Wellington Koo.
2. Jonatan Clements, *Wellington Koo: China* (London: Haus Publishing, 2008), 31.
3. Ibid., 19–20.
4. A 2018 study estimated there were 17 million deaths, but other estimates are higher: Peter Spreeuwenberg, Madelon Kroneman and John Paget, 'Reassessing the Global Mortality Burden of the 1918 Influenza Panademic', *American Journal of Epidemiology* 187(12) (2018): 2561–7.
5. Aisin-Gioro Pu Yi, *From Emperor to Citizen: The Autobiography of Aisin-Gioro Pu Yi, Volume 1* (Peking: Foreign Language Press, 1979), 33.
6. William de Bary and Richard Lufrano (comp), *Sources of Chinese Tradition: From 1600 through the Twentieth Century, Vol. 2* (New York: Columbia University Press, 2001), 322.
7. The amount to be paid, including interest, was more than 982 haiguan taels, the unit of account of the maritime customs, which was based on the value of silver. Because the amounts had to be paid in gold-based foreign currencies, the historian Frank King estimated that the actual amount to be paid, given the ratio of silver to gold value in the period 1902–40, was around 1.8 billion haiguan taels. Expressed in US dollars at the exchange rate of 1901 and adjusted for inflation, this would amount to approximately USD$ 40 billion in 2019. Frank H. H. King, *The History of the Hongkong and Shanghai Banking Corporation II: The Hongkong Bank in the Period of Imperialism and War 1895–1918* (Cambridge: Cambridge University Press, 1988), 323, footnote c.
8. Frans-Paul van der Putten, *Corporate Behaviour and Political Risk: Dutch Companies in China, 1903–1941* (Leiden: CNWS Studies in Overseas History, 2001), 23–5.

9 Ching-Hwang Yen, *Coolies and Mandarins: China's Protection of Overseas Chinese During the Late Ch'ing Period (1851–1911)* (Singapore: Singapore University Press, 1985), 333–4.
10 Clements, *Wellington Koo*.
11 For Liang's writings, see Peter Zarrow and Liang Qichao, *Thoughts from the Ice-Drinker's Studio – Essays on China and the World* (New York: Penguin Random House, 2024).
12 Orville Schell en John Delury, *Wealth and Power: China's Long March to the Twenty-First Century* (New York: Random House, 2013), 1105–107.
13 Ibid., 110–13.
14 Today, a plaque with Zhou's image hangs on the outside of the still-existing hotel commemorating his stay. The image was created by Paul Belmondo, artist and father of French film star Jean-Paul Belmondo.
15 Schell and Delury, *Wealth and Power*, 131.
16 Sun Yat-sen, *The International Development of China* (Shanghai: Commercial Press, 1920).
17 Bergère, *Sun Yat-sen*, 280–6.
18 Yat-sen, *International Development*.
19 Zheng Yongnian, *The Chinese Communist Party as Organizational Emperor: Culture, Reproduction and Transformation* (New York: Routledge, 2010), 55–63.
20 Schell and Delury, *Wealth and Power*, 134.
21 Chiang Kai-shek is the Western spelling of the Cantonese pronunciation of his name, and the form in which his name has become known internationally. In Mandarin, converted to Latin script, his name is Jiang Jieshi.

# 4

1 van der Putten, *Corporate Behaviour*, 110–11.
2 Bergère, *Sun Yat-sen*, 252–3.
3 van der Putten, *Corporate Behaviour*, 113.
4 The Nederlandsche Maatschappij voor Havenwerken, one of the forerunners of the Royal BAM Group.
5 Stalin sent another Comintern agent to China in 1932. This Otto Braun joined the CCP and in 1934 was part of the famous Long March.
6 van der Putten, *Corporate Behaviour*, 214–15.
7 Ibid., 139.
8 Jay Taylor, *The Generalissimo: Chiang Kai-shek and the Struggle for Modern China* (Cambridge: Harvard University Press, 2009), 155.
9 Vincent Chang and Yong Zhou, 'Redefining Wartime Chongqing: International Capital of a Global Power in the Making, 1938–46', *Modern Asia Studies* 51(3) (2017): 592–3.
10 An English translation of the book appeared in 1947 under the title *China's Destiny and China's Economic Theory*, from: Schell and Delury, *Wealth and Power*, 189–90.

11 Chiang Kai-shek, *China's Destiny and China's Economic Theory* (New York: Roy Publishers, 1947), 232.
12 'Declaration of the Four Nations on General Security', United Nations, 1943, https://archive.org/stream/unitednationsdoc031889mbp/unitednationsdoc031889mbp_djvu.txt.
13 'May I not hope that it is the resolve of Congress to devote itself to the creation of the post-war world? To dedicate itself to the preparation for the brighter future that a stricken world so eagerly awaits?'. Soon May-ling, 'Address to the US House of Representatives', Washington, DC, USC US-China Institute, 1943, https://china.usc.edu/soong-mei-ling-%E2%80%9Caddresses-house-respresentatives-and-senate%E2%80%9D-february-18-1943.
14 Taylor, *The Generalissimo*, 249.
15 Barbara W. Tuchman, *Sand against the Wind: Stilwell and the American Experience* (London: Macmillan, 1970), 410.
16 Office of the Historian, 'Foreign Relations of the United States: Diplomatic Papers, the Conferences at Cairo and Tehran, 1943', United States Department of State, 1943, https://history.state.gov/historicaldocuments/frus1943CairoTehran/d259.
17 Tuchman, *Stilwell*, 410.
18 David L. Boscoe, *Five to Rule Them All: The UN Security Council and the Making of the Modern World* (Oxford: Oxford University Press, 2009), 14–15.
19 Taylor, *The Generalissimo*, 256.
20 Ibid.

# 5

1 Hung Chang-tai, 'Revolutionary History in Stone: The Making of a Chinese National Monument', *The China Quarterly* 166 (2001): 465.
2 Zheng Yongnian, *The Chinese Communist Party as Organizational Emperor: Culture, Reproduction and Transformation* (New York: Routledge, 2010), 64.
3 Shu Guang Zhang, *Deterrence and Strategic Culture: Chinese-American Confrontations, 1949-1958* (Cornell: Cornell University Press, 1993), 96.
4 Shu Guang Zhang, *Deterrence and Strategic Culture*, 96–7.
5 Shu Guang Zhang, *Economic Cold War: America's Embargo against China and the Sino-Soviet Alliance, 1949-1963* (Stanford: Stanford University Press, 2002).
6 Kimie Hara, *Cold War Frontiers in the Asia-Pacific: Divided Territories in the San Francisco System* (Abingdon: Routledge, 2006).
7 Cited (English translation) in Zhang, *Deterrence and Strategic Culture*, 146.
8 Zhang, *Economic Cold War*, 273.
9 Stein Tønnesson, 'The South China Sea in the Age of European Decline', *Modern Asian Studies* 40(1) (2006): 1–57.
10 Vincent Bevins, 'What the United States Did in Indonesia', *The Atlantic*, 2017.
11 Peter Van Ness, *Revolution and Chinese Foreign Policy* (Berkeley: University of California Press, 1971).

12 Henry Kissinger, *On China* (New York: Penguin Press, 2011), 229–31.
13 On Kissinger's trip to China: Kissinger, 236–55.
14 Kissinger, *On China*, 260–1.
15 Ibid., 262.

# 6

1 Bill Keller, 'Gorbachev Visits Beijing for Start of Summit Talks', *The New York Times*, 15 May 1989.
2 Hung Chang-tai, 'Revolutionary History in Stone: The Making of a Chinese National Monument', *The China Quarterly* 166 (2001): 465.
3 Hong Bin, 'Deng Xiaoping's Perspective on National Interest', *Chinese Views of Future Warfare*, revised edition, Michael Pillsbury (ed.) (Washington, DC: National Defense University Press, 1998).
4 See Hong Bin, 'Deng Xiaoping's Perspective'.
5 Ezra Vogel, *Deng Xiaoping and the Transformation of China* (Cambridge, MA: Harvard University Press, 2011), 674.
6 Ramsey Fahs, 'How Coca-Cola Came to China, 40 Years Ago', *Los Angeles Review of Books China Channel*, 2019, https://chinachannel.org/2019/02/06/coke-in-china/; Lub Bun Chong, 'Chapter 4', *Managing a Chinese Partner, Palgrave Macmillan UK*, 2013; N. R. Kleinfield, 'Coca-Cola to Go on Sale in China as US and Peking Expand Ties', *The New York Times*, 1978.
7 Cary Huang, 'Yuan Geng: Chinese Guerilla Spy Turned Economic Pioneer, Dies at 99', www.scmp.com, 1 February 2016.
8 Katharina Buchholz, 'The Explosive Growth of 8 "Miracle" Chinese Cities – in One Chart', *World Economic Forum*, 2019, https://www.weforum.org/agenda/2019/09/infographic-the-explosive-growth-of-chinese-cities/.
9 Deng Xiaoping, 'Speech by Chairman of the Delegation of the People's Republic of China, Deng Xiaoping, at the Special Session of the U.N. General Assembly', Foreign Languages Press, 1974, https://www.marxists.org/reference/archive/deng-xiaoping/1974/04/10.htm.
10 Vogel, *Deng Xiaoping*, 86.
11 Richard McGregor, 'Forget Texas, China Came Out When Deng Tipped His Hat to Japan', www.scmp.com, 1 December 2018.
12 May Zhou, 'Visit Recalled Deep in Heart of Texas', www.chinadaily.com.cn, 4 January 2019; Ian Hutchinson, 'January 29, 1979 Performance of American Arts for Deng Xiaoping', *China Business Review*, 2019.
13 Jonathan Steele, 'America Puts the Flag Out for Deng', *The Guardian*, 30 January 1979.
14 Chenyi Wang, 'The Chinese Communist Party's Relationship with the Khmer Rouge in the 1970s: An Ideological Victory and a Strategic Failure', Wilson Centre, Cold War International History Project Working Paper Series, nr 88.
15 Vogel, *Deng Xiaoping*, 650.
16 Bonnie Girard, 'How 1980 Laid the Groundwork for China's Major Foreign Policy Challenges', thediplomat.com, 12 September 2018.
17 Qian Qichen, *Ten Episodes in China's Diplomacy* (New York: HarperCollins, 2005), 3.

18   Vogel, *Deng Xiaoping*, 495–504.
19   Chris Patten, *East and West: China, Power, and the Future of Asia* (New York: Pan Macmillan, 1998), 28.
20   Nicholas D. Kristof, 'Gorbachev Meets Deng in Beijing; Protest Goes On', *The New York Times*, 16 May 1989.
21   Cited in Kissinger, *On China*, 419.
22   Vogel, *Deng Xiaoping*, 651.
23   Cited in Kissinger, *On China*, 438.
24   Deng is said to have formulated the guideline as follows: 'Observe calmly, remain firm, react calmly and patiently, hide your skills and wait for your opportunity, hide your shortcomings and don't fall, never take the lead, make a difference' (冷静观察，稳住阵脚，沉着应付，韬光养晦，善于守拙，绝不当头，有所作为): Address by Foreign Minister Tang Jiaxuan on 15 June 2004: https://www.fmprc/cev.cev./cgrj/chn/zt/yjddsld/t132964.htm.
25   Qichen, *Ten Episodes*, 244.
26   Kissinger, *On China*, 438.
27   Ibid., 439.
28   Ibid., 477.

# 7

1   Minnie Chan, 'How a Luxury Hong Kong Home Was Used as Cover in Deal for China's First Aircraft Carrier', www.scmp.com, 19 August 2017; Minnie Chan, 'Mission Impossible: How One Man Bought China its First Aircraft Carrier', www.scmp.com, 18 January 2015; Minnie Chan, '"Unlucky Guy" Tasked with Buying China's Aircraft Carrier: Xu Zengping', www.scmp.com, 19 April 2015; Minnie Chan, 'PLA Brass 'Defied Beijing' over Plan to Buy China's First Aircraft Carrier Liaoning', www.scmp.com, 28 April 2015; 'A Naval Hero', Week in China, 250, 2014; Xinhua, 'Chinese President Attends Aircraft Carrier 'Liaoning' Handover Ceremony in Dalian', Qiushi, 26 September 2012, http://english.qstheory.cn/news/201209/t20120926_183622.htm.
2   'Hypersonic Weapons and Strategic Stability', IISS, 2020, https://www.iiss.org/publications/strategic-comments/2020/hypersonic-weapons-and-strategic-stability.
3   Jeffrey Bader, *Obama and China's Rise: An Insider's Account of America's Asia Strategy* (Washington, DC: Brookings Institution Press, 2012).
4   Ibid., 105.
5   Ibid.
6   William A. Callahan, *China: The Pessoptimist Nation* (Oxford: Oxford University Press, 2009), 69.
7   Ane Bislev, 'Nationalist Netizens in China: Online Historical Memory', *Journal of China and International Relations* 2(1) (2014): 117–36.
8   Callahan, *Pessoptimist Nation*.
9   Florian Schneider, *China's Digital Nationalism* (Oxford: Oxford University Press, 2018).
10   Bislev, 'Nationalist Netizens'.

11 Ties Dams, *De nieuwe keizer* (Amsterdam: Prometheus, 2018).
12 Ibid., 108.
13 Xi Jinping, speech, CCP party congress, 18 October 2017, 21 and 53.
14 On Great Harmony and *tianxia* in relation to China's role in the world, see: William Callahan, 'Harmony, Unity and Diversity in China's World', *IIAS Newsletter*, 2012, 22–3.
15 His family name is still internationally known thanks to his nephew Manfred, a talented pilot nicknamed 'the Red Baron' who shot down at least eighty Allied aircraft during the First World War before dying himself. He preferred to fly in a red-painted Fokker aircraft.
16 Sebastian Horn, Carmen M. Reinhars and Christoph Trebesch, 'How Much Money Does the World Owe China?', *Harvard Business Review,* 2020, https://hbr.org/2020/02/how-much-money-does-the-world-owe-china. Incidentally, the Chinese government also owns about $1 trillion in US government bonds, or about 6 per cent of US government debt. But in that case it is not about direct loans and there is no relationship with the New Silk Road.
17 Frans-Paul van der Putten, 'Harmony with Diversity: China's Preferred World Order and Weakening Western Influence in the Developing World', *Global Policy*, 2012.
18 Frans-Paul van der Putten, 'European seaports and Chinese strategic influence: The relevance of the Maritime Silk Road for the Netherlands', The Hague: Clingendael, 2019.
19 Jacob Funk Kirkegaard, 'Chinese Investment into the US and EU Has Plummeted since 2016, Peterson Institute for International Economics, 2019, https://www.piie.com/research/piie-charts/chinese-investment-us-and-eu-has-plummeted-2016#:~:text=In%202016%2C%20China%20invested%20%2446,percent%20of%20the%20country's%20GDP.
20 Mark Seal, 'How Donald Trump Beat Palm Beach Society and Won the Fight for Mar-a-Lago', www.vanityfair.com, 27 December 2016.
21 Jane Perlez, 'After Xi Leaves US, Chinese Media Assail Strike on Syria', www.nytimes.com, 8 April 2017.
22 The Chinese government responded with drastic countermeasures against Canada (but not against the United States), including accusing and imprisoning two Canadian citizens in China of espionage.
23 'John Bolton: Trump Sought Xi's Help to Win Re-Election', www.bbc.com, 18 June 2020.
24 Michael R. Pompeo, 'Communist China and the Free World's Future,' US Department of State, 23 July 2020, https://www.state.gov/communist-china-and-the-free-worlds-future/.
25 https://www.csis.org/analysis/biden-boycott-2022-beijing-winter-olympics Victor Cha, 'The Biden Boycott of the 2022 Beijing Winter Olympics', *Center for Strategic & International Studies*, 18 January 2022.
26 https://www.nytimes.com/2022/02/05/us/politics/russia-ukraine-invasion.html Selene Cooper and David E. Sanger, 'U.S. Warns of Grim Toll If Putin Pursues Full Invasion of Ukraine', *The New York Times*, 5 February 2022.
27 https://www.mfa.gov.cn/mfa_eng/zy/jj/bj2022/yswj/202406/t20240605_11377361.html. 'President Xi Jinping Held Talks with Russian President Vladimir Putin', The People's Republic of China MFA, 4 February 2022.

28 http://en.kremlin.ru/supplement/5770. 'Joint Statement of the Russian Federation and the People's Republic of China on the International Relations Entering a New Era and the Global Sustainable Development', President of Russia, 4 February 2022.
29 https://www.taipeitimes.com/News/editorials/archives/2022/08/22/2003783915.John J. Tkacik, 'Did US fighter Jets Escort Speaker Pelosi to Taiwan?', *Taipei Times*, 22 August 2022.

# Epilogue

1 Incidentally, he thought that there was nothing wrong with performing the *kowtow*: it was not intended to humiliate foreigners, because the highest Chinese officials also performed this ritual when they had an audience with the emperor. Diplomats simply had to adapt to local customs, Napoleon believed.
2 Barry E. O'Meara, *Napoleon in Exile, or a Voice from St Helena: The Opinions and Reflections of Napoleon on the Most Important Events of His Life and Government, in His Own Words II* (London: W. Simpkin en R. Marshall, 1822), 234.
3 Barry E. O'Meara, *Napoleon in Exile I* (Philadelphia: H.C. Carey and I. Lea, 1822), 304–5.

# RECOMMENDED READING

## General

For a general historical overview of China's role in international relations in the past few centuries, see Mark Mancall, *China at the Centre: 300 Years of Foreign Policy* (1984); Jonathan D. Spence, *The Search for Modern China* (1991); and Odd Arne Westad, *Restless Empire: China and the World since 1750* (2013). On China's historical relationship with Great Britain: Kerry Brown, *The Great Reversal: Britain, China and the 400-Year Contest for Power* (2024). On its relationship with the United States until the end of the twentieth century: Warren I. Cohen, *America's Response to China: A History of Sino-American Relations* (2000). In their book *Wealth and Power: China's Long March to the Twenty-First Century*, Orville Schell en John Delury (2013) examine the lives of Cixi, Liang Qichao, Sun Yat-sen, Chiang Kai-shek, Mao Zedong, Deng Xiaoping and others who have contributed to creating modern China. Henry Kissinger discusses China's geopolitical role in his books *On China* (2011) and *World Order* (2014).

## 1840–2

On an early phase of Sino-European geopolitical interaction: John E. Wills Jr, *Pepper, Guns and Parleys: The Dutch East India Company and China, 1662–1681* (2005). On China's response to the British attack during the first Opium War, see Mao Haijian (2018), *The Qing Empire and the Opium War: The Collapse of the Heavenly Dynasty*. Also on the Opium War: Stephen Platt (2018), *Imperial Twilight: The Opium War and the End of China's Last Golden Age*. For an overview of China's diplomatic relations with neighbouring states before the nineteenth century, see John K. Fairbank ed. (1968), *The Chinese World Order*.

## 1842–1912

For publications on the late Qing empire's diplomatic relations and conflicts with great powers: Jürgen Osterhammel, 'Britain and China, 1842–1914' in Andrew Porter and Roger Louis, eds, *The Oxford History of the British Empire III: The Nineteenth Century* (1999); S. C. M. Paine, *The Sino-Japanese War: Perceptions, Power, and Primacy* (2003); and Diana Preston, *The Boxer Rebellion: China's War on Foreigners, 1900* (2002). For a study of the early development of China's diplomatic representation abroad: Immanuel C. Y. Hsü, *China's Entrance into the Family of Nations: The Diplomatic Phase, 1858–1880* (1960). On the emergence of Chinese consulates: Yen Ching-Hwang, *Coolies and Mandarins: China's Protection of Overseas Chinese during the Late Ch'ing Period, 1851–1911* (1985). On Hong Kong during and after the nineteenth century: John M. Carroll, *A Concise History of Hong Kong* (2007).

## 1912–25

Biographies of some influential figures in this period are: Marie-Claire Bergère, *Sun Yat-sen* (1998); Jonatan Clements, *Wellington Koo: China* (2008); Jay Taylor, *The Generalissimo: Chiang Kai-shek and the Struggle for Modern China* (2009). On foreign interests and activities in China: Albert Feuerwerker, *The Foreign Establishment in China in the Early Twentieth Century* (1976); Ramon H. Meyers and Mark R. Peattie, eds, *The Japanese Colonial Empire, 1895–1945* (1984); Robert Bickers, *Britain in China: Community, Culture and Colonialism, 1900–1949* (1999); Frans-Paul van der Putten, *Corporate Behaviour and Political Risk: Dutch Companies in China, 1903–1941* (2001).

## 1925–43

For more insight into the developments leading up to the Second World War in Asia, including the role of economic sanctions: Akira Iriye, *After Imperialism: The Search for a New Order in the Far East, 1921–1931* (1969); by the same author: *The Origins of the Second World War in Asia and the Pacific* (1987); Nicholas Mulder, *The Economic Weapon: The Rise of Sanctions as a Tool of Modern War* (2022); Irvine H. Anderson Jr, *The Standard-Vacuum Oil Company and United States East Asian Policy, 1933–1941* (1975).

Books about China during the Second World War: Barbara W. Tuchman, *Sand against the Wind: Stilwell and the American Experience* (1970); Rana

Mitter, *China's War with Japan, 1937–1945: The Struggle for Survival* (2014).

# 1943–79

About the end of European interests in China: Robert Bickers, *Out of China: How the Chinese Ended the Era of Western Domination* (2017); Aron Shai (1996), *The Fate of British and French Firms in China, 1949–54: Imperialism Imprisoned*.

For an understanding of the US geopolitical position since the Second World War and its role in Asia: Stephen Wertheim, *Tomorrow the World: The Birth of U.S. Global Supremacy* (2020); Kimie Hara, *Cold War Frontiers in the Asia-Pacific: Divided territories in the San Francisco System* (2006).

On the establishment of the Security Council: David L. Boscoe, *Five to Rule Them All: The UN Security Council and the Making of the Modern World* (2009). For more on Mao Zedong and on the founding of the People's Republic: Jonathan Spence, *Mao* (1999); and Graham Hutchings, *China 1949: Year of Revolution* (2022).

For more about China's geopolitical position during the Cold War: Shu Guang Zhang, *Deterrence and Strategic Culture: Chinese-American Confrontations, 1949–1958* (1993); from the same author: *Economic Cold War: America's Embargo against China and the Sino-Soviet Alliance, 1949–1963* (2001); Peter Van Ness, *Revolution and Chinese Foreign Policy* (1971); Michael B. Yahuda, *China's Role in World Affairs* (1978); Samuel S. Kim, *China, the United Nations and World Order* (1979); Akira Iriye, *The Cold War in Asia: A Historical Introduction* (1974); and Chün-tu Hsüeh, ed., *Dimensions of China's Foreign Relations* (1977).

Specifically on US-China relations and the 1972 rapprochement: Rosemary Foot, *The Practice of Power: U.S. relations with China since 1949* (1995); and Margaret Macmillan, *Seize the Hour: When Nixon met Mao* (2007).

# 1979–2008

For a biography of the most influential Chinese politician in the late twentieth century: Ezra Vogel, *Deng Xiaoping and the Transformation of China* (2011). About China's international position in the early twenty-first century: Wang Gungwu and Zheng Yongnian, eds, *China and the New International Order* (2008); and Zheng Yongnian, ed., *China and International Relations: The Chinese View and the Contribution of Wang Gungwu* (2010). For a study of China's behaviour in border disputes: M. Taylor Fravel, *Strong Borders Secure Nation: Cooperation and Conflict in China's Territorial Disputes* (2008). On the early phase of Chinese activities in Africa: Chris Alden, *China in Africa* (2007).

## 2008–24

On China's identity and foreign policy: William A. Callahan, *China: The Pessoptimist Nation* (2009). On politics in Hong Kong: Tim Summers, *China's Hong Kong: The Politics of a Global City* (2019). Books about American China-strategy under Obama and Trump, respectively: Jeffrey Bader, *Obama and China's Rise: An Insider's Account of America's Asia Strategy* (2012); and Josh Rogin, *Chaos under Heaven: America, China, and the Battle for the 21st Century* (2021).

On China and great power rivalry: Graham Allison, *Destined for War: Can America and China Escape Thucydides's Trap?* (2018); Hugh White, *The China Choice: Why America Should Share Power* (2012); Nick Bisley, *Great Powers in the Changing International Order* (2012). About the United States and China in East Asia: Elena Atanassova-Cornelis and Frans-Paul van der Putten, eds, *Changing Security Dynamics in East Asia: A Post-US Regional Order in the Making?* (2014). On the Belt and Road Initiative and on Africa: Florian Schneider, ed., *Global Perspectives on China's Belt and Road Initiative: Asserting Agency through Regional Connectivity* (2021); Shao Binhong, *Looking for a Road: China Debates Its and the World's Future* (2017); Deborah Brautigam, *The Dragon's Gift: The Real Story of China in Africa* (2009).

On semiconductors and their role in US-China strategy: Chris Miller, *Chip War: The Fight for the World's Most Critical Technology* (2022); and Marc Hijink, *Focus: The ASML Way – Inside the Power Struggle over the Most Complex Machine on Earth* (2024).

# INDEX

ABN Amro 48
AEG 49, 78
Afghanistan 13, 139, 140, 142, 153, 154, 159, 171, 186
Africa 3, 11, 13, 58, 86, 87, 116–17, 119, 123, 170, 171, 174, 195
Aisin Gioro Minning *see* Daoguang Emperor
Aisin Gioro Puyi 36, 45, 76, *90*, 95
Aisin Gioro Zaitian *see* Guangxu Emperor
Alaska 10
Albania 119–20, 122, 123
Allison, John Moore 81
Amherst, William 195
Amoy *see* Xiamen
*Arrow* 23, 81
artificial intelligence (AI) 186, 188, 200
Asia-Pacific Economic Cooperation (APEC) forum 188
ASML 188
Assad, Anwar al- 161
Association of Southeast Asian Nations (ASEAN) 118, 163
Astana 170
*Athos,* sinking of, 1917 44
AUKUS 187
Australia 13, 28, 58, 187
Austria-Hungary 26, 33, 34, 44, 52

BASF 49
Batavia *see* Jakarta
Bayer 49
Beijing 8, 11, 13, 14, 22, 24–6, 29, 32, 33–5, *39*, *41*, 46, 47, 52, 54, 58, 70, 72–4, 80, 93, 95, 96, 99, 103, 104, 110, 112, 118, 121, 122, *125, 128*, 129, 130, 134, 136, 138, 141–3, 147, 150, 151, 154, *155*, 160–2, 166–8, 182–4, 189, *191–3*
Beijing Diplomatic Body 47
Beijing National Stadium 160, *191*
Belarus 59, 176
Belgium 6, 26, 33, 53
Belgrade 152, 153, 158, 165
Belt and Road Initiative (BRI) 172–8, 198
Berlin 22, 94
Biden, Joe 183, 186–9, 190, 191
Bilbao 175
Bird's Nest Stadium 183; *see also* Beijing National Stadium
Black Sea 158, 159
Blinken, Antony 189
Boeing 133
Bolton, John 181
Borodin, Mikhail 59, 60, 69, 78
Bosphorus 158, 159
Boxer crisis of 1900 32–5, 45, 53, 143, 167, 198
boycott 50–2, 56, 68, 72, 75, 79, 102, 164, 183, 197
Bremer, James 7, 8
Brezhnev, Leonid 119, 139, 140, 150
British American Tobacco Company (BAT) 49
Brunei 163
Burma (Myanmar) 9, 82–4, 104
Bush, George H. W. 138, 144–6, 153
Bush, George W. 160, 191
BYD 187

Cairo Conference of 1943 89
Calcutta (Kolkata) 24
Callahan, William A. 164
Cambodia 118, 138–40, 142
Canada 13, 180

Cantlie, James 21, 22, 58
Canton *see* Guangzhou
Cape of Good Hope 159
Cape Town 58
Carter, Jimmy 123, 137, 138
Central Intelligence Agency (CIA) 118, 138
century of humiliation 150, 169
Changsha 56
Chapdelaine, Auguste 24
Chaplin, Charles 77
Chevron 49
Chiang Ching-kuo 70, 80, 95, 126, 149
Chiang Fang-liang *see* Vachrava, Faina
Chiang Kai-shek 60–1, 68–70, 72, 74–7, 79, 80, 82, 84–6, 88, 89, *91*, 92, 93–6, 98, 99, 102, 107, 113, 114, 122, 123, *126*, 131, 134, 149, 150, 169, 197
China Merchants Steam Navigation Company (China Merchants) 31, 133–5, 175
Chinatown(s) 28, 51, 55
Chinese Communist Party (CCP): founding of, 1921 56
Chinese Exclusion Act of 1882 (United States) 50
Churchill, Winston 86–9, 92, 94, 106, 107, 141
Ciano, Edda 75
Citibank 48
Cixi 32–6, *40*
Clinton, Bill 145, 146, 151, 152
Clinton, Hillary Rodham 162, 163, 171, 178, 179, *192*
Club Med 177
CMA-CGM 175
Coca-Cola 133
COFCO 133
Columbia University 43, 70
Comintern 55–7, 59, 69, 78–80
Confucius 21, 69
consulates-general: Chinese, in Houston 182;
US, in Chengdu 182
contract workers 27, 28
Cornell University 150
COSCO 175–6
COVID-19 182, 183

Cowan, Glenn 121
Credit Agricole 48
Crimea 161
Cuba 28
Cultural Revolution 111–13, 117, 119, 120, 122, 124, 134, 136, 139, 167
Czechoslovakia 119

*Daini Tatsu Maru* 51
Dalai Lama 145
Dalian 74, 75, 105, 157, 159
Daoguang Emperor (Aisin Gioro Minning) 8, 9, *17*, 25, 142
Debenham, A. S. 67, 68
Democratic Progressive Party (DPP) 149, 190
Deng Xiaoping: address to the United Nations General Assembly of 1974 136;
visit to Japan of 1978 137;
visit to the United States of 1979 137
developing countries 116, 117, 119, 120, 123, 172–5, 198
Diaoyutai State Guesthouse, Beijing 183, *192*
Dinghai 5–8, 13, 14
Djibouti 174
Doihara Kenji 74–5, 96
Dutch East India Company (VOC) 6, 10–12
Dutch East Indies 56

East China Sea 107, 137, 165
East India Company (EIC) 6, 10, 12
Egypt 86, 88, 159
Eisenhower, Dwight 120
Elgin, Earl of (Thomas Bruce) 25
Elliot, Charles 6, 7, 13, 14
Europe 11–13, 22, 34, 44, 46, 48, 49, 53–7, 77, 82, 83, 86, 94, 97, 100, 101, 106, 110, 115–16, 119, 135, 142, 146, 162, 170, 171, 175–7, 184–8, 198, 200
European container terminal (ETC) 175
European Union (EU) 4, 176, 177, 185, 197, 200
Everson, Edward 68, 143
ExxonMobil 49; *see also* Standard Oil

Faina Vachrava 80, 149
Falklands War of 1982 141
Filoli estate 188, 190
First World War: China's entry into, 1917 43, 44
Forbidden City, Beijing 32, 34, 35, *41*, 45, 47, 73, 93, 95, 96, 129
Formosa *see* Taiwan
France 6, 12, 13, 15, 24, 25, 30, 33–5, 43, 53, 56, 57, 59, 60, *65*, 73, 78, 82, 86, 94, 99, 102, 114, 118, 132, 137, 177, 195, 196
*Fujian* (aircraft carrier) 160
Fujian (province) 26, 134, 160
*fuxing* 1, 169
Fuzhou 26–7, 51

G77 174
Gaza 186
Geely 170
General Electric 49
Georgia: war with Russia of 2008 160–1, 184
Germany 3, 12, 26, 31, 33, 34, 43, 44, 49, 52–4, 73, 78–80, 82–7, 89, 94, 99, 100, 119, 121, 132, 165, 171, 176, 177, 196
Gorbacheva, Raisa *155*
Gorbachev, Mikhail 129, 130, 142, 143, *155*
Great Britain 7, 10, 12, 13, 15, 23–5, 30, 34, 49, 53, 73, 76, 82, 83, 87, 89, 102, 106, 115, 132, 140, 145, 148, 195, 196; *see also* United Kingdom
Great Hall of the People, Beijing 129, 130, *155*
Great Leap Forward 110–12
Greece 53, 175
Guam 160, 189
*guandu shangban* 31, 172
Guangxu Emperor (Aisin Gioro Zaitian) 32, 36
Guangzhou 5–8, 10, 12, 14, 15, 21, 23–5, 30, 34, 46, 57, 60, 61, 67, 68, 134, 135, 147
Gulf of Aden 170
gunboat(s) 29, 46, 81, 157

Gu Weijun (Wellington Koo) 43–6, 53, 55, 66, 77, 94, 95

Hague, The 52
Haiphong 82
Hamas: start of Israel-Hamas War in 2023 186
Han Dynasty 171
Hankou (Wuhan) 68, 69
Hanoi 163
Harris, Kamala 189, 191
Hart, Robert 30, 33, 34, *39*
Harvard University 70, 121, 167
Hawaii 21, 28, 80, 83, 189
He Pengfei 158, 159
*hexie* 169
Hideyoshi Toyotomi 9, 10, 30, 82
Hitler, Adolf 78, 80, 82, 83, 94
Hong Kong: British handover to China, 1997 141;
  occupation by Great Britain, 1841 142
Hong Xiuquan 24
Honolulu 80
Houston 137, 138, 182
Hoxha, Enver 119, 122
HP 176
HSBC 48
Hua Guofeng 124
Huawei 180, 181
Hu Jintao 148–9, 153, 154, 157, 160, 167–9, 183
Huludao 75
human rights 144, 146, 173, 174, 183
Hunan 56
Hungary 119
Hutchison, CK 175
Hu Yaobang 130, 168

IBM 170
IG Farben 49
Imperial Chemical Industries (ICI) 49
India: border war with China of 1962 118, 138;
  under British rule 26
Indian Ocean 10, 116, 171
Indochina: independence from France, 1954 88;
  Japanese invasion, 1940–1941 82

Indonesia 56, 117, 118, 134, 162, 170, 171, 199
Intel 188
International Court of Justice (ICJ) (AU: Not found in text.)
International Monetary Fund (IMF) 114, 148, 172, 176
Inukai, Tsuyoshi 76–7
Iran 14, 162, 186
Israel 186
Italy 26, 33, 34, 53, 73, 119, 177
ITT 49

Jakarta 10, 170
Japan: invasion in Manchuria, 1931 157
  start of war with western allies, 1941 141
Jardine Matheson 48
Jiang Qing (Lan Ping) 113, 124, *127*, 131
Jiang Zemin 148, 150, 151, 152, 158, 168
Ji Shengde 158, 159

Kabul 13, 33
Kazakhstan 176
Kennedy, John F. 120
Khmer Rouge 138, 139
Khrushchev, Nikita 110, 119
Kim Il-sung 102, 104
Kissinger, Henry 4, 121–3, *128*, 144, 147, 151, 152, 182, 183, 201;
  first visit to China, 1971 123
Kolkata (Calcutta) 24
Kong Xiangxi (Kung, H. H.) 69, 77, 80, *95*
Korean War of 1950–1953 101
Kosovo War of 1999 152
kowtow 11, *195*
Koxinga *see* Zheng Chenggong
Kuala Lumpur 189
Kublai Khan 9
Kuka 177
Kung, H.H. *see* Kong Xiangxi
Kuomintang (KMT) 57, 59–61, 67–75, 77–82, 85, 86, 88, 94–9, 102, 111, 113–15, 122, 131, 136, 140, 149, 150, 164, 172, 196, 198; *see also* Nationalist Party
Kyakhta, treaty of (1727) 10

Lai Ching-te 190
Lan Ping (Jiang Qing) 113, 124, *127*, 131
Laos 118
Latin America 3, 13, 46, 116, 170, 171
League of Nations 53, 58, 73, 76, 86, 114, 170
Lebanon 186
Lee Teng-hui 149, 151, 152, 158
legation(s): Chinese legation in London 22
  foreign legations in Beijing 25, 32–4
Lehman Brothers 162
Lenin 55, 60, 75, 97
Lenovo 170
Liang Cheng 51, 52
Liang Qichao 54, 55, 59, 97, 129
*Liaoning* (aircraft carrier) 157–60, *193*
Li Hongzhang 28, 29, 31, 32, 34, 35, 38, 44, 51, 133, 172, 175, 197
Li Keqiang 167
Lin Biao 112
Lin Zexu 6, 14
Liu Shaoqi 112
Liu Yunke 26, 29, 51
London 21–3, 26, 28, 54, 67, 73, 83, 141
Longyu 45

MacArthur, Douglas 101–4, 107–8
Macau 10, 11, 15, 21, 23, 51, 105, 114, 135, 140–2, 150, 158, 159
Malaysia 118, 163, 189
Malta 43
Manchuria: Manchukuo 76;
  Manchus 8;
  South Manchuria Railway Incident, 1931 75
Mao Zedong 56, 59, 71, 79, 93, 97, 98, 110–13, 119, 121, 123, *125*, *127*, 130, 196, 197
Mar-a-Lago 178, *192*
Marco Polo Bridge Incident of 1937 80

Maritime Customs Service (Imperial, Chinese) 8, 29–30
May fourth protests of 1919 54, 56
May thirtieth incident of 1925 68
Melbourne, Viscount (William Lamb) 7
Mexico 180
Middle East 13, 100, 116, 153, 161, 170, 171, 184–6
Midea 177
Ming Dynasty 8, 116
missionaries 24, 25, 32, 46, 48, 49, 99
Mitsubishi 48
Mitsui 48
Mongolia 8, 58, 71, 112, 115, 140, 142
Moscow 22, 55–7, 70, 109, 110, 116, 139, 149
MUFG Bank 48
mujahideen 139
Mussolini, Benito 75
Myanmar *see* Burma

Nanjing: Massacre of 1937 81; treaty of (1842) 14
Napoleon (Bonaparte) 195, 196
Nationalist Party 57
National Museum of China 1, 129
Nazarbayev University 170
Nerchinsk, treaty of (1689) 10
Netherlands 10, 26, 33, 49, 52, 83, 188
Neumann, Vladimir 56
New York 28, 43, 58, 70, 81, 121, 136
Nicholas II, Tsar of Russia 36
Nixon, Richard 120–3, *128*, 129, 137, 180, 182, 183;
 first visit to China, 1972 180, 183
Nobel Peace Prize 36, 145
North Atlantic Treaty Organization (NATO) 152, 158, 161, 184, 187

Obama, Barack 161, 162, 165, 166, 171, 179, 186
Okinawa 190
Okura 48
Olympic Games: Beijing Summer Olympics of 2008 *191*;
 Beijing Winter Olympics of 2022 183;
 Tokyo Summer Olympics of 1964 137

O'Meara, Barry E. 195, 196
One Belt One Road (OBOR) *see* Belt and Road Initiative
opium: International Opium Convention of 1912 52
Opium Wars: First Opium War 1, 3, *19*, 23, 24, 27, 32, 51, 85, 106, 142, 147, 198;
 Second Opium War 22–5, 27, 31, 32, 35, 71, 81
Osterhammel, Jürgen 3, 29
overseas Chinese 27, 28, 54, 135

Pakistan 14, 121, 122
Palmerston, Viscount (Henry John Temple) 6–8, 12–15, *18*, 23, 24, 105, 106, 141, 147
*Panay* 81
Paracel Islands 114, 163
Paris, Peace Conference of 1919 52
Parkes, Harry 23–5, 30, 51
Partai Komunis Indonesia (PKI) 56, 118
Patten, Chris 142
Pearl Harbor, Japanese attack on, 1941 84
Pearl River 5, 6, 10
Peking *see* Beijing
Peking University 56
Pelosi, Nancy 189–90, *194*
Peng Dehuai 104, 112
Peng Liyuan 178, *192*
People's Republic of China, founding of, 1949 4, 113, 115, 122, *125*, 129
Peru 28
Philippines 10, 83, 101, 115, 118, 163, 165, 189
Philips 49, 78, 79
Piraeus 175–6, 178
Pirelli 177
Polo, Marco 80, 171
Pol Pot 138, 139
Pompeo, Mike 182
*Porthos* 57
Portugal 53, 142
Pottinger, Henry 14, 15, 23
Putin, Vladimir 160, 161, 183–6, 188, *191*, *193*
Pyongyang 102, 104

Qian Qichen 139, 150, 151
Qingdao 44, 52–4, 64, 73, 76, 159–60
Qing Dynasty 4, 8–11, 14–16, 21, 22, 24, 26, 28, 30, 31, 34–6, 44, 45, 51, 52, 70–2, 82, 99, 114, 115, 132, 140, 150, 195
Quadrilateral Security Dialogue (Quad) 187
quantum computing 186, 188

Rangoon(Yangon) 82
RCA 78
Reagan, Ronald 139, 144
Republic of China 2, 4, 58, 71, 93, 98, 100, 102, 108, 113, 115, 119, 122, 123, *125*, 129, 136, 137, *156*
Richthofen, Ferdinand von 171
Road to Rejuvenation (exhibition) 2
Roman Empire 171
Roosevelt, Franklin D. 84, 86–9, *92*, 94, 99–102, 106, 107, 199
Roosevelt, Theodore 36, 84
Rotterdam 175
Russia 4, 10, 12, 13, 24, 25, 33–6, 53, 55, 59, 60, 74, 75, 87, 144, 145, 154, 160, 161, 176, 183–5, 196, 198, 200;
    Russian Revolution of 1917 56
Russo-Japanese War of 1904–1905 36
Ryukyu 9

Saint Helena 195
Salamis 175
Samsung 188
San Francisco: treaty of, 1951 106
Scowcroft, Brent 144
Second World War 80–4, 86, 94, 96, 99, 100, 101, 106, 115, 119, 133, 135, 137, 139, 157, 163, 164, 197, 198
semiconductor(s) 78, 186, 188, 200
Serbia 53, 152
*Shandong* (aircraft carrier) 159
Shandong (province) 160
Shanghai 5, 14, 26, 29, 43, 47–9, 52, 56, 60, 68, 75–8, 80, 82, 83, 113, 135, 136, 139, 143, 147, 148, 167, 168
Shantou 135
Shell 49, 67, 68, 70, 81

Shenzhen 14–148, 135, 136
Siam 9, 26, 53; *see also* Thailand
Siberia 10, 35
Siemens 49, 78
Silk Road, New Silk Road *see* Belt and Road Initiative
Singapore 10, 83, 118, 132, 135, 171, 189
Sino-Japanese War: of 1592–1598 9; of 1894–1895 30; of 1937–1945 101
Six-Party Talks 184
Sneevliet, Henk 55–7, 59, 118
Song Ailing 69, 77, 95
Song Jiashu 69
Song Meiling 69, 77, 87–9, *92*, 95, *126*, 149
Song Qingling 62, 69, 77, 93, 95
Song Ziwen (Soong, T. V.) 70, 77, 94, 95
South Africa 58, 87
South China Sea 101, 114–16, 152, 153, 163, 165, 181, 189, 198, 200
Soviet Union 55, 59, 60, 69–71, 73–7, 79, 80, 82, 83, 86–9, 94, 96, 98, 100–2, 105–11, 115–20, 123, 124, 129, 130, 132, 137–42, 144–6, 157, 165, 184, 198
Spanish flu 45
Spratly Islands 114, 163
spy balloon incident of 2023 189
spy plane (Hainan) incident of 2001 152–3
Stalin 75, 76, 80, 83, 84, 86, 89, 96, 98, 100, 102, 104, 107, 109, 110, 119
Standard Chartered 48
Standard Oil 49, 67, 70, 81; *see also* ExxonMobil
Stilwell, Joseph 84, 89
Suez Canal 159, 171
Sumitomo 48
Summer Palace, Beijing *128*
Sun Yat-sen 21, 22, 28, 36, 45, 57–61, 62, 69, 70, 77, 85, 93, 95, 98, 109, 131, 148–50, 169, 170, 172, 197
Surinam 28
Sverdlovsk 80
Swatow *see* Shantou
Swire 48, 133

Syngenta 177
Syria 161, 179

Taipei 95, 140, 149, 189, *194*
Taiping Rebellion 24, 25, 35
Taiwan: crises of 1995–1996 151, 152; visit by Nancy Pelosi of 2022 189–90, *194*
Taiwan Semiconductor Manufacturing Company (TSMC) 188
Taliban 139, 186
Tanzania railway 117
tariffs 15, 50, 67, 72, 146, 180, 182, 187
Tehran 86, 89
Telefunken 78
Texaco 49, 67
Thailand 9, 118
Thatcher, Margaret 141, 144
Tiananmen Square: protests of 1919 (*see* May fourth protests of 1919); protests of 1989 129, 142–3
Tianjin 13, 24–6, 33, 34, 73, 76, 80, *90*
*tianxia* 9, 170
Tibet 8, 58, 71, 114, 115, 118, 150; Tibetans 71, 114, 115, 118
*Tien Kwang* 81
Tientsin *see* Tianjin
TikTok 187
Tito 119
Tokyo 22, 57, 96, 137
trade embargo 100, 105, 107, 109
trade war 76, 180, 181; between the United States and China, start in 2018 180, 181, 185, 186
Trans-Pacific Partnership (TPP) 163
tribute states 3
Truman, Harry 99–102, 105, 106, 108
Trump, Donald 1, 178–83, 186–8, 191, *192*
Tsai Ing-wen 178, 190, *194*
Tsinghua University 99, 167
Tsingtao *see* Qingdao
Turkey 158, 159

Ukraine, Russian invasion in, 2022 183–4
unequal treaties 26, 27, 31, 33, 43, 46, 52–4, 85, 87, 113, 197

Unilever 49
United Kingdom (of Great Britain and Northern Ireland) *156*, 187, 197, 200
United Nations (UN): General Assembly 104, 136, 174; Human Rights Council 174; Security Council 94, 100–2, 107, 108, 114, 115, 118, 123, 145, 173, 174, 199
United States (US): Congress 73, 144, 151; open door policy 99–100, 132; Pivot to Asia 165; restoration of diplomatic relations with China, 1979 123, 137; start of trade war with China, 2018 180, 185–7; start of war with Japan, 1941 141; war with China (*see* Korean War)
Uzbekistan 139

Vachrava, Faina (Chiang Fang-liang) 80, 149
Valencia 175
*Varyag* (aircraft carrier) *see Liaoning* (aircraft carrier)
Versailles, treaty of (1919) 53–5, 129
Victoria, queen of the United Kingdom 7
Vietnam: border war with China of 1979 166; Vietnam War of 1955–1975 123
Vladivostok 35
Voitinski, Grigori 56
Volvo 170

Wang Huning 168
warlord(s) 9, 11, 46, 56, 57, 59–61, 67–9, 71, 74, 75, 79, 82
Washington DC: Conference of 1922 72–3
Wellington Koo (Gu Weijun) 43–6, 53, 55, 66, 77, 94, 95
Wen Jiabao 148–9, 157, 167
Wilhelm II, Emperor of Germany 34
Wilson, Woodrow 53, 73
World Bank 114, 144, 148, 172

World Trade Organization (WTO) 114, 148
Wuhan (Hankou) 68, 69

Xiamen 7, 14, 135
Xi'an 79–80
Xianfeng Emperor 25, 32
Xi'an, incident of 1936 79
Xi Jinping 1, 16, 112, 134, 166–71, 173, 178, 179, 181, 183, 186, 188, 191, *192*, *193*, 197, 199;
  Museum address of 2012 1, 167
Xikou 60
Xingzhonghui 21
Xinhua News Agency 134
Xinjiang 10, 58, 71, 183;
  Uyghurs 114
Xi Zhongxun 112, 134, 167
Xuantong Emperor *see* Aisin Gioro Puyi
Xu Zengping 158, 159

Yang Jiechi 163
Yangon (Rangoon) 82
Yangtze 14, 24–6, 33, 46, 50, 70, 81
Yao Huaixiang 6
Yekaterinburg 80
Yellow River 82
Ye Mingchen 23
Yuan Geng 134
Yuan Shikai 35, 45, 53, 54, *63*, 67

Zambia railway 117
Zeebrugge 175
Zhang Xueliang 74–6, 79, *91*
Zhang Yimou 160
Zhang Zuolin 74
Zhejiang 26
Zheng Chenggong (Koxinga) 11
Zheng He 116
Zhou Enlai 57, 59, 60, 71, 79, 93, 103, 104, 112, 113, 117, 119, 121–3, 130, 137
Zhoushan 8
Zhuang Zedong 121
Zhuo Lin 137
Zhu Rongji 148, 158
Zinoviev, Grigory 55